# A Race So Different

D1546065

*Postmillennial Pop*

GENERAL EDITORS
Karen Tongson and Henry Jenkins

# A RACE SO DIFFERENT

## Performance and Law in Asian America

JOSHUA TAKANO CHAMBERS-LETSON

New York University Press

NEW YORK AND LONDON

NEW YORK UNIVERSITY PRESS
New York and London
www.nyupress.org

© 2013 by New York University.
All rights reserved

LIBRARY OF CONGRESS CATALOGING-IN-PUBLICATION DATA

Chambers-Letson, Joshua Takano.
A race so different : performance and law in Asian America / Joshua Takano
Chambers-Letson.
pages cm. — (Postmillenial Pop Series)
Includes bibliographical references and index.
ISBN 978-0-8147-3839-9 (cl : alk. paper)
ISBN 978-0-8147-6996-6 (pb :          )
1. Asian Americans—Legal status, laws, etc.—History. 2. Asian Americans and
mass media—History. I. Title.
KF4757.5.A75C43 2013
342.7308'73—dc23

2013017066

References to Internet websites (URLs) were accurate at the time of writing.
Neither the author nor New York University Press is responsible for URLs
that may have expired or changed since the manuscript was prepared.

New York University Press books

Manufactured in the United States of America
c 10 9 8 7 6 5 4 3 2 1
p 10 9 8 7 6 5 4 3 2 1

A book in the American Literatures Initiative (ALI), a collaborative
publishing project of NYU Press, Fordham University Press, Rutgers
University Press, Temple University Press, and the University of Virginia
Press. The Initiative is supported by The Andrew W. Mellon Foundation.
For more information, please visit www.americanliteratures.org.

*This book is dedicated to my Obāsan,*
*Tatsuko (Takano) Chambers.*
*She carried us across the ocean and continues*
*to carry us today.*

# Contents

# ACKNOWLEDGMENTS

In the LCD Soundsystem song "All My Friends," the song's narrator travels through a landscape of late nights, shifting intimacies, professional growth, and personal loss. In spite of all the changes, he states that in the end he "can still come home to this." This book was written in many houses and flats, in places that include Chicago, New York City, Los Angeles, the Inland Empire, Seoul, Tokyo, Kobe, Cincinnati, Connecticut, and Denver. But the comrades, friends, and family who gave me shelter these past years have been the *home* I come back to, and for this words cannot but fail to express my gratitude.

My colleagues in Northwestern University's Department of Performance Studies have done nothing short of changing my life, and their impact is everywhere in these pages. E. Patrick Johnson and D. Soyini Madison are every bit as impressive as scholars and artists as they are mentors and friends. Ramón Rivera-Servera makes me laugh to the same degree that he pushes me to challenge myself and to rethink my assumptions. Paul Edwards, Carol Simpson Stern, and Mary Zimmerman welcomed me to the department and inspire me on a regular basis. Words simply cannot articulate the joy it is to have my longtime comrade Marcela Fuentes with me on this adventure. Dina Marie Walters reminds me daily that I love my job, and Freda Love Smith kept me alive these past two years. I am so thankful to the School of Communication and Dean Barbara O'Keefe, who made this project possible. Immense gratitude goes to Northwestern's Asian American Studies Program, including

Carolyn Chen, Cheryl Jue, Jinah Kim, Shalini Shankar, Nitasha Sharma, and Ji-Yeon Yuh; and the Theater Department, including Reeves Collins, Tracy Davis, Sandra Richards, Liz Son, and Harvey Young. Across Northwestern, I am most grateful to Tom Bradshaw, Nick Davis, John Haas, Susan Manning, Dean Dwight McBride, Jacqueline Stewart, Joel Valentin-Martinez, Michelle Wright, and Michelle Yamada.

This project received generous support from Wesleyan University's Center for the Humanities during my Mellon postdoctoral fellowship. Jill Morawski was a fearless friend and leader, and Kathleen Roberts kept my head on straight while reminding me of the importance of standing up to the tyranny of squirrels. Beyond being one of the fiercest people I know, Kēhaulani Kauanui introduced me to Florence + the Machine, which became a central component of my writing ritual. Jonathan Cutler, Joe Fitzpatrick, and Miri Nakamura generously read and responded to earlier versions of this project, and their impact has been significant.

The English Department of the University of Cincinnati was a wonderful place to begin my career, and many of my interlocutors and colleagues fostered this work, including Myriam Chancy, Russel Durst, Jenn Glazer, Charles Henley, Emily Houh, Kristin Kalsem, Jon Kamholtz, Jana Leigh, Amy Lind, Furaha Norton, Stephanie Sadre-Orafai, Leah Stewart, Verna Williams, and Marisa Zapata.

I have learned so much from my students at all three institutions, especially the brilliant minds in my graduate seminars on Performing Racial Exception and Asian American Performance. I am particularly grateful to Kantara Soufrant and Mica Taliaferro, who provided invaluable research assistance for this book. I am so grateful to Meiver De la Cruz for being more of a miracle worker than a research assistant.

I do not think it is ever possible to repay the debt owed to one's teachers, and this is especially true in the case of the Department of Performance Studies at NYU. José Muñoz is more than a mentor to me. He has opened up worlds, training me in the pleasures of rigorous thinking and helping me to keep the horizon of the not-yet-here in my back pocket always. Karen Shimakawa's pedagogy, patience, and example continue to humble and inspire me. Ann Pellegrini challenged and encouraged me at every step, all the while reminding me that the best antidote to a sense of intellectual frustration is an hour or two with Judy Garland. Tavia Nyong'o set the bar high and continues to model a practice for surpassing it. Gayatri Gopinath and Kandice Chuh gave substantive critical feedback on the first incarnation of this project, and it is much the better for their impactful insights. Barbara Browning, Barbara

Kirshenblatt-Gimblett, Richard Schechner, and Peggy Cooper Davis were key in helping me to learn how to think about performance and law. I will always be grateful to Noel Rodríguez and Patty Jang for their support and assistance.

I have tried not to write *about* the artists discussed herein but rather *with* and *alongside* them. I only hope this work is in some way worthy of Frances Ya-Chu Cowhig, Ping Chong, Bruce Allardice and the crew at Ping Chong and Company, Dengue Fever and Josh Mills, Eric Owens, John Pirozzi, Hasan Elahi, and Emily Hanako Momohara. I would also like to thank the many institutions that assisted the realization of this book, including Jane Nakasako of the Hirasaki National Resource Center at the Japanese American National Museum, the Metropolitan Opera Archives, the Harry Ransom Humanities Research Center at the University of Texas at Austin, the Charles E. Young Research Library at UCLA, the New York Library of the Performing Arts, and the Tuol Sleng Genocide Center in Phnom Penh. I am also grateful to David Levin and the participants in the DAAD Faculty Summer Seminar at the University of Chicago.

An army of friends, comrades, and teachers acted as protective walls these many years. Jean Randich, Barrie Karp, and Judith Lane are three of the most remarkable teachers in the world. So much of what I have done in this book is a direct result of their influence. Christine Bacareza Balance, Alex Vasquez, and Shane Vogel are the greatest intellectual big siblings that a guy could have. I am also so grateful to Henry Abelove, Patrick Anderson, John Andrews, Sally Bachner, Anurima Banerji, Diego Benegas, Ricardo Bracho, Karen Bray, Katie Brewer-Ball, Nao Bustamante, Andre Carrington, Jamie Champlin, Erica Chenoweth, Patricia Clough, Michael Cobb, Jorge Cortiñas, Robert Diaz, Jennifer Doyle, Lisa Duggan, Keota Fields, Catherine Filloux, Diana Fox, Jane Guyer Fujita, Danielle Goldman, Raquel Gutiérrez, Kelly Haynes, Titcha Kedsri Ho, Stephani Hsu, Holly Hughes, Chloe Johnson, Joan Kee, Sue Kim, Nikki and Jocelyn Kuritsky, Esther Kim Lee, Deb Levine, Eng-beng Lim, Heather Lukes, Martin Manalansan, Anita Mannur, Uri McMillan, Shayoni Mitra, Ricardo Montez, Jeanne Moody, Charles Morcom, James Oliphint, David Pauley, Roy Pérez, Kenneth Pietrobono, Claire Potter, Jasbir Puar, Wallis Quaintance, Elliot Ramos, Joshua Roma, MJ Rubenstein, Sandra Ruiz, Russ Salmon, George Schein, Cathy Schlund-Vials, Shawn Schulenberg, Paul Scolieri, David Simon, Shante Smalls, Gus Stadler, Ryan Stubna, Alina Troyano, Jeanne Vaccaro, Hypatia Volourmis, Martin Waldmeier, Michael Wang, Phil Wells, Maya Winfrey, and Sam Wong.

Yves Winter is my favorite comrade and my best friend and is as a brother to me. So much of this book has been inspired by our exchanges, arguments, and rants. Katherine Lemons and Sonali Chakravarty, too, are everywhere on these pages, and I am so lucky to have them as part of my nonbiological family. I could not have asked for a better conspirator than Amy Tang. Miriam Petty's brilliance, friendship, and laughter ring throughout these pages; she has become my rock. Riley Snorton's generous feedback to various parts of this manuscript, his kinship, and our many conversations are woven across them. Jasmine Cobb astounds me with her intellect, and nothing else needs to be said beyond "I know." Ricky Rodríguez's mind amazes me, and I can think of no better friend with whom to keep the corner warm at Lil Jim's. Julia Steinmetz taught me to be a fit lay-dee. Trish Henley, my sister-wife in the attic, offered intellectual companionship and close friendship when it was most needed. Chris Gallahan is my favorite viper squirrel. Michelle Salerno has been a source of intellectual engagement and loving support for over a decade, and I am looking forward to many more.

NYU Press is the perfect home for this project. Eric Zinner is an amazing editor, and I do not know how he transformed these scraps of thoughts into a book, but I am so very grateful to him for it. Josephine Lee's work inspired me to enter the field, and I could not be more humbled to be the beneficiary of her amazing critical feedback. Another anonymous reviewer offered extraordinary advice, and I am ever in your debt. I am so lucky that Karen Tongson and Henry Jenkins were willing to take this project into their series. Karen's critical guidance has been invaluable throughout. Tim Roberts has been a great shepherd for this project, and Andrew Katz's eye is much appreciated. Finally, I am thankful to Ciara McClaughlin and Alicia Nadkarni for their wisdom and assistance.

This book is written under the sign of those who have gone before, including my late grandfather George Letson, Eve Sedgwick, and Randy Wray. Sam Pedraza sat in the Saloon, cried with me to Michael Jackson's "Will You Be There" after MJ's death, and was there in my darkest hours. Sam's death came in the last stages of preparing this book. He's taken an important part of my world with him. I wish that we could talk about it, but there, that's the problem . . . I will love and miss him forever.

Finally, whatever merits can be found herein belong entirely to my family. My parents, Shadi and Bill Letson, have nurtured and supported me at every turn in my life, and I simply cannot find the right way to express how much I adore and love them. May this book be a small token.

My grandparents Tatsuko and Cleo Chambers and Betty Letson are the reason that I write toward a better world: because they made this a better one for us. My precious Auntie and Uncle, Dr. Shadoan Chambers-Corkrum and Dr. Bob Corkrum, inspired me to pursue a PhD, and they are second parents to me. Although I wish I could name every member of my giant family, I am grateful in particular to Jeannie and Robin Ballard, Sonia, Jeff, and Chad Hinkley, Brenda and Tom Maw, Stacey and Dave Letson, Corey and Tammy Bendetti, Mika and Gabo Mateos, Takao and Mika Yoshikawa, Midori Ikemoto, Toshiko Morinaka, Gwen Chambers, and Christian and Derrick Hodge. Joshua Rains is my greatest source of support and the love of my life. You have filled my world with so much love and carried me when I could not walk any further on my own. Thank you is not enough. Momo is a welcome addition to our weird family. Lastly, the great and powerful Izumi is the best companion in the world, and I could not have written this without her encouragement, barking, and willingness to keep my feet warm as I worked. She is staring at me right now. We are going to take a long-deferred walk along the lake.

A different version of chapter 2 first appeared in *MELUS: Journal of the Society for the Study of the Multi-Ethnic Literature of the United States* 36, no. 4 (Winter 2011), edited by Tina Chen, and is reprinted by permission of the journal.

A version of chapter 5 first appeared in *Journal of Popular Music Studies* 23, no. 3 (2011), edited by Gus Stadler and Karen Tongson, and is reprinted by permission of the journal.

# Introduction: Performance, Law, and the Race So Different

Bashir, a former Guantánamo detainee from Pakistan, stands across the stage from Alice, his former interrogator. It is fifteen years after his time in Guantánamo. She does not recognize him, having taken pills to suppress the memories of her work in the prison. The stage is painted white, marked only by patches of distressed grays and scuffmarks from the actors' shoes. Bashir is short, with a slightly round body and thinning hair, and he wears a rumpled suit that lends an air of defeat to his figure. He stands upright and holds a bouquet of rose stems in front of him, after violently decapitating the flowers a few moments before. Alice leans up against the wall, arms drawn inward and her right hand nervously toying with fingers on the left. She is powerful, tall, and imposing, with brown hair pulled into a tight ponytail at the back. She leans back with one foot pushing against the wall behind her. Whereas Alice is healthy, living a comfortable middle-class life as a florist in Minneapolis, Bashir is stateless and ill, his body bearing the symptoms of hepatic encephalopathy. His fluttering hands serve as a constant reminder of a disease contracted and left untreated in the United States' most notorious prison. The light is dim, the sounds ambient, and the world seems suspended. Alice takes a breath and looks Bashir in the eye before she admits, "Iguanas. That's all I remember about Gitmo. Iguanas crossing the road. I was so scared of hitting one and having to pay a fucking ten thousand dollar fine." Bashir casually responds, "The iguanas were lucky. The Endangered Species Act was enforced."[1]

This scene takes place around the midpoint of the 2011 New York premiere of Frances Ya-Chu Cowhig's dark investigation of Guantánamo's legacy, *Lidless*. *Lidless* is a theatrical portrait of Bashir's racialization and subjectivation in Guantánamo. First workshopped in 2009 at the Lab Theatre of the University of Texas at Austin, before productions in Great Britain and Philadelphia, *Lidless* was presented by Page 73 Productions on the downtown Manhattan Walkerspace stage just a few weeks after the tenth anniversary of September 11. The first scene takes place at Guantánamo Bay in 2004 as Alice receives an executive memo authorizing sexual interrogation techniques before she proceeds with Bashir's interrogation. The rest of the play takes place fifteen years into the future, when Alice has placed her past in Guantánamo under erasure. She lives a seemingly normal life, running a Minnesota flower shop with her husband and daughter. This world explodes when Bashir arrives to confront his former interrogator and to demand a new liver to replace his failing organ. In encounter after painful encounter, he struggles to get Alice to remember him as he restages the scenes of their interrogation, places himself in stress positions, and ultimately coaxes Alice into playing her former role as a torturer. This reunion destroys Alice's family and highlights the intimate bonds that tie the two together. Throughout the play, law, performativity, and performance blur, blend, and collapse into each other across Bashir's body. Two scenes, in particular, emphasize the relationship between law and performance in the making of Bashir's racialized subjectivity: the initial interrogation in Guantánamo and Bashir's restaging of this interrogation in Alice's flower shop.

The play begins with the law. Before the interrogation, Alice unfolds an executive memo, which she describes as a "spankin' new strategy, straight from the top. Invasion of Space by a Female.'"[2] When warned by a colleague, "You don't have to do this," she responds, "But I'm allowed to. Dick Cheney says so.'[3] Throughout the play, *Lidless* reminds us that the law is much more than a statute or an executive order communicated in a memo. It is a process that comes to life through the interplay of juridical performativity and embodied action: the law's realization is inextricable from the performance of law.

During the interrogation scene, Alice identifies Bashir's racial difference as a Pakistani, Muslim man as a key factor in his detention at Guantánamo. Just before interrogating him, she exposes his genitals and remarks, "It appears those rumours about Asian men are lies your ladies tell to keep you to themselves."[4] The narrative repeatedly suggests that Bashir was innocent, like so many of the detainees at Guantánamo. He was incorrectly classified as an "enemy combatant" by a system of racial profiling that articulates the often conflated and/or misrecognized racial and religious difference of "Asian men" such as Bashir as tantamount to being a national security threat. As such a threat, Bashir is placed outside the law and rendered vulnerable to exceptional forms of interrogation, culminating in his rape by Alice.[5] Thus, his status as an Asian man circuitously justifies the exceptional legal status attached to his body: subject to the law but with less legal protections than an iguana.

The role of performance in Bashir's racialization and legal subjection is narrated with a theatrical vocabulary. At different points in the play, both Alice and Bashir refer to Alice's job at Guantánamo as "playing a role."[6] And when Alice cannot remember Bashir, he achieves recognition from her when he too begins to play his proper role. He assumes the choreography and even costume of the state: he covers his head with interrogation hoods, forges his body into stress positions, and offers to play a part in restaging the interrogation. Perhaps most horrifying, as Bashir later declares, he comes to identify with the very terms of the violence done to him in Guantánamo: "But the only way I kept from going crazy was by making myself love what they did to me."[7] Bashir's first performance of submission in Guantánamo is violently coerced, but the second, in the flower shop, exists in the confused space between coercion and a voluntary return to a script of subjection.

In *Lidless*, the state profiles, misrecognizes, and apprehends Bashir based on his racial difference as a Muslim and Pakistani man. His exceptional legal status is not entirely novel. It shares a familiar resemblance with the racialization of Asian immigrants and Asian Americans as potential national security threats who are subject to legal regulation while existing outside the universal assurances of the law.[8] In many ways, *Lidless* figures as a point of connection between the historical racialization of Asian Americans in the previous two centuries and contemporary forms of racialization in the era of the global war on terror (GWOT). *Lidless* is thus well situated within a tradition of Asian American plays that use the stage to document, interrogate, and complicate the processes of racialization in US law.[9]

*A Race So Different* is a study of the making of Asian American subjectivity. I argue that this process occurs through the intersection between law and performance in and on the Asian American body. As Robert S. Chang once wrote, "To bastardize Simone de Beauvoir's famous phrase, one is not born Asian American, one becomes one."[10] But what are the mechanisms by which this process takes place? In order to answer this question, this book takes seriously Michael Omi and Howard Winant's contention that "race is a matter of both social structure and cultural representation" but does so in a fashion that does not maintain the divide between the two.[11] A central contention of this book is that formations such as the law, politics, history, nation, and race are structured by and produced through overlapping and often contesting narrative and dramatic protocols akin to aesthetic forms of cultural production, representation, and popular entertainment. This book submits that aesthetic practices directly contribute to the shaping of these formations by serving as vessels for the mediation of legal, political, historical, national, and racial knowledge. *A Race So Different* analyzes racial formation through the lens of performance in order to historicize and explicate the legal and cultural mechanisms responsible for the production of racial meaning in and on the Asian American body. Bringing a performance studies perspective to bear on the study of Asian American racial formation, I suggest that it is in the places where "social structure" (the law) and "cultural representation" (performance aesthetics) become most deeply entangled on the body that they assume their greatest significance.

Interdisciplinary scholarship about law and performance has, to date, often distinguished the realm of legal ritual from the domain of aesthetic practices. Legal scholarship about performance traditionally focuses narrowly on First Amendment jurisprudence, copyright, or entertainment contract law, while theater and performance scholarship usually frames the law as either a narrative theme or part of the social/ historical background against which performance occurs.[12] This book joins an emerging body of performance studies literature that focuses on the intersection between state politics, law, and performance, most recently in the pathbreaking work of Tony Perucci and Catherine Cole.[13] Perucci's study of Paul Robeson's testimony before the House Committee on Un-American Activities demonstrates the ways in which performance can be mobilized by the state as "the field upon which politics is enacted" as well as the means by which a figure such as Robeson can deploy performance in order to disrupt "the containment of the theatrical frame secured and held at bay by" the government.[14] While the relationship between aesthetics and the performance of politics is important to Perucci's analysis, his primary focus is on the staging and disruption of political power, rather than the law as such. In turn, Cole observes that theater and performance scholars have generally approached the study of legal phenomena, such as South Africa's Truth and Reconciliation Commissions, by focusing "on theatrical or aesthetic representations of

the commission rather than on the commission itself as performance."[15]
She calls on performance studies scholars to bring their expertise to the
study of law *as* performance in order to open up a more robust understanding of legal procedure's social function. At the same time, by doing
so, Cole largely (and understandably) moves away from the analysis of
aesthetic objects.[16]

The present study insists that partitioned critical approaches that focus
on either legal ritual *or* aesthetic practices cannot adequately account for
the fact that (1) there is an aesthetics to the law, including performance
conventions and theatricality, and (2) performance, theater, and art
often function as agents of the law. Because performances are embodied
acts that occur in quotidian and aesthetic arenas, regularly blurring the
spaces between them, the performance studies approach of *A Race So
Different* allows us to understand the process of legal racialization without privileging the law over cultural production, or vice versa. That is,
through the lens of performance theory, we can begin to see how racialization occurs in the critical space where law and performance coexist
across the individual subject's body and in the cultural bloodstream of
the body politic. As such, this book demonstrates how a performance
studies approach to racial formation that accounts for the concurrence of
law, politics, and performance aesthetics can contribute to a more robust
understanding of the construction of social and racial realities in the
contemporary United States.

In the remainder of this introduction, I articulate the key terms and
concepts that frame this study. I show how the law is (1) performative,
(2) structured by acts of performance, and (3) mediated through aesthetic performance pieces. Like Bashir, Asian Americans are interpellated into a form of legal subjectivity that is figured as simultaneously
included within and excluded from the normative application of the law.
I describe this as a state of racial exception. I show how the law does
more than project this curious juridical status onto Asian American
bodies; it calls on the Asian American subject to perform in a fashion
that confirms his or her exceptional racial subjectivity. To be clear, this
book does not aim to prove the existence of racial exception. Theories of
a simultaneously interior and exterior national subjectivity have already
been established in the previous literature on Asian American racialization.[17] Rather, I take the racially exceptional status of Asian Americans
as a point of departure in order to demonstrate the mutually implicated
role of law and performance in the making of Asian American subjectivity as such. In doing so, I hope to show how the lens of performance can

help us to better understand Asian American racial formation in three key ways: (1) it gives us a frame for the historicization of the process of Asian American racialization; (2) it provides us with tools for complicating and contesting Asian American subjectification and subjection; and (3) it highlights the critical role that the racialization of Asian and Asian American subjects continues to play in the racial, political, and legal order of the United States.

## Performance Variations

Throughout what follows, I use the term *performance* in an expansive fashion to describe embodied acts of self-presentation. This use is aligned with Erving Goffman's definition of *performance* as "all the activity of a given participant on a given occasion which serves to influence in any way any of the other participants."[18] This broad definition allows us to think of a wide range of presentational and communicative behaviors as performance. This is particularly useful in a study of the law, given the law's reliance on forms of ritual or legal habitus. Of course, the law is also performative, which is to say that the law is structured by series of speech acts that produce a *doing* in the world. But this *doing* ties the performativity of the law to performance insofar as legal performativity is given form when the law manifests itself in and on the body through expressive acts. The spaces of everyday life are stages on which people perform for the law and, as such, become subject to the law. But if we are to think of performance in such a broad fashion, how can we differentiate between specific modalities of performance? How can we account for the difference between the representational acts of a lawyer before a military tribunal in Guantánamo and Cowhig's fictional representation of one Guantánamo detainee's life?

Even in the expansive use of the term *performance*, it carries a trace of its commonsense root: dramatic or theatrical aesthetics. This book does not set out to clarify the difference between quotidian forms of performance and aesthetic forms. Rather, it shows how the confusion between the two plays a significant role in the exercise of the law and in the making of legal and racial subjectivity. For definitional clarity, I describe everyday acts of self-presentation, including legal habitus, with the term *quotidian performance*. In turn, performances that are characterized by their nature as aesthetic works of cultural production are referred to as *aesthetic performances*. This includes theatrical works such as *Lidless* as well as performance art and popular music. The term is also used to discuss objects normally assessed within the frame of visual culture, such as a website or a series of photographs. Such objects may serve to document past performances or function as performances in their own right. Aesthetic performances are usually a step removed from everyday forms of self-presentation and are often self-consciously representational in nature. Audiences and spectators are meant to encounter them *as aesthetic experiences.*

This book is made up of a series of critical cross-maneuvers, navigating through various phenomena including legal performatives and legal rituals, acts of political and legal self-presentation by Asian American subjects, and Asian American aesthetic practices. In moving between and across these spaces, the reader will note that the distinction between quotidian performance and aesthetic performance is at times muddied and collapses entirely at other times. *A Race So Different* emphasizes the points at which the distinction between the legal and the aesthetic break down, pushing against the strict division or opposition of the two that is sometimes maintained by traditional disciplinary approaches in both the humanities and the social sciences. By organizing my study under a broad definition of performance, while attending to the specific impact of different modalities of performance, I aim to demonstrate not simply that the law has both a performative and an aesthetic dimension but that aesthetic performances often take on a legal function by serving as agents of the law. Before I can move forward with a discussion of the intersection of law and aesthetics (or performativity and performance) in the making of Asian American subjectivity, it is important first to articulate the specific conditions that define Asian American racialization.

## "A Race So Different"

Bashir's contention in *Lidless* that the "iguanas were lucky [because the] Endangered Species Act was enforced" translates the actual legal conditions that occurred in Guantánamo. It is indicative of a state in which the racialized subject is at once drawn into the regulatory apparatuses of the law while the law itself exists in a state of suspension. In the Supreme Court's landmark 2008 case *Boumediene v. Bush*, the High Court disappointed both Congress and the Bush administration by determining that Guantánamo detainees have the right to access and petition US courts for a writ of habeas corpus, or the right to appear before a judge and petition for release from detention.[19] Lawyers for the Justice Department asserted that Guantánamo, which is technically in

Cuba, is not a part of the United States and therefore not subject to US law. Two pages into a lawyer's brief filed on behalf of one of the detainees, a Jordanian national of Palestinian descent named Jamil El-Banna, El-Banna's lawyers refuted the government's position by simply stating, "U.S. law applies at Guantanamo."[20] In order to illustrate this contention, the brief cited the Endangered Species Act and explained, "Animals there, including iguanas, are protected by U.S. laws and regulations, and anyone, including any federal official, who violates those laws is subject to U.S. Civil and criminal penalties."[21] In other words, iguanas had more legal protections at Guantánamo than the prisoners did. So while the law "applies" in the prison, its force is suspended in relation to the bodies of the detainees. Translating this phenomenon into a theatrical medium, Cowhig's play gives this paradox flesh and form, allowing an audience to grasp some of its complex and contradictory implications.

This paradoxical legal status is not an invention of the GWOT. Rather, it has been a central feature of Asian American racialization in US law since the nineteenth century. The Japanese American concentration camps of World War Two, for example, bear a familiar resemblance to the suspension of the law at Guantánamo. Fred Korematsu, whose legal challenge to the Japanese American concentration camps is discussed in greater detail in chapters 3 and 4, states as much in an amicus curiae (friend of the court) brief filed in support of three men detained at Guantánamo in 2003. The brief submits that Korematsu's experience of detention "without a hearing, and without any adjudicative determination that he had done anything wrong," provides him with a "distinctive, indeed, unique perspective on the issue presented by the case."[22] Korematsu then concludes, "Although the specific legal issues presented in these cases differ from those the United States has faced in the past, the extreme nature of the government's position is all-too-familiar."[23] Tracing these familiar resemblances is one of the central critical imperatives of *A Race So Different.*

The title of this book is drawn from another example of the "all-too-familiar" suspension of the law in its application to the Asian / Asian American body. Dissenting in *Plessy v. Ferguson,* the infamous 1896 Supreme Court case in which the Court maintained the constitutionality of legal segregation for African Americans, Justice John Marshal Harlan famously opposed Jim Crow laws by arguing, "Our Constitution is color-blind, and neither knows nor tolerates classes among citizens. In respect of civil rights, all citizens are equal before the law."[24] As many critics of the color-blind Constitution have shown, Harlan's rhetoric of equality achieved the subordination of difference while maintaining a racial hierarchy that privileged whiteness as a neutrally central legal subject position.[25] But if Harlan believed that African Americans could be provisionally included within the definition of universal legal personhood protected by the Constitution, Harlan was quick to observe that the Chinese were "a race so different from our own that we do not permit those belonging to it to become citizens of the United States . . . [and who are], with few exceptions, absolutely excluded from our country."[26] As such, even with Harlan's limited expansion of constitutional protections to black subjects, the Chinese were produced as juridically exceptional limit figures against which the purportedly universal rights attached to US citizenship could be realized.

The problem, of course, is that Chinese people had not been "absolutely excluded" from the country. Or, more nearly, their legislative exclusion was relatively recent, having only been enacted with the 1882 Chinese Exclusion Act.[27] Chinese and other Asian immigrants had been entering the country for over half a century before the act was passed and upheld by the Supreme Court in *Chae Chan Ping v. United States*, a ruling for which Harlan was in the majority.[28] So while (on its face) the law simply *excluded* a group on the grounds of race and nation, the actual effect was far more complicated for Asian immigrants and Asian Americans *already within* the boundaries of the nation. Harlan's rhetoric posited this "race so different" as at once within the nation while being "absolutely excluded" from it. This juridical status, simultaneously included in and excluded from the privileges and protections of the universal assurances of citizenship on the basis of race, is understood throughout this book as a state of racial exception.[29]

This book does not aim to (re)prove the fact of racial exception, but it is worth explaining the ways in which this concept will function here. I theorize racial exception by drawing together established theories of Asian American racialization with political theories of the state of exception as a space in which the law is in force but suspended. The term *racial exception* is utilized to serve as shorthand for the specifically juridical construction of Asian American subjectivity as shuttling in and out of the law, figured as always already illegal. This theorization of Asian American subjectivity is not novel, in and of itself. However, by using a term that emphasizes the juridical status of Asian Americans as simultaneously located within and outside the law, I am able to maintain focus on the importance of the law as a key factor in Asian American racialization.

The diverse populations that make up Asian America have long been cobbled together by dominant racial discourses that treat Asian Americans as perpetually foreign, always already illegal, or an invading mob *and* model minority that is both included within and excluded from the national body politic. During the Asian exclusion era, the US cultural imaginary struggled to manage Asian populations already within the country through a process that David Palumbo-Liu describes as the interplay of introjection and projection, creating "an image of Asians located *not* 'in' Asia *nor* in the United States, but of shifting and often contrary *predications* of 'Asia' into the U.S. imaginary."[30] The Asian American body began to shuttle between inclusion and expulsion, or what Karen Shimakawa defines as "national abjection," whereby the abjection of the Asian body allows for the constitution of "stable borders/subjects."[31] As Shimakawa notes, national abjection "does not result in the formation of an Asian American subject *or* even an Asian American object," because the abject is neither subject nor object.[32] My use of *racial exception* thus serves two purposes. While relational to and compatible with introjection/projection and abjection, *exception* emphasizes the specific role that the law plays in the racialization of Asian Americans. Second, because the law requires a properly constituted subject in order for the body to be recognizable within legal discourse, *exception* explains the processes by which the law *makes* subjects out of bodies in order to apprehend them as such.

The concept of the *exception* has uniquely juridical valences born from a discussion between two Weimar-era theorists who existed on opposite ends of the political spectrum: Carl Schmitt, a conservative, Catholic jurist who ultimately joined the Nazi party, and Walter Benjamin, a Jewish, Marxist philosopher who committed suicide at the Franco-Spanish border when he could not escape the expanding sphere of Nazi occupation. Despite Schmitt's repulsive political biography, his diagnoses of law and politics remain illuminating, provocative, and descriptively correct. In 1922, Schmitt theorized the state of exception as a moment when, during a crisis, the normative juridical order is suspended in order to protect the long-term security of the state's constitutional order.[33] For Schmitt, the exception was at the core of sovereign practice, as the authority of the sovereign was defined by the ability to decide the exception.[34] Benjamin also defines the norm, or rule, as related to a category of exception. However, Benjamin describes the "state of emergency" as a perennial state characterizing the very existence of subordinated and subaltern groups. As he argued, "The tradition of the oppressed teaches us that the 'state of emergency' in which we live is not the exception but the rule."[35] For oppressed peoples taken as a whole, the state of exception is not simply a singular moment or decision but the very condition that characterizes subjection and subjectification. The norms prescribed by the dominant culture exist in dialectical relationship to this permanent state of emergency experienced by the oppressed masses. For the oppressed, the state of exception (or emergency) *is* the norm.

Racial exception is a combination of the preceding theories of Asian American racialization and the concept of a legal state of exception. Benjamin bridges the gap between these theories as he helps us to conceive of the ways in which certain subjects face a permanent state of exception, or at the very least the permanent possibility of its invocation.[36] It is this exigency that animates the historical frame of this book. The past 150 years have been characterized by repeated military conflicts, often as a result of the United States' imperialist agenda in the Pacific theater as well as in South Asia (Pakistan) and Central Asia (Afghanistan). If Asian-immigrant and Asian American subjects are figured as a threat to the ideal body politic because of their perpetually foreign status during times of peace, in times of war with Asian nations, the ethnic Asian in America becomes spectacularly understood as a national security threat. As a result, in the contemporary moment—which is otherwise casually celebrated as being "postracial"—ethnic Asian bodies within the sphere of US law continue to be produced as potential security threats and are thus subject to the law's capricious suspension.

*A Race So Different* offers a historicization of the present and the significant role that race continues to play in US law and politics. In doing so, I mean to emphasize the ways in which contemporary figurations of race within US law are built on the "all-too-familiar" juridical architecture designed to contain the threat posed by Asian-immigrant and Asian American difference throughout US history. This is the chief reason that I begin this book with the example of *Lidless*. *Lidless* allows us to open up a discussion of the significant points of connection between the racialization of Muslim and brown bodies (including Middle Eastern, South Asian, Southeast Asian, and Central Asian subjects) in the GWOT and the racialization of Asian immigrants and their descendants in the century and a half prior.[37] In anticipation of this argument, however, a brief discussion of the ways in which bodily difference was initially accounted for in US law is necessary in order to establish the unique role that exception plays in US racial formation.

From the inception of the republic, it attempted to articulate its ideal body politic as universally equal while at the same time defining it as racially homogeneous (white, colonial, Anglo-Saxon, Protestant), landed, and male. It was thus paradoxically founded on the simultaneity of Enlightenment ideals of egalitarianism and the stratified hierarchies of a settler-colonialist order structured by the interactive logics of bourgeois, white-supremacist patriarchy.[38] As disruptive but necessary presences, women, African slaves, free African Americans, bonded European servants, and Native Americans could not simply be wished away or ignored. As such, their political subjectivity was legally fragmented away from them, disaggregated from their bodies and placed back in the hands of their fathers/husbands, owners, and wards.[39] Legal fragmentation was central to the design of the Constitution and intended to settle the crisis that differently gendered, racialized, and classed bodies posed to the integrity of the state. As Supreme Court Justice Thurgood Marshall once observed,

> I [do not] find the wisdom, foresight, and sense of justice exhibited by the framers particularly profound. To the contrary, the government they devised was defective from the start.... When the Founding Fathers used this phrase ["We the People"] in 1787, they did not have in mind the majority of America's citizens. "We the People" included, in the words of the framers, "the whole Number of free Persons." On a matter so basic as the right to vote, for example, Negro slaves were excluded, although they were counted for representational purposes—at three-fifths each. Women did not gain the right to vote for over a hundred and thirty years. These omissions were intentional.[40]

Women, African Americans, bonded servants, and Native Americans were thus divided away from "the whole Number of free Persons" by virtue of their legally fragmented status. The legal fragmentation of racialized subjects continues to play a role in the maintenance of the state in the present day. As J. Kēhaulani Kauanui demonstrates, for example, Native Hawaiians are fragmented through the imposition of blood-quantum classification schemes that categorically decrease the number of "authentic" native subjects as "a condition for sovereign dispossession in the service of settler colonialism."[41] Legal fragmentation is thus inextricable from the identity of the United States as both a constitutional republic and a colonial empire.

In mapping out the definition and immediate effects of legal fragmentation, I mean to differentiate this form of subjection and racialization from what I am describing as exception. While fragmentation and exception are compatible, are structurally similar in some respects, and have shared outcomes (subordination, disenfranchisement, and/or genocide), fragmentation and exception function differently from a legal standpoint. Fragmentation is accounted for, written into, and even constitutive of the established legal order. In turn, the exception is invoked to manage subjects who are not otherwise accounted for or even anticipated by US law.

Historically, invocation of the exception allowed for the maintenance of the racial and social hierarchies put into place in the early law of the republic. In the nineteenth century, the emergence of global labor markets alongside US imperial expansion into and beyond both the Atlantic and Pacific introduced subjects who posed a threat to the US legal order in the form of Asian and Latino/a waves of migration. As Schmitt observed, "The exception, which is not codified in the existing legal order, can at best be characterized as a case of extreme peril, a danger to the existence of the state, or the like. But it cannot be circumscribed factually and made to conform to a preformed law."[12] While the US government initially experimented with the expansion of "preformed law" already in place for the management/subjection of Native Americans and African Americans, such attempts were fraught and often incomplete. New legal techniques had to be developed in order to manage the threat that Asian and Latina/o racial difference posed to the myth of a uniform and united "We the People."[13] Rather than simply doing away with the law, however, jurists began to strategically suspend certain provisions as applied to racialized subjects. This is what Giorgio Agamben describes as a legal ban, when the law is "in force without significance."[14] As I show throughout this book, Asian immigrants and Asian Americans from the nineteenth century to the present have often been drawn into the regulative sphere of US law at the very moment that its protections and assurances are suspended.

Racial exception was not reserved for Asian America alone, as it largely began to replace fragmentation as a legal technology for regulating racialized subjects after Reconstruction. The fragmented civic subjectivity of African Americans and women was arguably relinquished with the passage of the Fourteenth, Fifteenth, and Nineteenth Amendments. As is clear in the majority's ruling in *Plessy*, black bodies also began to meet with techniques of legal suspension.[45] And, like Asian Americans, Latino Americans and Latino immigrants were regularly met with a regime of legal suspension. Thus, as racialization often occurs within a comparative framework, much of my analysis throughout this book attends to the comparative racialization of different ethnic and racial groups in the United States. For minoritarian populations within the United States, the permanent possibility of the suspension of the universal assurances of the law is no longer the exception but the rule.

The question that animates this book is thus not whether racial exception exists for racialized subjects in the United States. What is of interest is the question of *how* exceptional racialization occurs: what technologies produce racial knowledge in and on the racialized body, and how might the historicization of this process help us understand the ongoing significance of the exception in contemporary racial formation? I submit that the key to this answer is a focus on the interplay of performance, performativity, and the law, because it is through the collapsing of these phenomena that racial knowledge takes hold of (inhabits, choreographs, and shapes) the raced body and makes it into a racialized subject. As such, this book is about the power of performance aesthetics insofar as performance is that which transforms legal performatives into embodied realities, as much as it can be the means through which the body disrupts the interpellative trajectory of the law in order to posit and present other alternatives. The remainder of this introduction thus attempts to break down the space between performance, performativity, aesthetics, and law in the context of Asian American racialization.

## Timorous Fiction: Legal Performativity and the Making of Asian Americans

So far, I have discussed the relationship of the law to performance, but I have only peripherally discussed the performativity of the law. The law is performative. It is composed of linguistic utterances and acts (statutes, policies, executive memos, judicial opinions) that do more than describe the world, because they produce a *doing* in it through their very utterance or inscription. In the language of J. L. Austin, Justice Harlan's declaration that the Chinese are "a race so different" is not constative; it is performative.[46] That is, Harlan did not in fact "'describe' or 'report' or constate anything at all," because in the uttering of the phrase, he achieved the *doing* of something.[47] Agents of the law do more than determine facts; they produce subjects through their performative utterances. As Austin observed, "a judge's ruling makes law; a jury's finding makes a convicted felon."[48] Harlan's declaration must thus be understood as part of a network of performative utterances that produced and confirmed the exceptional legal status of Asian Americans by naming and simultaneously "making" them into a "race so different." Although legal discourse masquerades as factual and descriptive, it is in fact central to the production of social meaning and reality through its enunciation.

Legal discourse forgets its own performative power, transforming a court's performative utterance into a codified reality. Whether or not the person subject to a jury's finding committed the felony, the jury's finding *makes* him or her a convicted felon as a fact of law unless and until a higher authority intervenes to overturn this determination. As Austin warned, "Of all people, jurists should be best aware of the true state of affairs. Perhaps some now are. Yet they will succumb to their own timorous fiction, that a statement of 'the law' is a statement of fact."[49] But the United States has a stare decisis system, whereby a decision in a given case will determine future application of the law. In such a system, a jurist may never have to succumb to this timorous fiction because a court that makes a factually erroneous determination transforms this error into a legal fact just by uttering it. Stare decisis allows a statement of law to retroactively become a statement of fact at the exact moment that a judge's ruling exceeds the constative function of a legal declaration in order to *make* law, to *make* a convicted felon, to *make* an enemy combatant, or to *make* Asian Americans into *a race so different*.

The law's misrecognition of Bashir as an "enemy combatant" in *Lidless* may well have been a fiction, but this was cold comfort to the man as he suffered in his Guantánamo cell. In many ways, little has changed since Thomas Hobbes issued his famous maxim, *auctoritas non veritas facit legem* (authority, not truth, makes the law), and this has grave consequences for racialized subjects when they are caught up within and misrecognized by the law. Because a legal declaration announces itself as the articulation of an established legal fact at the same time that it *makes* the law, the legal production of subjects is neither purely constative nor purely performative but both. As Jacques Derrida argued in his analysis of the US Declaration of Independence, it is precisely the "undecidability between, let's say, a performative structure and a constative structure, [that] is *required* in order to produce the sought-after effect" of giving simultaneous birth to a nation and the national subjects ("We the People") that authorize this event.[50] The law makes We the People, but, at the same time, it only comes into being as We the People play their properly cast role *as* We the People. In chapter 3's analysis of performances of patriotism in the Japanese American concentration camps of World War Two, I further demonstrate how it is in performance that the people realize the constitutional *being* and constitutive power of the state. This occurs through embodied acts that correlate with the formal ideals of the state, such as the Constitution or the law. Performance *makes* the nation. It is also what makes national and racial subjects.

The juridical performative can only go so far in making us into We the People or transforming Asian America into "a race so different." As a result, the interplay between legal performativity and embodied acts, or performances, is key to understanding how racialization occurs. By now the reader has hopefully noticed that we are gliding across the slippery ground between performativity and performance, or what Eve Kosofsky Sedgwick and Andrew Parker describe as a "generalized iterability, a pervasive theatricality common to stage and world alike."[51] The mechanisms productive of national and racial subjects are inherently theatrical, an assertion that I can best explicate through a close reading of a classic and paradigmatic example of subject production, Louis Althusser's "Ideology and Ideological State Apparatuses."

Describing "ideological state apparatuses" as the means by which the state reproduces a population's "submission to the ruling ideology," Althusser suggests that the state does not simply force itself on the subject but is most effective when it can seduce large masses of the people into willing submission.[52] Tellingly, he defines the law as *both* a repressive state apparatus *and* an ideological state apparatus (it is the only state apparatus that enjoys this dual status).[53] And as his paradigmatic example, he famously describes a "theoretical scene [*la scène théoretique*]" in which a police officer shouts out "hey you there," and the hailed person turns around.[54] Submitting to the recognition of the hail, "he [or she] becomes a *subject*" for the law.[55] The word *scène* in Althusser's description of interpellation translates as both "scene" and "stage," figuring the act of interpellation as a dramatic act, or a staged encounter between the law and the subject. Later, he even describes his illustration as "my little theoretical theater [*notre petit théâtre théoretique*]."[56] If we are to take seriously the metaphors by which he explains the process of interpellation, we see that "one becomes" or is "made" a subject through theatrical protocols.

Althusser is situated in a long tradition of Marxist criticism that relies on metaphors of performance. Marx himself describes commodities as circulating between "*dramatis personae*"; he refers to the market as a "stage," narrates the tale of a table that is "dancing of its own free will," and states that "the great events and characters of world history" occur as either "high tragedy" or "low farce."[57] But Althusser does more than simply invoke a rhetoric of theatricality to explain subject production; he shows us how subjection is itself a dramatic ritual. Elsewhere he even suggests that theatrical spectatorship can be a means for the making of a revolutionary, class-conscious form of subjectivity. In a short and oft-overlooked essay on the playwrights Carlo Bertolazzi and Bertolt Brecht, published in the decade before he wrote the essay on ideology, Althusser claimed that theater has the capacity for inspiring "the production of a new consciousness in the spectator" and, in the making of a new consciousness, a new mode of political subjectivity: "the play is really the production of a new spectator, an actor who starts where the performance ends, who only starts so as to complete it, but in life."[58] Through the experience of a truly revolutionary theater, Althusser's spectator becomes an "actor" who carries the momentum of the play out into the world, performing in a fashion that will realize the play's revolutionary ambitions, "but in life." The language of theatricality in the process of subjection conjures a similar image, as one is made a subject for the law by performing in response and accordance to its hail. Thus, subjection is both a legal and political process as well as a theatrical and aesthetic one. Subjection occurs through performance as the legal, the political, and the aesthetic mix together across the body.

But what is it that compels the subject to perform submission to the hail of the law? In *Lidless*, the law's misrecognition of Bashir as an "enemy combatant" because of his racial and religious difference tautologically results in a situation in which Alice (and, by extension, US law) treats him as if he were an enemy combatant. Fifteen years after leaving Guantánamo, the only way for him to become recognizable to Alice is by playing the role of the enemy combatant—that is, the torture victim. And, as he admits, this is a role that he has come to love in order to keep "from going crazy." Bashir's case exemplifies the ways in which legal interpellation can be perversely seductive. As Judith Butler remarks, in her assessment of the Althusserian scene, "This turning toward the voice of the law is a sign of a certain desire to be beheld by and perhaps also to behold the face of authority. . . . [It is] a mirror stage . . . that permits the misrecognition without which the sociality of the subject cannot be achieved."[59] In Bashir and Alice's twisted exchange, the *Lidless* audience is privy to Cowhig's restaging of this "theoretical scene." We watch as Bashir is made a subject for the law after his dominated body is seduced into performing the very subject position for which he was misrecognized in the first place.

Bashir describes the simultaneously seductive and coercive process of his interpellation as an "enemy combatant" by Alice thus: "When you were hard—when you screamed, ordered boards and chains—that was simple. I could go somewhere else. But when you were soft—when you touched my ears, my neck—my body had a will of its own. My own flesh, my own muscle, betrayed me."[60] Unwilling to hear more, Alice begs him, "Stop. No more. Please." Demonstrating the way in which the language of domination often finds its way into the mouth of the dominated, Bashir repeats her phrase but echoes it back to her with the urgency of a Guantánamo detainee during the act of torture: "Stop. No more. Please. I swear I'm an innocent man. I don't know Osama or Saddam or Khalid. I was studying at a mosque. I just wanted to be a good Muslim. Please, I beg you. Believe me."[61] He throws a bag onto the floor before asking once more, "Please." There is a long silence and then, as if something triggers a switch inside of her, she grabs him and wrenches his arms behind his back. She orders him, "Drop to your hands and knees. Now crawl. Go! There's a plastic bag by your feet. Pull the bag over your head and bend forward at the waist."[62] Bashir knows the choreography and positions his body into a stress position, waiting expectantly for the next order.

Alice only recognizes Bashir *after* he returns to the role scripted for him in the Bush administration memo. In other words, Bashir becomes a subject by performing a role for which he was cast by way of misrecognition. His subjectivity is brought into being through a performance of coercive mimeticism, a practice that Rey Chow describes by way of a revision to Althusser's *scène théoretique*:

> It is to say, "Yes, that's me" to a call and a vocation—"Hey, Asian!" "Hey, Indian!" "Hey, gay man!"—as if it were a crime with which one has been charged; it is to admit and submit to the allegations (of otherness) that society at large has made against one. Such acts of confession may now be further described as a socially endorsed, coercive mimeticism, which stipulates that the thing to imitate, resemble, and become is none other than the ethnic or sexual minority herself.[63]

In acts of coercive mimeticism, the minoritarian subject believes that by responding to the hail of minority status through self-referential performances, she is "liberating" herself from subordination. But while she may achieve some modicum of recognition and relief, she is inadvertently contributing to the maintenance of the dominant structures of ideology, interpellation, and racialization. This is particularly dangerous when the law is involved because, as Antonio Viego observes, "If misrecognition is a serious harm, then we must be concerned that legal recognition may go wrong, misrecognizing already subordinated groups and codifying that misrecognition with the force of law and the intractability of stare decisis, . . . [whereby] the price of protection is incarceration."[64] If Bashir demands recognition from Alice for his time in Guantánamo, the price extracted in the preceding scene is his figurative return to the interrogation chamber. In other words, when we perform as properly situated subjects in order to be recognizable as such by the law, we run the risk of transforming our bodies into prisons.

## Between Performance and Law

That subjection occurs through the enactment of protocols that are theatrical in nature is unsurprising given that the law and dramatic performance both radically blur the space between law and the aesthetics of performance. My understanding of the law as a living entity, one that is realized through legal habitus and interpretive performances, is indebted to a progressive strand of US jurisprudence that conceives of the law as, in the words of a young lawyer who later became Supreme Court Justice Louis Brandeis, a "living law."[65] But it is equally influenced by Schmitt's argument that "all law is situational law."[66] If legal positivism conceives of the law as a system of closed norms, a legal realist and/or critical race theory approach submits that the law is messy, imprecise, imperfect, and always relational to the situation or context in which it is enacted and applied. Because "the legal idea cannot translate itself independently," writes Schmitt, it requires an intermediary (in the form of the judge, lawyer, or law enforcement officer), which amplifies the always already political nature of legal determination.[67] In this way, the legal functionary's job has a familiar resemblance to that of an actor.

Because the law is an embodied art, theatricality is a constitutive component of the law. Judges and legal functionaries interpret the law in much the same way as an actor interprets (and necessarily improvises) a script or character. In some ways, constitutional and statutory law, as well as administrative policy, is not unlike a dramatic text. Just as *Lidless* does not become a performance until the script is given a production, the executive memo "straight from the top" only becomes law in its fullest sense when an agent of the law (Alice) enacts it. As Hobbes wrote, "law is a command, and a command consisteth in declaration, or manifestation of the will of him that commandeth, by voice, writing, or some other sufficient argumentation of the same."[68] The law should thus be properly understood as the union of performance and performativity.

The law has become no less theatrical in the transition from monarchial sovereignty to popular democracy. This is primarily because democracy retains and even amplifies the representational aspects of monarchism. Hobbes provides us with a particularly useful explanation of the theatrical nature of representative politics by describing two forms of persons: the "natural" person (someone "considered as his own") and the "feigned or artificial person."[69] He notes that the term *person* is rooted in the Latin *persona*, which "signifies the *disguise*, or *outward appearance* of a man, counterfeited on the stage."[70] Hobbes surprisingly declines the antitheatrical sentiment common to Western political thought (paradigmatically modeled in Plato's *Republic*), as neither the terms "counterfeited" nor "outward appearances" are used in a pejorative fashion.[71] Instead, he draws a clear equivalence between the mode of artificial personage that occurs in a legal setting and that which occurs on the stage:

> And from the stage, [person] hath been translated to any representer of speech and action, as well in tribunals, as theaters. So that a *person*, is the same that an *actor* is, both on the stage and in common conversation; and to *personate*, is to *act* or *represent* himself, or another; and he that acteth another is said to bear his person, or act in his name; (in which sense Cicero useth it where he says, *Unus sustineo tres personas; mei, adversarii, et judicis,* I bear three persons; my own, my adversary's, and the judge's;) and is called in divers occasions, diversely; as a *representer*, or *representative*, . . . an *actor*, and the like.[72]

Whether the representative is monarch or a member of the House of Representatives, this political figure realizes the unity of the state through the representative practice of *acting* on behalf of the state's subjects: "A multitude of men, are made *one* person, when they are by one man, or one person represented."[73] Read thus through Hobbes, political theater and legal theatrics should not be understood as a distraction from the real stuff of law and politics. Performance and theatricality are central components of both.

The theatricality of the law is distinctly important in the case of the US justice system, an importance intensified by the historical events that inspired *Lidless*. The US political and legal system is, for better or worse, representative: politicians and lawyers act as representatives of their constituents or clients. So if Hobbes observed a blurring between the theatrical and the legal forms of representation, the lawyer's art *as a performer* becomes a key means for countering forms of critical injustice. Take for example Guantánamo advocates Mark P. Denbeaux and Jonathan Hafetz's introduction to a volume of interviews with Guantánamo lawyers: "[The detainees] were all held in secret and denied communication with their families and loved ones. Most, if not all, were subjected to extreme isolation, physical and mental abuse, and, in some instances, torture. Many were innocent; none was provided an opportunity to prove it. These are their stories. The stories are told by their lawyers because the prisoners themselves were silenced."[74] The prisoners, who are "silenced" by the US state, have no immediate recourse to speak their own stories to the general public, to their families, or even in a court of law. The situation necessitates the imperfect solution of having others perform in their stead, revealing representational advocacy to be a limited form of artificial personage that might realize greater conditions of justice for the detainees. That Denbeaux and Hafetz conceive of the lawyer's art in the language of narrative storytelling is important because they seem to suggest that the narrative conventions employed by the advocates are equally important to their job as the factual record that they are presenting to both the public and the courts. In this sense, aesthetic practices (narrative, dramatic structure, character) can play powerful roles in a representative act meant to intervene in and reformat the conditions produced within the law. This power is not only the province of the lawyer, who adopts aesthetic traditions in the execution of his or her representative act, as the artist can deploy/wield it as well.

A Race So Different distinguishes itself from previous interdisciplinary approaches to law and aesthetics that commonly note that the primary difference between the two is that the law has a "real" impact on the world, while aesthetics registers as less impactful. For example, in Juana María Rodríguez's otherwise beautiful analysis of an asylum hearing in a US court, she argues, "Both law and literature are intrinsically concerned with language, interpretation, and reception. . . . Put succinctly, literary criticism and legal treatises are both involved with constructing credible subjects, narratives, and readings. Yet law is discourse with a difference; the stories and characters are real and the interpretations have long-lasting consequences."[75] Rodríguez correctly observes that the events that inspire legal cases are drawn from real-world events. However, anyone who has ever been represented by a lawyer will tell you that by the time one's experiences are translated into legal discourse and entered into a court record, they feel as foreign as would be a fictionalization of their story in a "ripped from the headlines" episode of *Law and Order*. This casts a dubious shadow on the notion that the stories and characters translated into the law are necessarily more consequential (or real) than those that are translated onto the dramatist's stage.

Nor am I convinced that the law is especially imbued with a capacity to produce more "long-lasting [real-world] consequences" than are dramatic and literary narratives or other forms of aesthetic production. After all, most people have probably gleaned more legal knowledge from a show such as *Law and Order* than they have from reading actual legal texts. Culture shapes reality, sometimes confirms it, and at times supplants it. After all, people generally believe that Julius Caesar was killed in the Roman Senate, where Shakespeare placed the act, rather than in a side chamber of the Theater of Pompey, where he was actually assassinated. Mass forms of cultural production including, and especially, theater, film, popular music, and TV often function as thinly veiled ideological state apparatuses. These "culture industries" are thus what Max Horkheimer and Theodor Adorno called "instrument[s] of domination."[76] Aesthetic narratives can have "long-lasting consequences" that become real over time. As an aesthetic medium that gives embodied form to narrative, representational modes of performance (such as theater, performance art, or even film and TV) lend legal discourse an embodied verisimilitude that helps to transform a "statement of law" into a "statement of fact" within the popular consciousness of the audience. Popular aesthetic performances function as agents of the law, circulating legal narratives through the bloodstream of popular culture.

At the same time, in making a case for the power of aesthetics as legal agents, I do not want to idealize aesthetic practices *over* the law. In a discussion of the role of tribunals in response to the trauma of the Holocaust, Shoshana Felman seems to do as much when she writes, "Law is a discipline of limits and of consciousness. We needed limits to be able both to close the case and to enclose it in the past. Law distances the Holocaust. Art brings it closer. We needed art—the language of infinity—to mourn the losses and to face up to what in traumatic memory is not closed and cannot be closed."[77] Felman acknowledges a need for the law but figures the law as that which "encloses" a traumatic event in the past. She suggests that art's function is to provide a closer proximity to such events, arguing that it is in the "slippage between law and art" that traumatic memory is negotiated. On this latter point, we are in agreement—it is in the slippage between law and aesthetics that real cultural work can be done to rectify past injustices. But to accept a definition of the law as "a discipline of limits and of consciousness" is to displace the slippery, "situational," and performative nature of the law. This ignores the familiar resemblance and formal relationship between law and performance and sidesteps the fact that both, being equally reliant on the "independently determining moment" of embodied action, give way to the "language of infinity." As such, while the law and aesthetic performances may both serve to "distance us" from the truth of a historical injustice, they also have the fecund potentiality to open up and rethink these injustices as we rehearse and stage the possibility of a more just future.

## "A Rehearsal for the Example": The Possibilities in Performance

In the preceding section, I sought to unsettle the line between aesthetics and the law as well as a critical rubric that would significantly privilege one over the other. In doing so, I had to sever some of our preconceptions about the causal nature of either law or performance. Or, to be more specific, while I acknowledge that both law and performance may inspire specific effects, these effects cannot necessarily be causally predicted. As I argue in chapter 4 in particular, the indeterminacy of the aesthetic encounter is precisely what allows for aesthetic performances to be a primary medium for disrupting the political and legal subjection of Asian Americans. The political power of performance is in its ability to enact, in Jacques Rancière's terms, "an unpredictable interplay of associations and dissociations."[78] Aesthetic performances are spaces that, as much as they may be used to reify dominant racial ideology, also threaten to undo the formal "associations" between, say, dominant knowledge about racial difference and the body of the racialized subject.

Aesthetic performances are the spaces in which we can stage and experience incompleteness and openness that challenges the limits and closures of racialization and racialized subjectivity. Keen to this fact, Asian American artists have long used the stage as a space to work with the audience to challenge the racialization of Asian America. As Shimakawa argues, "the dramatic space is one where audiences are arguably willing to relax those otherwise punitively enforced restrictions on bodily identity and so may afford if not a complete repudiation of those imposed identities then at least (and at its best) a problematization of or critical engagement with them."[79] Aesthetic acts of performance, precisely because of their indeterminacy, are spaces that unleash a range of possibilities that can show how there are multiple ways of being in the world beyond the identity that the dominant culture imposes or projects onto the racialized body.

In performance, we can rehearse, stage, and materialize the stuff of a better world. Performance provides us with the means to interrupt the conditions of reproduction that reify the inequities of the present. In taking this position, I mean to signal to the reader that this book should be understood as openly situated within the tradition of Marxist cultural criticism. *A Race So Different* conceives of performance in the terms of Frankfurt School philosopher Ernst Bloch, who understood the stage as "a paradigmatic institution" in the process of imagining and enacting social change.[80] Like the law, dramatic experiences require a decision, not only on the part of the performer but also on the part of the spectator: "They demand that the spectator make decisions, at the very least a decision as to whether he likes the performance as such."[81] Through decision, action is realized, and it is in action that a new politics emerges. Additionally, aesthetic performances have the unique capacity to imagine and give temporary form to otherwise impossible realities. In doing so, the stage becomes a "rehearsal" for dreaming the new and making it a reality: "As soon as the rehearsal for the example is staged the goal is clearly visible, but the stage, being experimental, that is, being a state of anticipation, tries out the ways in which to behave in order to achieve."[82] Performance at its best, by insisting on and demonstrating that *something better* is possible, verifies that this possibility can in fact become a reality.

If the space between law and aesthetics is one that is constantly traversed, blurred, and breaking down in the making of Asian American subjectivity, this book submits that both quotidian and aesthetic forms of performance can be deployed by Asian Americans as a "rehearsal for the example." As Dorinne Kondo writes, in theater and performance "Asians and Asian Americans can 'write our faces,' mount institutional interventions, enact emergent identities, refigure utopian possibilities, and construct political subjectivities that might enable us to effect political change."[83] In many ways, this is a sentiment that is shared by many of the scholars of Asian American performance who have inspired this book, including Kondo, Shimakawa, Josephine Lee, Esther Kim Lee, Sarita Echavez See, Lucy Mae San Pablo Burns, and Christine Bacareza Balance.[84] Many of the sites studied in *A Race So Different* are proof of the fact that Asian American performance can create spaces in which we model strategies for critiquing and complicating the racialization and subjection of Asian Americans, while staging otherwise impossible potentialities that push against the limits of the present.

The structure of this book is loosely chronological, tracing the production of exceptional juridical subjectivity for Asian America from the Asian-exclusion era into the GWOT. The first two chapters consider how stage performances can act as legal functionaries in their own right. In chapter 1, I return to a critical text in Asian American studies, *Madame Butterfly*, with a comparative study of the three original versions of the narrative: John Luther Long's 1898 novella *Madame Butterfly*, David Belasco's 1900 theatrical spectacle adapted from the novella, and Giacomo Puccini's 1904–7 opera *Madama Butterfly*. I read the ways in which *Madame Butterfly* functions as an agent for the dissemination of exclusion-era jurisprudence about Asian racial difference, suggesting that as a work that remains popular for contemporary audiences, it continues to influence the making of legal subjectivity for Asian Americans today. In chapter 2, I study Ping Chong and Company's 1995 experimental performance piece *Chinoiserie*, a staged history of Chinese America. If much of the history of Chinese American encounters with the law has been tainted by injustice, Ping Chong and Company use the stage to enact what I describe as "reparative justice." *Chinoiserie* engages with the legal history of Chinese America in order to restore erased Chinese American stories to history and to rethink the possibilities for emergent forms of justice for the future.

Chapters 3 and 4 turn to the realm of quotidian performance with a study of the Japanese American concentration camps. In chapter 3, I look to everyday performances of patriotism in the camps, attending to the interplay of legal performativity and embodied performance in the manifestation of racial subjectivity in and on the Japanese American body during the war. I consider how performances of patriotism had the potential to reify and sometimes disrupt the state's claim to incarcerated Japanese Americans. Chapter 4 studies the political performativity of objects, reading a scrapbook of contraband photographs of camp life taken by a Heart Mountain internee. Demonstrating the ways in which the state, and immigration law in particular, deployed a visual logic to compel Asian American subjects to perform for the state's optic, I argue that the internee's photographs pose a performative intervention into the visual surveillance and regulation of Japanese America while raising significant questions about the limits of visibility as a strategy for liberation.

The final section of the book turns to the racialization of Asian immigrants and Asian Americans from the period of the Vietnam War to the GWOT. Chapter 5 studies the performance practices of Cambodian/American band Dengue Fever in order to trace the precarious position constructed for Cambodian refugees of the Vietnam War in US law. Studying Dengue Fever's centralization of the figure of the "illegal immigrant" in its performances, I argue that the band draws attention to and interrupts the vulnerable position of Cambodian immigrants and Cambodian Americans who are subject to new forms of state violence in the era of the GWOT. In conclusion, I offer a brief meditation on racial profiling within the GWOT and on Hasan Elahi's digital performance project *Tracking Transience*. Doing so, I offer suggestions for the role that scholarship about Asian American performance might contribute to criticizing, historicizing, and potentially transforming current conditions of racialization in the era of the national security state.

Racial subjection is most successfully realized when the state is able to seduce and compel racialized bodies to perform as raced subjects. That is, when the state inspires the subject to do as Bashir did, when he learned "to love what they did" to him. Studying sites where we can see the point at which law and performance meet in and on the Asian American body, this book documents some of the central technologies by which racialized subjectivity comes into being. It is offered as a contribution to the project of understanding and historicizing the technologies of Asian American racialization in order to critically dismantle them and to bring about greater conditions of social justice. Most importantly, however, by analyzing and documenting a series of Asian American performances, the following pages make up a record of resilience and possibility. For if performance is the means by which racialization comes into being in and on the body, performance can also be a radical practice for rehearsing and realizing the long-deferred promises of justice and emancipation.

# 1 / "That May Be Japanese Law, but Not in My Country": *Madame Butterfly* and the Problem of Law

Tuan Anh Nguyen spent most of his life in the United States. He was born in Vietnam to a US American father and Vietnamese mother in September 1969. His mother abandoned Nguyen and his civilian contractor father, Joseph Boulais, when he was only a few years old. In 1975, Boulais returned to the United States with his six-year-old son, whom he continued to raise. At the age of twenty-two, Nguyen pleaded guilty to two counts of sexual assault on a minor in a Texas state court. A few years later in 1996, while serving out the terms of his eight-year sentence, Congress passed the Illegal Immigrant Reform and Immigrant Responsibility Act (IIRAIRA). IIRAIRA mandates the deportation of aliens convicted of a felony charge. As a result, the Immigration and Naturalization Service initiated deportation proceedings against Nguyen, and an immigration judge subsequently ordered his deportation to Vietnam. Despite having a citizen father and being raised by this father in the United States, the US government considered him to be an alien and targeted him for deportation to a place he hardly knew.

Nguyen's legal status was written nearly thirty years before his birth, at the height of the Korean War and the US military's occupation of Japan. In 1952, Congress passed the McCarran-Walter Act, heavily revising the section of the US code that regulates immigration and naturalization. As part of the act, the legislature clarified citizenship eligibility for children born abroad to unwed parents when only one parent is a US citizen. While children born to citizen mothers automatically receive citizenship retroactive to birth, children born to citizen fathers must meet three additional requirements for citizenship eligibility. Nguyen appealed his case, arguing that the differential burden violated both fathers' and sons' equal protection rights. (Unaware of the differential burden, Boulais had not registered his son as a citizen within the statute of limitations.) Justice Anthony Kennedy's Supreme Court opinion in *Nguyen v. INS* affirmed the constitutionality of the law, counterintuitively arguing that the three-part bar—despite the fact that it made it three times easier for fathers (often US servicemen) to escape responsibility for illegitimate children born overseas—forwarded a legitimate government interest in the "facilitation of a relationship between parent [father] and child."[1]

In a 2009 *New York Times* interview, Justice Ruth Bader Ginsburg (who was among the dissenting Justices) described *Nguyen* (and a similar case, *Miller v. Albright*) in terms that directly associated it with the legacy of US imperialism in Asia. In a surprise move, she did so by suggesting that the majority's ruling was written under the sign of a popular Orientalist opera: "They [the majority] were held back by a way of looking at the world in which a man who wasn't married simply was not responsible. There must have been so many repetitions of *Madame Butterfly* in World War II. And for Justice [John Paul] Stevens [who voted in the majority in *Nguyen* and penned the *Miller* opinion] that was part of his experience."[2] Ginsburg's interview implies that the impact of *Madame Butterfly* extends beyond the proscenium arch, insinuating itself into the high court's interpretation of the law. At the same time, she evidences the ways in which Western audiences regularly mistake the fiction of *Madame Butterfly* for a reality. As if the opera were a template for actually occurring incidents, she muses, "there must have been so many repetitions of *Madame Butterfly*." Somewhere in the middle of *Nguyen* and *Madame Butterfly*, the difference between a legal reality and an onstage theatrical spectacle collapses.

In 1907, Giacomo Puccini premiered *Madama Butterfly* at the Metropolitan Opera in New York City.[3] It is a tragic story of a Japanese bride in nineteenth-century Japan who is married to and ultimately abandoned by her US American husband, ending in the young bride's suicide. Since its debut, *Madama Butterfly* has become a centerpiece of most major opera companies' repertories, and by some accounts it is one of the most produced operas in the world. Due to its iconic and canonical status, *Madama Butterfly* has contributed significantly to the shaping of cultural stereotypes of Asian difference and Asian femininity. As such, the Butterfly narrative is a central critical object for the field of Asian American studies.[4] But how is it that *Madame Butterfly* has come to influence

FIGURE 1.1. Geraldine Farrar in the 1907 Metropolitan Opera premiere of *Madama Butterfly*. Courtesy of the Metropolitan Opera Archives.

the writing of American law, and in what surprising ways does the narrative itself function as a vessel for the transmission of knowledge produced about Asian racial difference in US law?

This chapter argues that the legal management of Asian and Asian American difference is not simply the historical background against which the various versions of Madame Butterfly were written but that the Butterfly narratives themselves function as agents for the law's codification and transmission. Madame Butterfly is a product, manifestation, and ultimately a representative of exclusion-era jurisprudence; it is part of the dominant culture's juridical unconscious. This term is a legally focused amendment to Fredric Jameson's description of literature as part of the "political unconscious," whereby "master narratives have inscribed themselves in the texts as well as in our thinking about them; such allegorical narrative signifieds are a persistent dimension of literary and cultural texts precisely because they reflect a fundamental dimension of our collective thinking and our collective fantasies about history and reality."[5] As I will demonstrate, the Butterfly narrative neatly aligns with exclusion-era jurisprudence in areas of the law ranging from the immigration code to courtroom procedure and child custody. As a work of popular entertainment, it codified and represented these narratives, giving them the verisimilitude of flesh-and-blood presence onstage while confirming and embedding them within the national culture. Furthermore, as Ginsburg's comment suggests, Madame Butterfly's legal force is not contained in the twentieth century. Due to its continued popularity, it still functions as part of the nation's juridical unconscious. It acts as a medium for the continued transmission of exclusion-era ideas about Asian racial difference, projecting these ideas onto the contemporary Asian American body.

Before continuing, I need to make one key point about my intervention into critical analyses of the Butterfly narrative. In the compendium of critical work published about the narrative, few scholars have critically interrogated the role of law in Madame Butterfly. But the law is everywhere in the heroine's tale, including lengthy discussions of the marriage contract that binds Cho-Cho-San to her US American husband, legal counsel provided by her friends after she is abandoned, and a stunning scene in which the heroine imagines herself performing before a judge in a US court. Important Asian Americanist analyses of the narrative have often overlooked the legal theme in their studies of the Orientalist configurations of gender and the spectacle of US empire in the Butterfly narrative. While some of the studies have focused on the opera, many

more have turned to works inspired by the opera, including two semi-
nal works that premiered in 1989: David Henry Hwang's Broadway play
*M. Butterfly* and Claude Michel-Schönberg and Alain Boublil's musical
*Miss Saigon*.[6] Much less attention has been paid to the two texts on which
the opera is based, John Luther Long's 1898 novella and Long and David
Belasco's successful Broadway adaptation of this work in 1900.[7] The
three original versions of *Madame Butterfly* were, like their descendants,
popular and commercial successes, but few contemporary studies offer
a comparative analysis of all three. If one looks at each version individually, the law seems simply to be an otherwise random incident of plot,
which might account for the literature's critical oversight of this factor.
However, when the versions are read comparatively, it becomes clear that
the law is a consistent concern that is central to and survives every early
iteration of the story.

A focus on the problem of law in *Madame Butterfly* is necessary insofar as it supplements a missing piece of the Butterfly puzzle. My interest
in the problem of law does not offer an alternative to critical investi-
gations of race, gender, and empire in *Madame Butterfly* so much as it
builds on this body of scholarship in order to offer a robust example of
the ways in which these phenomena are produced at the intersection of
law and performance in the narrative. It should be observed that one
of the notable exceptions to the paucity of scholarship about law and
*Madame Butterfly* is an article written by family law scholar Rebecca
Bailey-Harris. Bailey-Harris's 1991 article is a study of the "conflict of
laws" posed by *Madame Butterfly* and analyzes the recently codified
Meiji reforms of 1898 in Japan in relation to US jurisprudence of the
same time.[8] While the author provides a precise accounting for each and
every legal question that *Madame Butterfly* raises regarding both US and
Japanese law, her approach is avowedly guided by a mechanistic attention to the "issues of concern to a lawyer in the audience [that] arise from
the plot." Bailey-Harris goes so far as to ask whether the heroine would
have been "better advised to refrain from so drastic a step [her suicide]"
given the likelihood that both the United States and Japan would have
recognized her marriage.[9] Like Ginsburg, Bailey-Harris treats *Madame
Butterfly* as if it were a possible historical reality, exhibiting little critical
interest in the fact that the heroine is a fictional construct structured
by bourgeois, racist, sexist, and imperialist aesthetic conventions. As
an alternative, I offer a close reading of the problem of law in *Madame
Butterfly*, one that attends to *both* the questions of law and aesthetics,
in order to demonstrate the legal function of an aesthetic performance

which works alongside the law to transmit and codify Orientalist notions about gendered, racial difference for Asians and Asian Americans.

This chapter is divided into three parts. After mapping out the cultural significance and the historical development of the three versions of *Madame Butterfly*, I trace the alignment between Long's novella and Asian-exclusion legal discourse. Part 2 expands this analysis to focus on the legal theme within *Madame Butterfly* as it reflects Asian American jurisprudence in the late nineteenth century. Part 3 brings us into the present with a focus on Trouble, the mixed-race progeny of Pinkerton and Cho-Cho-San's love affair. I thus conclude with an assessment of the ways in which this mixed Asian figure becomes manifest as a problem for contemporary law and culture.

## Prologue: A Brief History of the Three Butterflies

It is little coincidence that the publication and dissemination of the various versions of *Madame Butterfly* occurred during a period of increased anxiety about the threats posed to national and racial borders by Asian bodies flowing in and out of the sphere of the US empire. Long's novella was published in 1898, sixteen years after the passage of the Chinese Exclusion Act and the same year that the United States officially began both the colonization of the Philippines and the illegal annexation of Hawai'i. At the end of the nineteenth century, US border definition was threatened by the empire's territorial expansion outward and the need to draw foreign bodies inward in order to satiate the needs of expanding capital.[10] Legal and cultural apparatuses thus began to mark Asians as the exception to national, legal, and cultural forms of theatrical as a means of managing and containing the crisis that they posed to the constitution of ideal borders and national subjects. As a representative of the dominant culture's juridical unconscious, *Madame Butterfly* exemplifies Lucy Mae San Pablo Burns's assertion that US American popular culture is "part of the ideological state apparatus that extend[s] U.S. cultural hegemony" and empire.[11] It manifests and embodies the racial ideology of the dominant culture through aesthetic means.

The short synopsis of all three narratives is this: a US officer, Benjamin Franklin Pinkerton, is stationed in Nagasaki, Japan. Beset by boredom, he takes a fourteen-year-old Japanese wife—Cho-Cho-San (or Cio-Cio-San in the opera). Eventually Pinkerton abandons his Japanese child-bride, who remains steadfast in the belief that he will return. In his absence, she raises their son, curiously named Trouble. Importantly,

Trouble was born after Pinkerton's departure and without his knowledge. Pinkerton's friend Sharpless, a US consular officer, remains concerned for the young woman and her son and attempts to convince the girl to remarry. She declines, believing that her marriage is protected by the laws governing marriage in the United States and that she will be able to press her case in a US court, if necessary. Pinkerton eventually returns from the states but—to Cho-Cho-San's great horror—with a white (US American) wife. As a result, Cho-Cho-San kills herself in the hopes that Pinkerton will claim and raise his son.

John Luther Long never set foot in Japan, and according to opera historian Arthur Groos, much of his narrative was pieced together from collaboration with Long's elder sister, Jennie Correll. Correll lived in Nagasaki for a number of years as a missionary before returning to the United States in 1897.[12] The centrality of the question of law in the three versions of *Madame Butterfly* may have been an accident of autobiography, as Long did not make his living as a novelist and dramatist but as a lawyer.[13] The story first reached the upper- and middle-class audience of *Century Magazine* in January 1898. It proved so popular that the magazine published a reprint in book format and in 1903 released a "Japanese edition" with illustrations. The general excitement with which the story was received was, no doubt, aided by the fact that, as noted earlier, 1898 was a significant year in the history of US imperial expansion into the Pacific.

Audiences in the United States were hungry for exotic stories of the Far East, and shortly after the book's publication, Long collaborated with theater impresario David Belasco to adapt the story into a one-act play. A one-act version of *Madame Butterfly* premiered at New York's Herald Square Theater at 10:00 p.m. on May 5, 1900, with a production price of $4,000.[14] The play's literary merits are less impressive than its historical and cultural significance, and it was a success primarily because of Belasco's trademark technological innovation. The production received rave reviews and wowed audiences with its incorporation of emergent visual technologies made possible by the shift from gas to electric lighting. Belasco fused novel design elements with extreme naturalist conventions to produce an air of authenticity, convincing audiences that they were seeing an accurate representation of Japan and Japanese femininity.

Belasco wanted to use the magic of the theater to transport audiences into an exotic and otherworldly Japan. Reviewers reveled in the technological sophistication of the show, beginning with the opening moment in which, according to one review, a "drop curtain arose, disclosing another curtain split in the middle and bearing typical Japanese figures."[15] This gave way to a series of lushly painted screens depicting scenes from Japanese country life, described in the *New York Times* thus: "Beautifully illuminated views of the land of cherry blossoms in the time of cherry blossoms are shown. The setting sun illuminates the dome peak of Fujisan. There is one lovely water view. Thus, gradually, one is taken to Cho-Cho-San's dainty little cottage, which is a perfect picture in all its details."[16] The set was a stunning performance of what Belasco imagined a Japanese home to be: walls lined with *shoji* screens, murals covering the fixed internal walls, and rich light pouring in from all angles. Another reviewer wrote, "Its pictures of Japanese life and domestic customs, . . . its brilliant display of color, its changing light effects, combine to make it a show that will be much talked about and that many persons will want to see."[17] This assessment proved correct, and audiences flocked to the production.

One of the primary draws of the evening was the technological simulation of the passage of time in an extended scene in which Cho-Cho-San waits through the night for Pinkerton's return. The success of this spectacle *must* have been at least somewhat compelling, as actress Blanche Bates held the audience rapt for no less than *fourteen minutes* as she sat perfectly still in absolute silence as lighting effects evoked the breaking dawn amid the sounds of singing birds.[18] As columnist Alan Dale waxed, "Even if I forget the story of 'Mme. Butterfly' the picture of Cho-Cho-San standing at the window from evening till night and from night till morning will remain impressed upon my memory."[19] The success of the production resulted in the transfer of an expanded three-act version of the play to London's West End a few months later.

In London, the narrative architecture of Long's story was once more kept in place, and most of the expansions aimed to give the characters increased psychological heft or to give audiences more of the exciting design elements that made the production a hit in New York. It starred ingénue Evelyn Millard in the title role, whose appearance was greatly anticipated in the press and was featured in a cover story for the *Illustrated Sporting & Dramatic News*.[20] Opera composer Giacomo Puccini sat in one of the audiences of the London production and soon after attained Belasco's permission to adapt the story/play into an opera. *Madama Butterfly* debuted to a mixed reception at La Scala on February 17, 1904, with a libretto by Luigi Illica and Giuseppe Giacosa. After various revisions, a robust version returned to New York with a premiere at the Metropolitan Opera House on February 11, 1907, with famed soprano

FIGURE 1.2. Metropolitan Opera premiere of *Madama Butterfly*, 1907. Courtesy of the Metropolitan Opera Archives.

Geraldine Farrar in the title role.[21] Again, the narrative remained fairly intact, with the majority of the adaptations made to accommodate Puccini's lush Orientalist score. Shortly after this, Puccini completed revisions on what was to become the standard version of *Madama Butterfly*.

*Madama Butterfly* remains one of Puccini's most popular operas in the United States and across the globe. Although my analysis of Belasco's dramatization will reconstruct sections of the original one-act production that debuted in New York in 1900, my descriptions of the opera are drawn from the Met's 2006 production, directed by the late Anthony Minghella. I turn to this particular production for a number of reasons. The production is part of the Metropolitan Opera's recent mission to update its repertoires to draw in new audiences. This mission is based on the presupposition that classical operas, such as *Madama Butterfly*, maintain their cultural relevance and social importance in the twenty-first century. To promote the opera, the production was broadcast live in Times Square. It continues to be broadcast to movie theaters throughout the country and, indeed, the world. It is also available for purchase in DVD format or for viewing on the Met's website for a small fee. If the argument can be made that *Madama Butterfly* is a relic of another era, I would suggest that the Met's mediated promotion and hyperdistribution of Minghella's production refutes this assumption. In other words, Butterfly has not left the building, and she does not show signs of doing so anytime soon.

## Act I. "American Hardware": Exclusion in Long's House on Higashi Hill

As a manifestation of the United States' juridical unconscious, one could say that Long's 1898 novella is a text in which a US American lawyer imagines a Japanese woman imagining herself as she performs in response to US law. But even before Cho-Cho-San begins her fantasied journey into US jurisprudence, the domestic relations that structure her marriage to Pinkerton are neatly representative of dominant conceptions of US sovereignty in the early period of Pacific expansion. The novella begins with a domestic dispute about the exclusion of Cho-Cho-San's family from Pinkerton's home. This argument mirrors the legislative debates about Asian exclusion occurring in both federal and state legislatures and courtrooms at the turn of the century.

In the opening sequence, Cho-Cho-San asks her new husband, Benjamin Franklin Pinkerton, to explain the hybrid construction of their home:

> Some clever Japanese artisans then made the paper walls of the pretty house eye-proof, and, with their own adaptations of American hardware, the openings cunningly lockable. The rest was Japanese.
>
> Madame Butterfly laughed, and asked him why he had gone to all that trouble—in Japan![22]

This early sequence is significant of two concerns that run throughout the narrative: an attempt to define and demarcate the territory of US sovereignty beyond US borders, and the crisis of subject constitution posed by figures and spaces that exist between and across both the United States and Japan.

Pinkerton's response to Cho-Cho-San's question is instructive: "'To keep out those who are out, and in those who are in,' he replied, with an amorous threat in her direction."[23] I will return to the first half of his answer later, but here I want to emphasize his "amorous threat" as that which announces the sexual and imperial valences of the narrative. The locks on the house (with "openings cunningly lockable") function as something of a chastity belt that locks Pinkerton's sexual conquest away from the rest of the world. It simultaneously describes the US military's adventures in the Eastern Hemisphere, with expansion into Asian-Pacific sovereignties and territories. This was exemplified by Commodore Matthew Perry's 1853 expedition to Japan, when Perry forced the Tokogawa Shogunate into a trade agreement with the threat of a naval attack on Nagasaki. Michio Kitahara, working with concepts adopted from Erving Goffman, argues that Perry's mission was explicitly staged as a performance: "Since the Japanese were not accustomed to deal[ing] with the Americans, the skillful presentation of 'appearance,' 'manner,' 'setting,' and 'personal front' by Perry's squadron [allowed] the 'performance team' [to] manipulate the Japanese effectively, control their definition of the situation, and make them open the country."[24] It can hardly be incidental that Pinkerton is a naval officer stationed in this same city. Indeed, the imaginary figure of Cho-Cho-San reflects the concurrent feminization of Asian nations that were seen as rife for conquest and dominance by the masculine US military that is represented by Pinkerton.

Just as Pinkerton and Cho-Cho-San stand in for an aggressive US military and passive Japan, the "American hardware" on the Japanese doors can be seen to reflect the US assertion of extraterritorial jurisdiction, the practice of claiming US sovereignty within Asian countries. In the novella, this occurs by way of a link to domestic structures of normative heteropatriarchy. On the one hand, a struggle over the exclusion of Cho-Cho-San's Japanese relatives (those "who are out") is an opportunity for Pinkerton to assert the sovereign right of exclusion, while it is also a means for taking possession of his wife. As Teemu Ruskola observes, the US assertion of extraterritorial jurisdiction in Asia (and China specifically) fundamentally transformed previous notions of sovereignty as being contained within the nation-state because "in China, among other places, American law did not attach to US territory but to the *bodies* of American citizens—each one of them representing a floating island of American sovereignty."[25] Pinkerton and his home mirror practices of extraterritorial jurisdiction performed by the United States, whereby sovereignty is delinked from the geographic boundaries of the nation and attached to the traveling body of the US agent abroad. His assumption of a home "in Japan!" with "American hardware" and his quick exclusion of Cho-Cho-San's Japanese relatives neatly reflects the

US government's imperial practices of extraterritorial jurisdiction and exclusion as a means of constructing the nation and national identity.[26] The result is that the space of sovereign exercise, which is to say the territory of US legal and cultural independence and self-determination, is dominated by Pinkerton, while transforming Cho-Cho-San into a figure that exists inside the United States from outside its borders, cut off from Japan while inside Japanese territory. Properly speaking, she is neither a US American nor Japanese subject. As such, she emerges as a transnational figure that floats between and is denied a proper place in both.

In defining the term *transnational*, Aihwa Ong places emphasis on *trans* as that which "denotes both moving through space or across lines, as well as changing the nature of something."[27] The transnational body is not only in a state of flux as she moves between spaces; she carries the potential to "change the nature" of the spaces that she traverses. This highlights the fact that, as Ramón H. Rivera-Servera and Harvey Young argue, a border must be conceptualized "as simultaneously a geographical locale and a condition/form of movement."[28] The border is realized through performance as the body moves between, across, and in relation to its often-porous limits. The body in performance thus poses a threat to the border because, "when bodies walk, drive, sail, or fly, their movements blur the *here* and *there*, constantly reorganizing the spatial relations and negotiating the consequences (political, social, economic, cultural) of their crossings."[29] In order to manage this threat, immigration law choreographs the immigrant's body, placing limits on her range of movement or even her ability to cross into the geographical territory of the nation. For the Asian subject in the United States, this took the form of an exceptional juridical regime that was developed to control the threat of her perceived dance across borders. Cho-Cho-San's figuration in Long's novella and the struggle over who, precisely, is excluded from Pinkerton's home is significant of this fact.

After Pinkerton explains his reason for installing the locks, Cho-Cho-San happily performs the mantle of authority created by the decision to exclude. This performance is quickly disrupted, however, when she learns just who it is that her husband wants to keep out: "She was greatly pleased with it all, though, and went about jingling her new keys and her new authority like toys,—she had only one small maid to command,—until she learned that among others to be excluded were her own relatives."[30] Cho-Cho-San repeatedly petitions Pinkerton to allow for her relatives to enter the home. However, he dismisses the family as "a trifle wearisome" and definitively rejects her attempts to bring the outside in.[31]

It should be noted that while much of the early exclusion legislation specifically targeted the Chinese, these technologies were expanded to similarly exclude other immigrants. And while US legislators were worried that targeting Japanese immigrants would offend the Japanese government, thus resulting in largely administrative means for securing Japanese exclusion (such as the Gentlemen's Agreement of 1907), there was a general domestic consensus that all Asian immigration was undesirable by the turn of the century.[32] Reading a narrative about a Japanese character alongside Chinese exclusion law and jurisprudence can be a useful exercise insofar as it helps to clarify the ways in which the domestic dispute in Long's novella functions as an "allegorical narrative" significant of the national and legal debates born from "collective thinking" and, more specifically, collective anxieties about Asians in America. Long's readers would have been well aware of the general anti-Asian sentiment that pervaded the country. During the late 1870s and early 1880s, the nation was engaged in vigorous debates over what to do about a perceived influx of Chinese, Japanese, Korean, and Indian immigrants. As Shirley Hune argues, "the division within Congress and especially the conflict that took place between the legislative and executive branches over the Chinese issue centered largely over the *means* and not upon the goal of restriction itself."[33] With Asian immigrants figured as a threat to the national order, only a very small minority voiced support for a pluralist embrace of Chinese immigrants. Pinkerton's desire to "keep out those who are out" would have resonated with popular sentiment about Asian subjects in general at the time.

*Madame Butterfly* was published nearly a decade after the US Supreme Court upheld Congress's right to enact the first Chinese Exclusion Act.[34] By the time that Long's story hit the masses, it is likely that most readers would have been aware of the Court's decision, *Chae Chan Ping v. United States*, which itself became something of a national drama. Indeed, media outlets turned to the rhetoric and narrative form of dramatic melodrama to report on the case, demonstrating the powerful role that aesthetic conventions play in mediating legal knowledge about Asian immigrants. The *New York Times*, writing about Chae Chan Ping's deportation in 1889, described him thus: "The name of Chae Chan Ping is now familiar to American ears. He is a Chinese gentleman who has given the United States courts a great deal of trouble in his endeavors to force his unwelcome presence upon the citizens of this fair and free country."[35] Demonstrating the ways in which legal spectacles take on the conventions of fictional narrative forms, his legal battle is framed with the language of literary or theatrical melodrama. He is cast as an aggressive villain struggling to "force his unwelcome presence" on an innocent victim, "the citizens of this fair and free country."[36] The judiciary, in turn, is figured as a heroic patriarch, instructing him to "pack up his traps and be off."[37]

In *Chae Chan Ping*, Justice Stephen Johnson Field issued the first articulation of Congress's plenary power to, in Pinkerton's words, "keep out those who are out": "That the government of the United States, through the action of the legislative department, can exclude aliens from its territory is a proposition which we do not think open to controversy. Jurisdiction over its own territory to that extent is an incident of every independent nation. It is a part of its independence."[38] Thus, Field understood the right of exclusion as a fundamental component of the constitution of sovereignty and the composition of national independence.

Three years later, the Supreme Court reaffirmed this principle in a case that applied the *Chae Chan Ping* holding to an ethnic Japanese petitioner in *Nishimura Ekiu v. United States*.[39] This 1892 case involved a woman who immigrated to the United States aboard a steamer, pursuing a husband who had previously arrived in the country. Resonating with Cho-Cho-San's ultimate foreclosure from national belonging and reflecting the particular will to keep Asian women from immigrating to the United States (discussed in greater detail in the next chapter), she was denied entry. Once more, the right of exclusion was defined as a foundational power of the state. But the *Nishimura Ekiu* court, even more than in *Chae Chan Ping*, reveals the border as performance by focusing not on territory but instead on the regulation and choreographing of the immigrant's body as it moves into and across the national space. As Justice Horace Gray wrote, "It is an accepted maxim of international law, that every sovereign nation has the power, as inherent in sovereignty, and essential to self-preservation, to forbid the entrance of foreigners within its dominion, or to admit them only in such cases and upon such conditions as it may see fit to prescribe."[40] In both *Chae Chan Ping* and *Nishimura Ekiu*, the act of exclusion produces, defines, and protects the identity of the sovereign nation through the law's control of the immigrant's movement across borders. But acts of legal choreography were not enough to manifest and police these borders. Aesthetic practices supported and, in the case of the theater, manifested flesh-and-blood figurations of Asian difference that would confirm and justify these actions in the minds of national audiences.

As we saw in the *New York Times* reportage on the *Chae Chan Ping* case, Congress and the courts were described as loving patriarchs, doing away with the villainous threat of Asian invaders with a protective deci-siveness. This figuration is not at all dissimilar from the characterization of Pinkerton's own management of his domestic sphere. Pinkerton's will to "keep out those who are out" and the "American locks" both reflect the dominant consensus that Asian bodies *should* be excluded from the nation. At the same time, the United States was grappling with Asian bodies already within national borders. So if Cho-Cho-San's family can be understood as representative of the "yellow hordes" that had to be excluded, the sanctioned presence of Cho-Cho-San's "one small maid" (Suzuki) in Pinkerton's home is significant of this other political dilemma.

Exclusion was often too late because the vacuum of both capitalism and imperialism had already drawn large numbers of Asians into the United States. In a concession to industries and employers who wanted to continue to exploit the labor of Chinese immigrants already within the country, the Chinese Exclusion Act allowed Chinese immigrants who entered before 1882 to leave the country and return, so long as they received a certificate of identification. Shortly before *Chae Chan Ping*, the Supreme Court issued a ruling in *United States v. Jung Ah Lung*.[41] The case involved a Chinese laborer who left the country with just such a certificate but lost it (reportedly stolen by pirates) before reentry. The justices ruled that this certificate was not the only piece of identification necessary for reentry.[42]

Not unlike Jung Ah Lung, as a domestic laborer, Suzuki moves in and out of Pinkerton's house at ease, but this movement should not be confused with absolute inclusion. Her presence is emblematic of a long and ongoing history of the racialization of certain bodies whose status as exploitable labor sources allows them to pass through spaces that are otherwise explicitly closed to them, so long as they carry out the dances of domestic servitude and un(der)compensated labor. But such figures were and often are not to be understood as proper citizens or even sub-jects of the nation. While the Chinese Exclusion Act allowed Chinese laborers who entered the country prior to 1892 to exit and reenter the country, their presence was juridically figured as illegal. Justice Louis Brandeis observed this fact in *Ng Fung Ho v. White*, a 1922 case involving Chinese petitioners subject to the mandates of the Chinese Exclusion Act: "One who has entered lawfully may remain unlawfully."[43] In other words, some Chinese laborers were paradoxically tolerated because the state would not always remove them, but their presence was always already illegal in theory of the law. As I discuss in chapter 5, this is a status that continues to attach itself to Asian immigrants in the present. As we shall now see, Cho-Cho-San's own sanctioned presence in the Pinkerton home explodes into a legal problem of tragic proportions.

## Act II. Madame Butterfly and the Problem of Law

### SCENE 1. BETWEEN INTERIOR AND EXTERIOR IN LONG AND BELASCO'S 1900 PLAY

If Long's novella manifests the juridical unconscious of the dominant culture in narrative form, Belasco's 1900 theatrical adaptation embodied it, giving audiences the rare chance for a flesh-and-blood, theatrical encounter with the exotic and mysterious body of the Asian Other. Turning now to the dramatic adaptation, Long and Belasco's onstage representation of Cho-Cho-San as a character that blurs clear national and racial distinctions was of particular interest and consternation for audiences and reviewers alike. With white women such as Blanche Bates and later Valerie Bergere and Evelyn Millard playing the role of Cho-Cho-San in yellowface, spectators demonstrated significant angst over whether what they were seeing on the stage was an authentic representation of Japanese femininity.[44] The *Times* complained, for example, "Bates' portrayal is human and its imitations of Japanese manners and characteristics is facile."[45] Despite the *Times*'s complaint, it seems the actresses were relatively successful in convincing audiences of their character's authenticity.

In 1904, Bergere gave an interview in which she described her decision to remain in costume after a performance of the play. A pair of tourists caught view of her and declared, "I tell you it can't be. She must be a Jap. No white woman could ever play such a role."[46] Bergere kept up the façade, as the tourists followed her through the streets of Times Square, before eventually disclosing her whiteness, to their great disappointment. There is little doubt that Bergere looked completely ludicrous shuffling down Broadway near midnight in what she described as the "short, quick steps of the Japanese," dressed in a kimono while speaking in "broken English."[47] The spectacle onstage was probably no less stupid. However, the audience's refusal to acknowledge what was no doubt a clear act of racial mimicry evidences a regulation of the color line so staunch that audiences believed that "no white woman could ever play such a role."

Belasco's dramatic adaptation eliminates the debate over the exclusion of Cho-Cho-San's family. It begins after Pinkerton has already abandoned Cho-Cho-San, as she earnestly awaits his return. Again, the importance of the locks are highlighted as in the opening scene, in which Cho-Cho-San explains to Suzuki why her husband put the locks on the door: "to keep out those which are out, and in, those which are in. Tha's me."[48] "Tha's me" identifies Cho-Cho-San's confused status between interior and exterior, Japan and the United States, linking the regulation of Asian female sexuality to the practice of constituting proper national and racial borders. This form of racial and national confusion between interior and exterior is lifted from Long's novella and brought to life before the audience's eyes in the form of the set, described in the script thus: "Everything in the room is Japanese save the American locks and bolts on the doors and windows and an American flag fastened to a tobacco jar. Cherry blossoms are abloom outside, and inside."[49] The symbolic blend between interior and exterior is represented by potent symbols of US and Japanese nationalism (the US flag and the *sakura*) cohabiting the home. This confusion of cultural and national distinction is embodied in a less harmonious form by the character of Cho-Cho-San. This is specifically realized through her spoken dialogue.

Linguistic utterance becomes a primary method by which Cho-Cho-San's confused status between the United States and Japan is performed. It is the medium through which the audience can identify her inability to properly perceive her exclusion from both spaces at the very moment she attempts to perform her inclusion in them. The structure of the dialogue signifies the peculiar place of the gendered Asian-immigrant and Asian American subject as always, somehow, located outside the United States. In the opening scene, for example, Cho-Cho-San insists that Suzuki speak English only:

MADAME BUTTERFLY: (*Reprovingly*) Suzuki, how many time I tellin' you—no one shall speak anythin' but those Unite' State' languages in these Lef-ten-ant Pik-ker-ton's house? (*She pronounces his name with much difficulty.*)[50]

She speaks in a pidgin that draws on and embellishes the dialect spoken by the heroine in Long's novella. Her insistence on English is at once significant of a desire to enter the United States and indicative of her cultural inability to properly perform ideal US subjectivity. In the novella, she explains that Pinkerton has insisted that she speak "United States' languages" in his absence.[51] If she does this, upon his return, she claims, "he go'n' take us at those United States America."[52] Cho-Cho-San's failed attempt to speak in "Unite' State' languages" reinforced dominant arguments in support of exclusion: namely, no matter how much Asians in America may attempt to perform ideal US subjectivity through the guiles of cunning and artifice, their innate racial, national, and cultural difference marks them as incapable of fully assimilating into the dominant white culture.

Popular media in the nineteenth century, from news reportage to stage shows such as *Madame Butterfly*, commonly represented Asian subjects as speaking broken English. The figuration of Asian immigrants burdened with accented English was shorthand for Asian racial difference as that which impedes proper assimilation or the performance of proper national subjectivity. Thus, representations of broken English were inherently tied to the narration of Asian subjects as those that *should* be excluded from the national body politic. Take, for example, the *Times*'s description of the final words of Chae Chan Ping, just before his removal from the United States: "He said in pigeon [*sic*] English: 'I don't want to go back to China; I want to stop in California.'"[53] Emphasizing his "pigeon" (a spelling error that figures him as both foreign *and* animalistic, or at least less than human) at the exact moment that he decries his removal from the nation confirms the article's insistence that the Chinese *must* be removed and excluded from the United States. Like Cho-Cho-San, his "pigeon" is a means of representing the racialized Asian immigrant's inability to perform as a proper national subject. It thus justifies his or her exclusion.

The use of dialect to mark the inferiority of racialized bodies was not new. Cho-Cho-San's dialect, in both Long's and Belasco's treatments, is reminiscent of the "darky dialect" central to blackface minstrelsy. This form of dialect was also widely popularized in representations of African Americans in nineteenth-century US American melodrama and literature. As Eric Lott argues, blackface minstrelsy was significant of both a practice of domination and the desire for the dominant white culture to consume black racial difference.[54] "Darky dialect" represented African Americans as unintelligible, inferior racialized subjects who were ripe for domination, while staging such subjects as projection screens onto which fantasies about the "liberties of infancy" could be displayed.[55] The adoption of similar forms of dialect for the representation of Asian and Asian American subjects achieved similar ends and highlights the ways in which Asian racialization occurred across the differentiated representational landscapes of race in the United States.

That Long's and Belasco's adoption of a dialect that was at the very least referential to the dialects of blackface traditions is in keeping with the comparative racialization of Asian and African American subjects in both aesthetic and legal traditions of the era. Krystyn Moon shows how US composers in the nineteenth century, eager to satiate audience desires to consume exotic sounds of the "Orient," turned to familiar "musical representations of difference" found in blackface minstrelsy: "By combining African American traditions with European Orientalism and transcriptions of Chinese music, they again played to notions of difference and inferiority and expanded on the conflation of the non-Western world."[56] This form of racial triangulation was similarly present in the law, most notably in Harlan's *Plessy* dissent, figuring nonwhite racial difference as that which could be simultaneously consumed and excluded in the construction of ideal (white) national subjectivity. Thus, as Julia H. Lee observes, "the figure of the Asian was vital in mediating the relationship between blackness and American national identity, and in turn . . . blackness was key in imagining Asian racial difference in relation to the nation."[57] While the outcomes and effects of such processes were varied for different minoritarian groups, their mutually subordinate construction by the dominant culture bolstered the stability of whiteness as an ideal national subject position.

White audiences reveled in the ability to consume Cho-Cho-San's dialect as that which signified the fetish of her exotic racial difference, while confirming the subordinate position projected onto racialized bodies by the logic of white supremacy. Her speech patterns thrilled the cosmopolitan New York crowd, as documented by one newspaper reporter who described Bates's "delivery of Mr. Long's curious patois as exceedingly interesting."[58] But they also confirmed the fact that she was utterly incompatible within the parameters set by the dominant culture to define ideal national subjectivity. The charming naïveté of Cho-Cho-San's assumption that the language she is speaking would in any way pass for English is encapsulated by her failure to name it properly. She refers to English erroneously in the plural as "Unite' State' languages." Her radically incommensurate relationship to the United States is thus figured through her speech, which breaks down and becomes incomprehensible as her status between Japan and the United States grows increasingly and tragically confused. Spectacularly exhibiting this contention, her final lines in the play are nearly gibberish: "Well—go way an' I will res' now. . . . I wish res'—sleep . . . long sleep . . . an' when you see me again, I pray you look whether I be not beautiful again . . . as a bride."[59] Belasco and Long make Cho-Cho-San a tragic figure that is confused and confusing, broken, neither here nor there, incomprehensible and thus impossible. It is this incomprehensibility, her incompatibility with US culture and, ultimately, US law which results in Cho-Cho-San's destruction.

The heroine's tragic end is prefigured in each version of *Madame Butterfly* with a legal contract that is beyond her comprehension: the contract establishing Pinkerton's rental of the home and his marriage to Cho-Cho-San for a period of 999 years. What the audience is told via Pinkerton in all versions and what Cho-Cho-San does not grasp, however, is that Japanese law (according to Long, Belasco, and Puccini) allows Pinkerton to simply walk away from both the house and the marriage without penalty. Looking back to Long's 1898 novella, for example, we find a detailed discussion of the legal terms that structure the purchase of Pinkerton's wife and the rental of his home:

> With the aid of a marriage-broker, he found both a wife and a house in which to keep her. This he leased for nine hundred and ninety-nine years. Not, he explained to his wife later, that he could hope for the felicity of residing there with her so long, but because, being a mere "barbarian," he could not make other legal terms. He did not mention that the lease was determinable, nevertheless, at the end of any month, by the mere neglect to pay the rent.[60]

The metonymic relationship between Cho-Cho-San and the house is established by way of the legal contract. (By the time we get to the opera, this distinction is dissolved, and both the bride and house are rented for 999 years.) Pinkerton, for his part, is protected by his mastery of the law. Understanding the legal limits placed on him by his status as a foreign "barbarian," Pinkerton manipulates this status to set up a seemingly permanent arrangement that is entirely predicated on his ability to walk away from the house and wife at any point.

The play begins after Pinkerton's abandonment, and in the first scene, we find Cho-Cho-San pacing the stage and hemorrhaging the limited funds left to her care by her husband on a rent that is beyond her means. She does so believing that (a) she is required to keep up the 999-year lease signed by her husband in his absence because (b) the lease is proof (to her) of his intention to return home. As she declares in the opening scene, while Suzuki counts the dwindling amount of money they are left, "If he's not come back to his house, why he sign Japanese lease for nine hundred and ninety-nine year for me to live?"[61] Belasco inaccurately stages Japan as a state of capricious lawlessness, suggesting that it is the fact that Japanese society exists without the benefit and securities of the

US legal contract, and not Pinkerton's abandonment of Cho-Cho-San, that is the root of the tragedy.[62] The burden of blame is further shifted onto the heroine, as she is responsible for ultimately failing to grasp her proper position with regard to national and juridical categories of ideal subjecthood. Put clearly, she fails to comprehend the fact that she is hardly a subject at all but more nearly an object for exchange between nations and men.

All three versions of *Madame Butterfly* include a crucial scene in which the abandoned Cho-Cho-San is given harsh advice by Sharpless, Pinkerton's friend who remains concerned with her well-being. In his endeavor, the marriage broker (Gobo) and a Japanese suitor (Yamadori) accompany Sharpless. Each man encourages her to move on and marry again. They assure her that remarriage would be legal given her circumstances. As they attempt to explain to her that her marriage is not binding under Japanese law, Cho-Cho-San rejects their counsel, curiously insisting that she is not subject to Japanese law. She claims, instead, that she is a subject of US legal jurisdiction.

In the dramatic adaptation, the scene unfolds thus:

YAMADORI: According to the laws of Japan, when a woman is deserted, she is divorced. (*Madame Butterfly stops fanning and listens.*) Though I have traveled much abroad, I know the laws of my own country.

MADAME BUTTERFLY: An' I know laws of my *husban's* country.

YAMADORI: (*To Sharpless*) She still fancies herself married to the young officer. If your Excellency would explain . . .

MADAME BUTTERFLY: (*To Sharpless*) Sa-ey, when some one gettin' married in America, don' he stay marry?

SHARPLESS: Usually—yes.

MADAME BUTTERFLY: Well, tha's all right. I'm marry to Lef-ten-ant B.F. Pik-ker-ton.

YAMADORI: Yes, but a Japanese marriage!

SHARPLESS: Matrimony is a serious thing in America, not a temporary affair as it often is here.[63]

This exchange demonstrates the proper orientation of a national subject, which is embodied by the two men. The thoroughly Japanese Yamadori knows "the laws of [his] own country," and the unflinchingly US American Sharpless knows the laws of his. That proper subjectivity is tied to gender is amplified by the fact that unlike Cho-Cho-San, Yamadori

speaks impeccable English. Furthermore, Belasco hierarchically organizes Japanese marital legal conventions as inferior, lacking the "serious"
nature of marriage in the United States. We also encounter an implicit
critique of US imperialism as Sharpless suggests that marriage is "a serious thing" in the United States (effectively condemning the behaviors of
his colleague Pinkerton, who has behaved as if it were not). This is less a
critique of US imperialism than of its execution by irresponsible agents
like Pinkerton. Sharpless stands in as the ideal model of how US empire
*should* function; he is a stable and responsible moral authority. What is
without a doubt, however, is that Cho-Cho-San is confused with regard
to both, applying what she understands of US law to herself. Adopting
the laws of her "*husban's* country," Cho-Cho-San disavows the laws of
Japan, while failing to recognize that she would be completely illegible in
the theater of US law.

## Scene 2. The Scene of Exception in Puccini's Opera

The heroine's crisis is that from a legal and a cultural perspective, she
makes no sense. She is neither Japanese nor US American, and within
the rigidly segregated logic of the turn of the century, this makes her
altogether impossible. This impossibility is temporarily negotiated by
the heroine as she shuttles between subjecthood and an objecthood that
Long describes as an Oriental curio: "After all, she *was* quite an impossible little thing, outside of lacquer and paint."[64] Her disavowal of her
legal status as a Japanese subject and insistence on her impossible status
as a US subject is even more explicit in the same scene in Puccini's 1907
opera.

In Minghella's 2006 production of *Madama Butterfly*, the "serious"
nature of US law is counterpoised against the childlike and silly nature
of Japanese law. In this scene, the characters inhabit a primarily empty
stage, save a wall of white *shoji* screens behind them. Cio-Cio-San is
clad in a preposterous kimono of shocking pink and neon green, and
the other Japanese characters wear equally ridiculous colors and towering hats and flap fans as if they were chicken wings. Sharpless grounds
the scene with the sobriety of a staid diplomat, wearing a professional,
earth-toned suit, sitting patiently on a Western-style chair, as the Japanese characters argue over Cio-Cio-San's legal status:

GOBO:     But the law says.
BUTTERFLY: (*interrupting him*) I know it not.

GOBO:        (*continuing*) For the wife, desertion
             Gives the right of divorce.
BUTTERFLY: (*shaking her head*) That may be Japanese law,
             But not in my country.
GOBO:        Which one?
BUTTERFLY: (*with emphasis*) The United States.
SHARPLESS: (Poor little creature!)[65]

The heroine's confused legal status is emphasized as the "Star Spangled Banner" makes an appearance, flowing under her lilting glissando. Here, the lyric—"La legge giapponese . . . [The Japanese Law . . .]"—and the anthem are placed in counterpoint against each other, suggesting their incompatibility. Then, as she sings, "non gia del mio paese [is not the law of my country]," the anthem meets her melody, and they join together for a brief moment as she sings this lyric in place of the phrase "by the dawn's early light."[66] The anthem abandons her immediately after Gobo asks, "Which one?" She responds, "The United States," and the strings cascade into a lower register that broaches an ominous minor-key tonality, setting up Sharpless's hushed utterance, "Poor little creature!" This statement, rendered as an aside, emphasizes the fact that *this* is the tragedy of Cio-Cio-San's situation (from the opera's point of view): because she is incapable of grasping the concept of territorial jurisdiction, and her exclusion from the United States, she is incapable of properly situating herself as a Japanese legal subject/object.

Cio-Cio-San's problem is that she has attached herself to an improper and impossible love object (Pinkerton and, by extension, the United States). The Asian-immigrant and Asian American subject's desire for a place in the United States is thus figured as an inappropriate amorous attachment. This narrative trope was a convenient way of affirming the myth of US exceptionalism (as a place that all people purportedly desire to be a part of), while maintaining firm boundaries regulated by the practice of exclusion. In the *New York Times*'s coverage of Chae Chan Ping's deportation, his relationship to the United States is similarly described as an illicit, forbidden, and ultimately one-sided love affair: "Ping's love of country is confined to this country."[67] Like Cio-Cio-San, his relationship to the state is discursively staged as a failed marriage: "He was . . . *wedded* to the fascinations of Chinatown, and remained there until the indignant howl of an ever vigilant press awakened the authorities to a realization of the fact that Ping had brought his knitting and intended to stay."[68] Pitiable as Chae Chan Ping or Cio-Cio-San's romantic national convictions may be, the final solution is unmistakable: negation through exclusion (or death). Locked in a one-way romance, both appealed to the majesty of US justice in the hopes that the state would ultimately recognize their marriage to the United States. Unsurprisingly, both lose their case.

Cio-Cio-San invokes rights that she imagines she has gained through marriage. In all three versions of *Madame Butterfly*, an exchange occurs in which she paints a detailed portrait of the scene of justice. She describes the ritual of going before a US judge in order to appeal for relief from the injustice of Pinkerton's abandonment. In each case, she assumes that the judge will perceive her as a subject of US law and protect her accordingly. In the opera, this sequence directly follows the previously discussed scene. After Cio-Cio-San declares herself subject to the laws of the United States, the strings slide into a playful lilt. This is accompanied by tremolos in the wind section that give the scene an air of childlike playfulness. Like the dialect in Long's and Belasco's versions of the story, Puccini's orchestration frames Cio-Cio-San as naïve, foolish, and infantile.[69] This is particularly acute when she flutters around the stage with an enthusiastic euphoria as she earnestly lectures Gobo on the nature of US law and her assumed place within it. She complains about the tenuous nature of Japanese marriage, calling on Sharpless to authenticate her critique: "But in America, that cannot be done. (*to Sharpless*) Say so!"[70] Sharpless attempts to interject, "(*embarrassed*) Yes, yes—but-yet," and we can assume that he would continue to explain that Cio-Cio-San cannot claim the protections of US law. She will not permit him to continue, however, and sings with august sincerity:

MADAME BUTTERFLY: There, a true, honest
And unbiased judge
Says to the husband:
"You wish to free yourself?
"Let us hear why?—
"I am sick and tired
"Of conjugal fetters!"
Then the good judge says:
"Ah, wicked scoundrel,
"Clap him in prison!"[71]

On the one hand, because Butterfly is clearly wrong, we can interpret the scene as a critique of the bias of the judicial system in the United States. The aria explicitly acknowledges the gendered injustice of a system that would deny the basic claims for justice that a petitioner like Cio-Cio-San might put before a judge. At the same time, Cio-Cio-San's embodiment reduces her to a stereotype of racialized, gendered subjectivity that is incapable of understanding the complicated vicissitudes and implications of engagement with a justice system that, ultimately, does not recognize her as a proper juridical subject.

As Cio-Cio-San delivers this aria, she bounds around the stage. When she embodies the judge, she stands behind Sharpless's chair and issues the orders into his ear. As the beseeching husband, she bends on one knee in front of him and begs for release from his "conjugal fetters." She stands and once again moves behind the chair, delivering the judge's order with masculine authority, before melting into the opera's rote physical manifestation of Japanese female sincerity: eyes batting and feet shuffling. (Over a century after the first production of Belasco's play, it seems directors and performers still turn to Bergere's "short, quick steps of the Japanese" to signify Japaneseness.) In every way, the scene stages not only the sexist trope of the incapacity of Cio-Cio-San to understand the gravity of her confused legal status but also the ridiculousness of her assumption that she would be perceived by a US judge as a fully recognized subject of US law.

As Cio-Cio-San performs for her imaginary judge, the audience in the theater is given the opportunity to take on another role: that of a jury weighing the merits of her case. In this sense, the scene draws on the classical Athenian roots of Western theater. As J. Peter Euben notes, for the Athenians of antiquity, "drama was as much a political institution as the law courts, assembly, or boule."[72] Indeed, the theater could be a unique place for working through the political debates of the day because it lacked what Carl Schmitt described as the juristic decision that is the determining moment in the law's realization.[73] As Euben observes, "Freed from the urgency of decision which marked other political institutions, drama encouraged inclusive and reflective thinking about contemporary issues."[74] Thus, we locate one of the unique political and legal functions of aesthetic performances in the nineteenth and early twentieth centuries, which carry a trace of their historical ancestors in the Theater of Dionysus.

As reflective of the juridical unconscious of its time, *Madame Butterfly* encourages the audience-as-jury to weigh the different exigencies behind the case. Unquestionably, the audience is meant to feel sympathy for the heroine. But this sympathy is not necessarily driven by the revelation of an unjust system that excludes her from the sphere of national belonging or the protection of US law. Instead, this sympathy—expressed in

Sharpless's "Poor little creature!"—is colored by condescension. The tragic irony that attaches itself to Cio-Cio-San is born from the fact that Puccini's Western audience, like Sharpless, knows that she has no place in the United States. It is thus Cio-Cio-San's infantile inability to grasp this fact (infantile *because* she is a woman *and* Japanese) that causes the tragedy. Weighing the evidence, the audience-as-jury is encouraged to reject Cio-Cio-San's deposition. They are given every reason to rule that the heroine is tragically beyond the jurisdiction of US law. Having been given the opportunity to sympathize with her, however, the liberal sensibilities of the audience can remain intact while the juridical exclusion of Cio-Cio-San proceeds apace.

If we can imagine the evidence leading the audience, however sympathetic, to reject Cio-Cio-San's plea, we *know* that the courts of the period most certainly would have. Turning to a set of cases dealing with the question of Asian testimony in US courts shows just how closely the Butterfly narrative functions as a representative of this jurisprudence. It is important to understand how the problem for a subject like Cio-Cio-San was not simply the lack of a "true, honest, and unbiased" judge. Rather, bias was the constitutive element for the exercise of law over the Asian-immigrant and Asian American body. Cio-Cio-San's fantasy of testifying before a judge against her Caucasian American husband was simply impossible. An evolving jurisprudence in California and the Pacific Northwest was quickly defining Asian bodies as exceptional to the law's application with regard to questions of due process. This process was helped by the comparative racialization of other racial minorities.

At first, the state tried to manage the threat of Asian racial difference by turning to previous technologies developed to control African American and Native American racial difference, attempting to make the Asian American body "conform to a preformed law."[75] In 1851, for example, the California Congress banned African American and Native American witnesses from testifying against white parties.[76] In an 1854 case, *People of California v. Hall*, the Supreme Court of California considered whether the ban on testimony would extend to Chinese witnesses. Chief Justice Hugh Campbell Murray delivered an astonishing opinion in which he determined that because Christopher Columbus landed in the Americas in an attempt to travel to India, the term *Indian* as misapplied to Native Americans must also now apply to descendants of Asia: "We have adverted to these speculations for the purpose of showing that the name of Indian, from the time of Columbus to the present day, has been used to designate, not alone the North American Indian, but the whole of the Mongolian race, and that the name, though first applied probably through mistake, was afterwards continued as appropriate on account of the supposed common origin."[77] If Columbus erroneously transformed Native Americans into Asians, the Murray ruling applied a reversal that retroactively transformed Asians into Native Americans. But this alone was not enough, requiring the development of a practice of legal suspension to adequately manage the surprise that Asian racial difference posed to the unity of the ideal body politic.

In two Oregon cases from this period, the Supreme Court of Oregon ruled that Chinese persons could be allowed to stand as witnesses against other Chinese defendants. However, both courts declared that Chinese testimony could only be accepted after suspending the formal requirements of due process. In *State of Oregon v. Mah Jim*, the court issued a *per curium* opinion which reasoned that Chinese witnesses against other Chinese parties, though permissible, must be observed with the utmost suspicion: "Experience convinces every one that the testimony of Chinese witnesses is very unreliable, and that they are apt to be actuated by motives that are not honest. The life of a human being should not be forfeited on that character of evidence without a full opportunity to sift it thoroughly."[78] In *State of Oregon v. Ching Ling*, a murder case two years after *Mah Jim*, Judge Andrew Jackson Thayer similarly suggested that evidence against a Chinese defendant did not need to live up to the same standards of evidence required for a white defendant. The irreducible racial difference of the Chinese was proffered as the primary reason for this decision: "The testimony was not sufficient to have had any weight whatever as against white persons. . . . As to Chinamen, however, it is different."[79] This difference did not register the Chinese as totally beyond the reach of the law but placed the Chinese body in an exceptional position at the law's limit: "An attempt to apply strict technical rules in such cases is too apt to result in a sacrifice of substance to form. The law was instituted to secure justice, and its design and purpose should not be suffered to be defeated by a strict adherence to formal rules in its administration. In cases of homicide among these Chinamen, it is almost impossible to ascertain who the guilty parties are."[80] As the court would not apply the "technical rules" of due process to the Chinese, the Agambenian legal ban was realized through law that appears to be in force but suspended.

For the West Coast courts, the notion that an Asian subject would have full standing before a US judge was simply impossible. This is a conceit that is replicated in the opera via Sharpless's assessment of Cio-Cio-San's fantasied performance before a US judge. Yamadori asks him, "You hear her?" and the consular officer responds, "I am grieved at such hopeless blindness."[81] The judges and Sharpless deploy a rhetoric of rationalist pity, which allows the audience-as-jury to receive a callous injustice (the suspension of due process, or Cio-Cio-San's foreclosure from US justice) as a testament to the universal greatness of the US American way of life and law. This is manifest in the altruistically concerned figure of Sharpless, who is representative of a paternalistic US concern for Cio-Cio-San that stops short of giving legitimacy to the "hopeless blindness" of Cio-Cio-San's petition for incorporation. For the courts, the very fact that they were willing to lower the exalted glory of US law to the base and trivial nature of a Chinese man's murder was a testament to the universal objectivity and success of the rule of law in the United States. As Thayer declares, "If we were disposed through a dislike of the race to consider the life of a Chinaman as a trivial matter, still we would have no right to immolate justice upon the altar of our prejudice."[82]

Both *Mah Jim* and *Ching Ling* placed the Asian body at the limit of the law's application. Like Cio-Cio-San and Suzuki, these figures were understood to be subject to the rule of law but without the protections of citizenship or due process. Significantly, the justifications proffered by the courts were rooted in the belief—mirrored in the three versions of *Madame Butterfly*—that Asian subjects are nothing if not constantly engaged in theatrical deception. In *Mah Jim*, the court describes the Chinese as dubious and inscrutable: "No one can tell what the class of persons [Chinese] may have in view. Their practices are very peculiar and mysterious, and the court, in no such case, should adopt a refined, technical rule as to the admission of evidence tending to show what their motives may be."[83] In *Ching Ling*, an accident of history further realizes the conceit of perfidious Chinese theatricality because the murder itself occurred in the Chinese Theater of Portland. This situational irony is woven throughout the opinion as Thayer defines the Chinese as performers skilled at "artifice and cunning," making it impossible for courts to be "stolid and persistently adhere to [the] formality [of due process]."[84] Thayer's description of the Chinese as skilled actors is thus not unlike Pinkerton's own assessment of Cho-Cho-San's family in Long's novella. When they come to petition for entrance into the home, he dismisses them with the observation, "you look exactly like a lacquered tragedy mask I have hanging over my desk."[85] So just as Cho-Cho-San's family is described as resembling dramatic masks, the West Coast courts understood Asian and Asian American subjects as perpetual, inscrutable performers whose untrustworthy nature placed them outside the normative bounds of US law. This is a trope that is also fully personified in Cho-Cho-San's attempts to perform the role of a US American wife.

The theatrical presentation of self within Cho-Cho-San's domicile becomes one of the central means through which she negotiates the movement between and across the United States and Japan in Long's novella:

> American women, we are told, assume more fearless attitudes in the security of their boudoirs than elsewhere. Japanese women, never. Their conduct is eternally the same. It must be as if someone were looking on—always. There is no privacy for them short of the grave. They have no secure boudoirs.
>
> But Madame Butterfly (through the courtesy of her American husband) had both these. It will therefore be argued, perhaps, that she is not a typical Japanese woman.[86]

Japanese femininity is figured as the mark of difference against which bourgeois forms of Western domesticity and gender are defined. Similar to Ann Laura Stoler's observation about European colonial techniques for regulating sexuality in Southeast Asia, Cho-Cho-San's boudoir performance is significance of the fact that "the cultivation of bourgeois sensibilities were inextricable from the nationalist and racial underpinnings of them."[87] For Long's narrator, Japanese subjectivity is always already theatrical, and Japanese women ceaselessly perform "as if someone were looking on—always." Because Japanese women must present themselves with the knowledge that they will never have "privacy . . . short of the grave," they are denied even the smallest of liberties achieved by US American women, who perform with "a more fearless attitude in the security of their boudoirs." And since liberty or freedom is one of the core ideals of the United States, Japanese women such as Cho-Cho-San are figured as incapable of incorporation into the nation.

The courts constructed a portrait of Asian immigrants and Asian Americans as perpetual performers, masters of disguise who were otherwise unrecognizable to the normative stability of US law. Works of popular cultural production, such as *Madame Butterfly*, could bring these narratives to life, affirming them as authentic for the audiences that consumed them. As "quite an impossible" subject who challenges the distinction between national, racial, and cultural boundaries, Cio-Cio-San's repeated turn to the law can only fail her. Bodies like Butterfly's that attempted to move across the geographical and cultural borders of the US nation and into the ranks of the body politic punctured holes in the story that the dominant culture was telling itself about its firmly defined boundaries. By the dictates of this story, US borders were clearly defined, were territorially bounded, and contained a body politic that was purportedly white, properly gendered, and defined by enlightened morality and bourgeois, Protestant ideals. Attempts to shore up the holes, whether in law or aesthetics (and I mean to suggest that the division between the two is blurry at best, during this period), required ambivalent and often violent acts of foreclosure. This occurred either through the suspension of civic status (as with the suspension of due process in *Hall*, *Ching Ling*, and *Mah Jim*) or through acts of brutal anti-Asian violence.[88] In the case of the Butterfly narrative, it is both.

## SCENE 3. "SHE DIES"

In *Ching Ling*, the court suggested that all parties might be guilty, retroactively assigning guilt to the Chinese victim (Lee Yick). Like the *Ching Ling* court, the three Butterfly authors solve Cio-Cio-San's legal crisis through her murder by suicide. Whatever critiques of US imperialism may have been intended by Long, Belasco, and especially Puccini and whatever social taboos they sought to stage through the dramatization of an interracial romance are ultimately subordinated to the reification of dominant/normative national, racial, cultural, and juridical categories. In the words of Josephine Lee, "The theatrical treatment of taboos such as interracial sex can arouse audiences and make the playwright seem politically progressive, yet result in a dramatic outcome in which racial boundaries are ultimately reinforced."[89] The death of Cio-Cio-San is so emblematic of this process that it is one of the primary paradigms for understanding the foreclosure of Asian and Asian American female difference.

While Cio-Cio-San's suicide is an Orientalist fantasy of Japanese feminine honor, one of the sexist tropes of the tragic opera heroine, and a popular convention in turn-of-the-century naturalist drama (such as Ibsen's *Hedda Gabler*), it can also be read as a kind of death sentence handed down to her as a way of managing the crisis she poses to national and juridical borders. Her death is significant of what James Moy observes when he writes, "Although increased contact between Asia and America offered an opportunity for real understanding and exchange, American dramatists, with the characteristic provincialism of the Eurocentric colonialist way of looking at the world, began killing off Asians—as if to articulate an unwillingness, an impatience, or simply a lack of desire to understand."[90] Against this, one might argue that Cio-Cio-San's death is simply a convention of the tragic form, but this is tautological. The tragic form has long relied on the violent foreclosure of women and ethnic subjects as a central component of tragedy, and so it can hardly excuse itself by saying that tragedy as such has propensity for falling back on racism and sexism to achieve its narrative ends. Cio-Cio-San's suicide is certainly in keeping with the conventions of tragedy. But the grand spectacle of Cio-Cio-San's death suggests that the "killing off [of] Asians" was indicative not only of a refusal to understand difference but of a perverse pleasure that audiences were invited to indulge in by watching bodies such as Cio-Cio-San's bleed out. At the very least, her suicide offered a no-fault, definitive solution to the threat of her potential entry into the national family of the United States. As such, it is important to take a moment to trace the three versions of Cio-Cio-San's suicide.

It is possible that the heroine does not die in the 1898 novella, as textually her fate is uncertain. Long's final chapter describes her suicide attempt with lurid details. In her decision to kill herself, she is returned to a properly Japanese status, as "she placed the point of the weapon at the nearly nerveless spot in the neck *known to every Japanese*, and began to press it slowly inward."[91] Long's description of the scene is just as much a narrative of the suicide as it is an erotic meditation on the spectacle of Cho-Cho-San's breasts: "But presently she could feel the blood finding its way down her neck. It divided on her shoulder, the larger stream going down her bosom. In a moment she could see it making its way daintily between her breasts. It began to congeal there. She pressed on the sword, and a fresh stream swiftly overran the other—redder, she thought."[92] Her blood doubles as a kind of ejaculate ("a fresh stream swiftly overran the other"), shooting over Cho-Cho-San's body ("down her neck," "down her bosom," "daintily between her breasts") not once but twice, after the sword's penetration. This erotic description of the suicide is evidence of my earlier claim that the audience in fact desired to witness her death. Even Cho-Cho-San wants to be a spectator to her death, as she grabs a mirror to watch herself die. Ultimately, the maid puts the baby in the room, and the distraught heroine drops the sword "dully to the floor."[93] The blood congeals, and she weeps as the maid wraps her wound. However, Long withholds a definitive word as to whether she dies. Instead, in the last line of the novella, she simply disappears: "When Mrs. Pinkerton called next day at the little house on Higashi Hill it was quite empty."[94]

The final stage direction of Belasco's 1900 play is, succinctly, "She dies."[95] In this version, Sharpless finally returns to the stage, screaming Cho-Cho-San's name, just before her death. That audiences experienced pleasure by watching her die is evidenced by the *Times*'s rapturous description of the scene: "*This is a thrilling moment*, when she blindfolds the baby and cuts an artery in her neck with the sword of her honorable parent."[96] A century later, Minghella's 2006 production of Puccini's opera continued the tradition of making the death scene a sensuous spectacle. She stands on a pitch-black stage, wearing a glistening white kimono with a blood-red *obi* and a giant red poppy in her hair. She raises the knife in a slow, protracted gesture but hides it as her son enters the stage in puppet form. She delivers her final, heart-wrenching aria explaining that her suicide is a sacrifice for the child's benefit, before blindfolding the child and commanding him to play. A line of black-clad, *kuroko*-style stagehands stand at the back of the stage. Behind them, a dim red scrim casts their bodies in silhouette. Cio-Cio-San raises the knife and dramatically plunges it into her neck. At this exact moment, and for no discernable reason, the stagehands open giant golden fans and hold them in front of their already concealed faces—perhaps signaling a chain of sunsets. As Cio-Cio-San sinks to the floor, two *kuroko* stagehands enter and slowly begin to unravel the sanguine *obi*. The floor is made of black lacquer, as is a panel floating above the stage. In this lighting, the shiny black ceiling takes the place of the mirror in Long's novella. Instead of Cio-Cio-San watching the blood flow into her bosom, the audience is treated to the slow-motion spectacle of a river of fabric blood spreading out in all directions from her body, amplified by the reflection floating above the stage. In this stage picture, Cio-Cio-San's body becomes a neatly unified symbol of Asian bodies spreading out across the world, her death suggesting a possible solution to the crisis of US national constitution posed by such as diaspora. The lights turn a bright sanguine red before fading to darkness. The audience explodes into wild applause.

## Act III. The Trouble with Trouble

If Butterfly's suicide resolves the question of her impossible national and racial subjectivity, the extraordinary ambivalence projected onto Asian-immigrant and Asian American bodies by the legal and cultural

FIGURE 1.3. Death scene from David Belasco's *Madame Butterfly*, featuring Blanche Bates, Frank Worthing, and Little Kittie. Courtesy of the Harry Ranson Humanities Research Center at the University of Texas at Austin.

narratives that we have been discussing do not resolve the problem completely. There remains, after her death, a character whose body, even more than his mother's, threatens the boundary between interior and exterior. He is situated between the United States and Japan, so disturbing to the limits of racial and national belonging that his name is "Trouble." It is the significance of this figure that I discuss for the remainder of this chapter. It is also through this figure that I show how *Madame Butterfly*'s codification and circulation of the forms of legal subjectivity scripted for Asian subjects across the courtrooms and stages of the nineteenth century comes to impact the juridical subjectivity of Asian Americans in the contemporary era.

The turning point in the narrative, leading to Cio-Cio-San's tragic demise, is her steady realization of Trouble's nationally and racially confused status. In all three narratives, the scene between Butterfly, Sharpless, and the matchmaker results in an uncomfortable moment in which the matchmaker points out that the infant will have no place in the United States or among the Japanese. While the crisis posed by Cio-Cio-San's confused subjectivity is brought to narrative conclusion as she takes her life, Trouble comes into being as a subject that is not quite foreclosed but is no less disruptive than his mother.

I begin my study of Trouble by returning to the 1898 novel, in which the child is never officially named. Since Pinkerton does not know about his son, Cho-Cho-San assigns the name "Trouble" as a temporary appellation, to be rectified upon the father's promised return: "She was quite sure he [the absent Pinkerton] would like the way she had named him [the baby] Trouble—meaning joy. That was his [Pinkerton's] own oblique way. As for his [Trouble's] permanent name,—he might have several others before,—that was for him [Pinkerton] to choose when returned."[97] The passage is confusing in every sense: Trouble is confused with joy, but the reader is unsure if the confusion is the result of Cho-Cho-San's inadequate grasp of English or whether she experiences "trouble" with a kind of perverse pleasure (as it is implied that Pinkerton does in his "own oblique way"). He is also denied the right of proper name or proper identification. His naming is suspended in both the play and the opera and is also in keeping with the grammatological traditions of political exclusion, in general, and US racism, in particular.

The tradition of withholding a proper name as a means of negating a being's political subjectivity has a long history in Western political thought. Nicole Loraux has shown, for example, how early myths and records of the founding of Athens celebrate the name of the autochthonous ancestor of all Athenians, Erichthonios, while withholding or only begrudgingly affording a name for the first woman. The refusal of a proper name and political disenfranchisement are directly related. There is no word in Ancient Greek for "Athenian woman," which Loraux describes as a purposeful omission intended to appease Poseidon for losing control of the city to the goddess Athena "by depriving women of their power and their name."[98] This example is particularly salient in Trouble's case insofar as Athenian citizenship was based on the Periclean law, which required bilateral parentage. Thus, citizenship standing was denied to subjects born to mixed parents, even if born and raised in Athens. There is a familiar resemblance between the Periclean order of citizenship and the US American model that denied citizenship to Tuan Ahn Nguyen.

The withholding of names also has significance in relation to the racial ordering of the modern US American civic imaginary. Hortense Spillers argues that the act of withholding and denying proper names from ethnic subjects forecloses the possibility of subjectivity by denying the ethnic body a place in the terminology of the nation. She notes that through the refusal to name gendered black subjects *as* subjects, black women in the US slave trade were transformed from persons into quantities, inhabiting subjectivity under erasure: "Those African persons in 'Middle Passage' were literally suspended in the oceanic, if we think of the latter in its Freudian orientation as an analogy on undifferentiated identity: removed from the indigenous land and culture, and not-yet 'America' either, these captives, without names that their captors would recognize, were in movement across the Atlantic, but they were also *nowhere* at all."[99] To be clear, I do not mean to collapse three historically different figures: women in classical Athens, enslaved black women in the Middle Passage, and the mixed-race child of a white, US American father and Asian mother. Instead, I cite Loraux and Spillers to highlight the transhistorical practice of withholding names as a technology of patriarchal and racial domination in Western political and legal traditions. The refusal to recognize the subject's name is thus a means of suspending the gendered and ethnic body in the space between interior/exterior, person/quantity, and citizen/alien. This practice dislodges the subject from the terrain of proper civic being. Trouble is neatly representative of this crisis.

Long's Cho-Cho-San refuses to accept what is supposed to be her proper orientation within the law; Trouble is incapable of doing so because he has no proper place, signified by his lack of a proper name. The result is that, returning to Spillers, if "the loss of indigenous name/ land marks a metaphor of displacement for other human and cultural features and relations," the lack of a name at all marks the displacement of Trouble from the proper terrain of subjectivity writ large.[100] This produces him as a limit figure against which the properly named national subjectivity of Sharpless or Pinkerton's white American wife (Adelaide/ Kate Pinkerton) is defined. That Cho-Cho-San has deferred the ultimate assignation of a permanent name for Trouble by placing the responsibility on her absent US husband suggests that the only way that Trouble can become a properly named subject is by gaining his father's acceptance (or the embrace of his "fatherland," the United States). Because this will never happen, the narratives each resolve the crisis of Trouble's national status by transforming him into an object, an exotic commodity to be traded by Western consumers.

The primary dramatic tension in the latter half of Long's narrative is born from the question of who will take custody of the baby. But Mrs. Pinkerton's interest in raising the baby does not transform Trouble from an object into a subject so much as it confirms his exceptional status as simultaneously object and subject. Pinkerton returns to Nagasaki with his wife but quickly leaves for a temporary work assignment. When Adelaide Pinkerton catches sight of the child, she telegraphs her husband immediately: "Just saw the baby and his nurse. Can't we have him at once? He is lovely. Shall see the mother about it tomorrow. Was not at home when I was there to-day. Expect to join you Wednesday week per *Kioto* [*sic*] *Maru*. May I bring him along? ADELAIDE."[101] Adelaide Pinkerton's desire to possess the child is, in this respect, not terribly different from her husband's "rental" of Cho-Cho-San. Just as Cho-Cho-San is an object of exchange between men and nations, the child doubles as a commodity for domestic exchange between women and nations.

The moral dimension of Trouble's possession is more fully fleshed out in the 1900 dramatic adaptation, in a scene in which Mrs. Pinkerton (renamed Kate) suggests that it will be to the child's benefit to leave Cho-Cho-San's care and enter into her own:

KATE:               Let us think first of the child. For his own
                    good . . . let me take him home to my coun-
                    try. . . . I will do all I would for my own.
MADAME BUTTERFLY: (*Showing no emotion*) He not know then—me—
                    his mother?
KATE:               It's hard, very hard, I know, but would it not be
                    better?[102]

If Trouble is to have any meaningful place in the world, it requires the extreme measure of removing him from Cho-Cho-San's care—as the possibility of Cho-Cho-San entering into the United States with her son is foreclosed from the start. Mrs. Pinkerton's solution is to instigate a forced forgetting of Trouble's Japanese mother, extinguish the etiolating effects of Japanese cultural difference, and to place him in the civilizing care of the properly married (and, thus, legally recognized) white wife of his father.

As with the characterization of Cho-Cho-San's jurisdictional crisis, the problem of custody for Trouble efficiently represents jurisprudence about the status of mixed-race Asian children and Asian orphans during the period of Chinese exclusion. The foreclosure of mixed-race children from national status was clearly established in a 1909 ruling (*In re Knight*) that determined that mixed white, Japanese, and Chinese petitioners were not eligible for naturalization due to a bar that proscribed citizenship for nonwhite subjects.[103] Furthermore, Mrs. Pinkerton's and Sharpless's desire to take responsibility for the moral future of Trouble is entirely reflective of the jurisprudential concern for the status of Chinese children already in the United States.

In an 1890 case, *In re North Pacific Presbyterian Board of Missions v. Ah Won and Ah Tie*, the Oregon Supreme Court approached just such a question. The case involved whether two Chinese orphans should be placed in the custody of Chinese relatives (who intended to return the children to their grandmother in China) or a religious organization run by white women, the Woman's North Pacific Presbyterian Board of Missions (WNPPBM). Judge Thayer (the author of *Ching Ling*) noted that the Chinese appellants had a justifiable interest in seeing that the children "might be raised in accordance with the customs of their father."[104] He did so, however, only after defining the "customs" of the Chinese thus: "Chinamen such as we have among us can rarely be trusted. . . . Those of the race who have come to this coast have generally exhibited a total disregard of virtue, candor, and integrity, and have shown such a propensity to cunning, deception, and perfidy, that if they were to engage in an effort to accomplish an apparently meritorious object a strong suspicion would arise that there was some covert sinister scheme at the bottom of it."[105] Thayer's construction of Chinese cultural difference as malignant and averse to altruistic pursuits served as a foil for the benevolent nature of US culture. Again, describing the Chinese as "cunning," "covert," and "deceptive," the ruling aligns with the Butterfly narrative's characterization of Asians as skilled, and therefore untrustworthy, performers.

Against Thayer's definition of Chinese cultural difference, the court constructed an image of ideal national culture in the United States, one that was unmistakably yoked to white, bourgeois, Protestant subjectivity. By comparison, this ideal subject was signified in the Butterfly narratives by fictional figures such as Sharpless and Mrs. Pinkerton. As with Mrs. Pinkerton's attempts to adopt Trouble, the court took the position that it would be in the interests of the children's welfare to be raised by white women rather than their Asian relatives: "If these children are allowed to remain under [the WNPPBM's] control and influence, their mental, moral and physical condition will be greatly improved."[106] The justification for this choice was nothing less than the defense of the ideal body politic: "Experience has proved that the body politic cannot be maintained and upheld, nor the progress of the world influenced, unless learning is propagated, morality inculcated, and a knowledge of the practical affairs of life extended to the constituent parts which make up the great whole."[107] Effectively, if Chinese American children were going to insist on being born, thus threatening the firm borders of the body politic, the best solution was to excise them from their Chinese families whenever possible and to deliver them to the care of white women who promised to kill their racial and cultural difference for the betterment of society.

As noted earlier, in the 1898 novella, Trouble, Suzuki, and Cho-Cho-San simply disappear. In the 1900 play, the child stands by his mother, made a puppet of her defeat, as stage directions indicate that "she waves the child's hand which holds the [US] flag."[108] In the 2006 production of the opera, however, he literally *is* a puppet. Whereas most productions of *Madama Butterfly* face the significant challenge of incorporating child actors into the opera's staging, Minghella's production opted instead to produce Trouble as a Westernized manifestation of traditional Japanese *bunraku* puppetry. Various elements of "traditional Japanese arts" make their way into the performance, which includes a strange fan-dance prelude inserted before the opening of Puccini's score and the *kuroko* stagehands mentioned earlier. But Trouble stands out as the only puppet onstage in the entire production.

Just before the Met premiere in 2006, the *New York Times* ran an interview with Minghella that defined his choice to cast a puppet as the child as a "solution to a problem."[109] Minghella explained his turn to puppetry as an aesthetic approach to staging the opera that would embrace the fantasy of *Madama Butterfly*, simultaneously disavowing attempts at verisimilitude. The production was unapologetic in its desire to represent Trouble as both a *thing* and a person. For example, Cristina Gallardo-Domas, who played Cio-Cio-San, celebrated the benefits of using a puppet: "It's a big change not to have a baby, a boy, a human being. . . . But it amazed me to see how strong a presence the puppet is. . . . Whatever my feelings are, the puppet interprets them, articulates them. He gives me concentration."[110] The result is that the rendering of the character as "a baby, a boy, [and] a human being" and simultaneously an inanimate object both negates the character's humanity and intensifies the Butterfly fantasy.

The opera's 1907 stage directions command Sharpless to pick up the child after the father rushes onstage to discover Cio-Cio-San's body. However, this sheds no light on Trouble's fate because the father, still, has not claimed the child as his own before the curtain drops. While US American arms may momentarily embrace Trouble, nothing about Pinkerton's character thus far leads us to believe that he will take responsibility for the child. Trouble's name and national status remain ambiguous, as the narrative ends without his proper location beneath the name of the father. Minghella's staging does away with the conceit altogether, leaving Trouble alone, blindfolded, and waving the flag back and forth as his father and the audience take in the rapturous spectacle of Cio-Cio-San's death. In light of a case such as *Nguyen v. INS*, discussed at

FIGURE 1.4. *Madame Butterfly*, Cio-Cio San (Patricia Racette), produced by Anthony Minghella. Photo by Marty Sohl. Courtesy of Marty Sohl and The Metropolitan Opera.

the beginning of this chapter, one might be compelled to read the Met's contribution to the Butterfly narrative as another moment in the collaboration between *Madame Butterfly* and the law in the performative production of Asian racial difference as that which is to be met with exceptional ambivalence and potential foreclosure.

## Coda: War Baby Problems

Exactly one hundred years after the first publication of Long's *Madame Butterfly* in *Century Magazine*, the Supreme Court continues to write Trouble's story. Minghella's objectification of Trouble was a "solution to the problem" of his fraught subjectivity. This ultimately resulted in his foreclosure. The Court's 1998 ruling in *Miller v. Albright* approached a similar quandary. Justice Stephen Breyer described *Miller* as being concerned with "the 'war baby' problem—the problem created by American servicemen fathering children overseas and returning to America unaware of the related pregnancy or birth."[111] In a case that ultimately determined the Court's ruling in *Nguyen* a few years later, the ruling justices denied the citizenship application of Lorelyn Peñero

Miller. Miller was born in the Philippines in 1970 to a Filipina mother and US citizen father. Her parents met when her father was stationed in the Philippines as a member of the US Air Force. He departed before Lorelyn's birth, unaware that her mother was pregnant. As the narration of Asian racial difference in the three original versions of *Madame Butterfly* aligned with, codified, and circulated the racist knowledge that was produced in tandem with the jurisprudence of the Asian-exclusion era, contemporary productions of the opera run the risk of continuing this fated collaboration. Minghella's figuration of Trouble as an object slated for ambivalent foreclosure ultimately performs alongside the Supreme Court's similar treatment of subjects such as Miller and Nguyen. Both resurrect the tradition of the Periclean law, foreclosing the civic subjectivity of children with mixed parentage. And both continue the tradition of foreclosing Asian and Asian American subjects as a means of perpetuating the national amnesia that marks the imperial past and present of the United States.

Whereas many of the cases discussed in this chapter are largely forgotten, *Madame Butterfly* continues to be one of the most popular performance works of contemporary culture. It is constantly rearticulated and reincarnated in a variety of forms. Justice Ginsburg may have meant her criticism of *Madame Butterfly*'s influence on her male colleagues' worldview as a rhetorical flourish. Understanding *Madame Butterfly* as part of the judicial unconscious, however, her complaint rings all too true. In Aihwa Ong's now classic study of globalization and transnational Asian subjects, she comments on the continued popularity of Orientalist operas including *Madama Butterfly*. Noting the operas' clear gendering of Asian nations as a female space ripe for Western domination, Ong wryly quips, "Sooner or later, Asian women get invited by American dates, despite their Vietnam-era angst, to see these operas (or, God forbid, *The Mikado*) as harmless fantasies about the East."[112] Observing that the Butterfly narrative "must inform or resonate with worldly New Yorkers' attitudes toward 'the Orient,'" Ong suggests that it continues to exert significant power in the process of representing collective thinking and collective fantasies about Asian (and Asian American) racial difference.[113] For people such as Tuan Anh Nguyen and Lorelyn Peñero Miller, the damage done by the Butterfly narrative is far from a harmless fantasy. *Madame Butterfly*, in permutations discussed here and beyond, surfaces at the place where law and performance blend together, continuing to contribute to the racialization of Asian Americans as outside the law and deserving of a place outside the nation.

# 2 /   "Justice for My Son": Staging Reparative Justice in Ping Chong's *Chinoiserie*

On the morning of October third, 2011, Private Danny Chen arrived at a guard tower in Afghanistan to report for duty. Upon arrival, he realized that he forgot to bring his helmet. A superior officer sent Chen, the only Chinese American soldier in his unit, to retrieve his gear and ordered him to crawl back, burdened down by his gear, across over one hundred meters of gravel. Two fellow officers threw rocks at him as he crawled, before a superior dragged him the rest of the way up the tower steps. This was not the first time that Chen's unit subjected him to this type of treatment. For six weeks, members of Chen's unit forced him to do demeaning and physically painful acts while calling him racist epithets including "gook," "chink," and "dragon lady." During one incident, he was forced to dress in a green helmet and shout in Chinese to a battalion that included no other Chinese American soldiers. Alone in the tower on October third, at approximately 11:03 a.m., Private Danny Chen shot himself in the head. In black ink, Chen wrote a single sentence on his arm: "Tell my parents I'm sorry."[1]

In the months that followed, Chen's working-class parents voiced suspicion that their son's case would not receive judicious attention from military investigators. When the military announced that eight soldiers, all white, would be charged in connection with Chen's death, his mother, Su Zhen Chen, responded with a hopeful and hesitant surprise: "It's of some comfort and relief to learn that the Army has taken this seriously."[2] Pentagon spokesman Captain John Kirby was far less tentative, placing absolute faith in the justice system: "There's a justice system in place to deal with it. And that's what we're seeing here in the case of Private Chen."[3] Indeed, the family's hope was dealt a blow two months later when a military investigator recommended that the most serious charge be dropped against the first of the soldiers to stand trial. As the *New York Times* reported, representatives of Chen's family "expressed concern that the military would not investigate the case thoroughly."[4] On July thirtieth, 2012, a military jury acquitted Sergeant Adam M. Holcomb, the first of eight men charged with negligent homicide, reckless endangerment, communicating a threat, and hazing.[5]

This chapter begins with the Chen family's suspicion that the military's investigation would not result in justice for their son. For those attentive to the history of racial violence in the United States, Su Zhen Chen's teary address to the US media is marked by an uncanny familiarity. Twenty years before Danny's suicide, another Chinese-immigrant mother briefly captivated the cameras of the national news media with a plea for justice. In 1982, two white Detroit autoworkers beat Vincent Chin to death with a baseball bat in a McDonald's parking lot because he was Chinese American. Pursuant to a plea bargain reached with the state, both men received extremely lenient sentences that were largely diminished, if not overturned, upon appeal. Throughout the proceedings, Lily Chin, Vincent's mother, was documented in national news media, tearfully begging for justice for her son. Both Lily Chin and Su Zhen Chen articulate what many of us experience as a shared concern that, for Asian Americans subject to forms of racial violence, justice is hardly the ironclad assurance that Captain Kirby takes for granted. In this chapter, I want to take this call for justice seriously and consider how aesthetic performance might be deployed to respond to it.

One of the intentions of *A Race So Different* is to complicate the distinction between performance and law, demonstrating the aesthetic nature of the law and the legal function of aesthetics. This presupposition does not, however, rest on the naïve idea that there is simply no difference between legal exercise and cultural production. Both have capacities and limits that are unique. The law is often rightly conceived of as one concrete path toward existing understandings of justice, however imperfect and at times inadequate this path may be. But it is also structured by limits and evidentiary procedure that reproduce and reify forms of social domination by the ruling classes.[6] Critical race theorists have long contended that the rules of law can be biased toward the dominant culture, making the law a source of racial injustice.[7] If we are compelled to assume a racialized subject position that is recognizable to the state in order to petition a redress of grievances, is it not possible that our attempt to attain justice may result in the reification of the very institutions that fostered the injury in the first place?

Aesthetics and cultural production emerge as one possible alternative to the turn toward the law in a struggle for justice. Performance in particular can be a space for the rehearsal and enactment of new forms of justice. As Lisa Lowe argues, "if the state suppresses dissent by governing subjects through [the rationalist and legal discourse of] rights, citizenship, and political representation, it is only through culture that we conceive and enact new subjects and practices in antagonism to the regulatory locus of the citizen-subject, by way of culture that we can question those modes of government."[8] Because of aesthetic performance's emphasis on the body, it is a uniquely effective method for "conceiving and enacting new subjects and practices in antagonism" as it rehearses and brings them to life in the presence of the collective community of the audience. In this way, performance is also a prime medium for the rehearsal and enactment of new practices in justice. In this chapter, I explore the ability of aesthetic performance practices to stage forms of justice that lie beyond the limits of the law and the constraints of legal procedure.

I want to emphasize that I am not suggesting that aesthetic practices are always the *best* means of pursuing justice. Instead, I am suggesting that aesthetics have the capacity to rehearse and enact *new forms* of justice that are otherwise unavailable within the given limits of law. A major difference between law and aesthetics is that law is governed by rationalist limits that dictate the rules of evidence and procedure, which in turn govern outcomes. These limits may be negotiated, but only to a point. Thus, a judge's decision to exclude a specific piece of evidence from a trial, for example, may be bound by the law of evidence. Certainly, a great deal of discretion is involved in juristic decision, but there are some constrictions so carefully defined by the law that the interpretive act can only go so far. The limits that govern the law are neither neutral nor lacking in ideological or political viewpoint. But this does not make these rules any less of a limit from a legal standpoint. An artist, on the other hand, has relatively free range to include and represent whatever information/material he or she chooses. An artist may meet with forms of convention and limit but has a great deal more latitude to negotiate and even reject them. Because of this greater range of movement, aesthetics have the capacity to repurpose legal discourse in ways that stage new forms of justice that simply cannot exist within an official legal context.[9]

In order to illustrate this claim about aesthetics, I turn to Ping Chong and Company's experimental theater piece *Chinoiserie*. *Chinoiserie* debuted in 1995 and is a multimedia performance that Chong later characterized as a "collage [made] from the detritus of East-West relations."[10] In *Chinoiserie*, Chong, four actors, and three musicians perform a dramatic history of Euro-American–Chinese relations. Chong describes *Chinoiserie* as made up of the "detritus" of history, and much of this detritus survives in the form of legal documents and events such as a treaty between China and Great Britain, the passage of the Chinese Exclusion Act, and the trial of Vincent Chin's murderers. In this chapter, I argue that *Chinoiserie* uses the imaginative space of the stage to work with this legal source material in order to enact new forms and practices of justice that might address the calls of Lily Chin and Su Zhen Chen.

*Chinoiserie* stages a practice of justice that functions not through the negation of the law but by using performance to disassemble and repurpose the objects of the law in order to make reparation for Chinese America. I draw the concept of reparation from the work of psychoanalytic theorist Melanie Klein and queer theorist Eve Kosofsky Sedgwick.[11] Klein articulated reparation as a process that occurs after a subject acts out on aggressive impulses against a parent figure (often in fantasy/phantasy). Because this violence occurs against a phantasy of the parent who has been introjected into the subject, the violence is psychologically injurious and even fragmenting to the subject him- or herself. The "desire to make reparation" is indicative of a desire to "make good the injury psychologically done to the [parent] and also to restore [the subject] herself."[12] In a discussion of Klein, Sedgwick defines making reparation as an attempt to "use one's own resources to assemble or 'repair' the murderous part-objects into something like a whole—though ... *not necessarily like any preexisting whole.* Once assembled to one's own specifications, the more satisfying object is available both to be identified with and to offer one nourishment and comfort in turn. Among Klein's names for the reparative process is love."[13] If the history of Chinese America has been fragmented and torn apart by official US practices of exclusion, violence, and exception, Ping Chong and Company's *Chinoiserie* does not simply disavow the law and culture of the United States. Rather, it draws them inward, working with these fragmented objects in order to assemble and repair Chinese American history into "something like a whole." Doing so, it rehearses and stages a response to the call for justice for Chinese America.[14] *Chinoiserie* is thus significant of "the many ways selves and communities succeed in extracting sustenance from the objects of a culture—even of a culture whose avowed desire has often been not to sustain them"—in order to repair the past in pursuit of a just future.[15]

## Chinoiserie

*Chinoiserie* is the second installment in a four-part, staged interrogation of collisions and points of connection between Europe, the United States, and Asia. This series, comprehensively titled *The East/West Quartet*, began with *Deshima: A Poetic Documentary* (organized around Japan), followed by *Chinoiserie* (China), *After Sorrow: A Work in Four Parts* (Vietnam), and *Pojagi* (Korea). Chong is a multimedia artist who began as a dancer with Meredith Monk, and much of his work preceding *The East/West Quartet* relied on devised theater practices. For the first two installments of the quartet, however, Chong worked with his longtime collaborator, Dominican American artist Michael Matthews, to write a script before heading into rehearsals. *Chinoiserie* debuted on September twenty-second, 1995, at the Lied Center for Performing Arts in Lincoln, Nebraska, before receiving its New York premiere as part of the Brooklyn Academy of Music's Next Wave Festival later that year. This was Chong's last collaboration with Matthews, who passed away due to AIDS complications in early 1996.

Like *Deshima*, *Chinoiserie* might be understood as a "poetic documentary." Describing the structure of the earlier work, Theodore Shank writes, "Although incorporating historical material and figures, the structure of *Deshima* is nonlinear and multilayered, allowing for ironic contrasts and comparisons between events from different periods."[16] *Chinoiserie* departs from the spectacular theatricality of *Deshima*, however. *Deshima* relied heavily on scenic elements, elaborate costumes, and a relatively large cast of nine actors—which included Matthews as a narrator / master of ceremonies. In turn, *Chinoiserie* features a sleek, minimalist aesthetic, pared down to a few costumes and a stationary set. At the back wall of the stage are four lattice-framed panels, and at the center is a large, rectangular white carpet. Four metal music stands and stools are upstage left. The narration is divided between a multiracial collective of actors who also perform a range of characters (mostly drawn from history): Shi-Zheng Chen, Aleta Hayes, Michael Edo Keane, and Ric Oquita. They remain onstage, behind the music stands, for virtually the entire performance. Their scripts are displayed before them, and they are dressed in neutral black outfits with white jackets. Although most of the dramatic action occurs behind the music stands, with the actors shuttling at a rapid pace from one role to the next, extended scenes (often involving complex choreography and self-conscious theatricality) occasionally occur on the carpet at the stage's center.

Before I begin my analysis of the reparative engagement with history and law in *Chinoiserie*, a key element of its mise-en-scène deserves further explanation. Throughout the performance, the actors portray a range of characters with racial and gender identities that do not conform to their own bodies. Hayes, for example, is an African American woman and shares the role of British envoy George Macartney, portrays a white woman in an excerpt from a nineteenth-century melodrama, and completes the performance in the role of Vincent Chin's Chinese immigrant mother, Lily Chin. While one might casually describe the casting strategies of Ping Chong and Company as "color-blind," this determination would be inaccurate. Rather than ignoring the racial difference of the actors from the roles that they play, *Chinoiserie* routinely and strategically emphasizes it.

The concept of color-blind casting takes its name from Justice Harlan's *Plessy* dissent. Like Harlan's color-blind Constitution, this popular conceit runs the risk of eliding difference in an attempt to "celebrate" it. In many ways, the US judiciary has established Justice Harlan's concept of the color-blind Constitution as the preferred doctrine for responding to invidious forms of discrimination.[17] In the introduction, I suggested that the color-blind Constitution (and one might even say the concept of equal protection itself) is haunted by traces of white chauvinism and Asian exclusion. Today, rather than providing courts with the complex tools needed for dismantling systemic and historically produced forms of discrimination, color-blind rhetoric is deployed by courts in ways that flatten out difference and even reify or reproduce the very institutions that the doctrine of blind equality hoped to abolish.[18] A similar risk is attached to the practice of color-blind casting.

In Angela Pao's illuminating study of the various deployments of and debates about color-blind or nontraditional casting, she notes that one popularly held definition of such practices is the casting of minoritarian subjects in roles for which the race, gender, or ethnicity of the character is not central to the play's or character's development.[19] One benefit of color-blind casting is that it gives talented minoritarian actors the opportunity to portray roles that are otherwise denied to them by a limited view of what a Hamlet or a Nora Helmer looks like. At the same time, it can often play into a liberal vision of a world in which the mark

FIGURE 2.1. Michael Edo Keane and Aleta Hayes in *Chinoiserie*, by Ping Chong and Company. Photo by Glenn Halvorson. Courtesy of Walker Art Center.

of race does not, in fact, produce meaning in and on the body, displacing history and the way that it hurts. Color-blind casting runs the risk of subordinating difference by simply pretending that the role of Hamlet does not signify differently when it is portrayed by an actress of color, as if the history that has resulted in her subjectification as a woman of color, or the racist and sexist culture that shaped the different viewing practices of the audiences, can cease to matter.

If racial difference has been used to subordinate different groups throughout US history, Ping Chong and Company capitalize on the textured materiality of the stage to provide a reparative alternative. The racial difference of the actors from their characters is always on display in *Chinoiserie* as the company reconfigures the mark of racial difference in and on the actor's body to new "specifications" as a means of challenging the bodily logic of racism. That is, the gap between the bodies of the actors and the roles they play is not placed under erasure through color-blind staging. Instead, as I will show, this difference is strategically emphasized, allowing the audience to make important connections about the process of racialization and the way it works differently on differently raced or gendered bodies. Emphasizing the best possibilities in nontraditional casting, such practices invite the audience to encounter the changing nature and performativity of social identity. "This perpetual state of flux," writes Pao, "entails a constant renewal of concepts, categories, and practices that not only reflect but actually constitute new cultural identities."[20] In *Chinoiserie*, the often-fragmenting effects of racialization are not subordinated to color-blindness; they are repaired so as to open up new possibilities for social and cultural meaning in and on the raced body.

## Political Theater: "The Center(s) of the Civilized World"

History has to be broken apart if it is to be reconfigured, repaired, and put back together. *Chinoiserie* stages history as a dramatic palimpsest, showing the audience how historical formations such as race, nation, and political power have been performed into being in a contradictory and overlapping fashion not unlike a dance drama. As a result, *Chinoiserie* demonstrates how form can be just as important as narrative in the making of both nations and good theater. Additionally, it shows how aesthetic performance's familiar resemblance to the theater of global politics makes it a prime medium for the restoration and reparation of Chinese America to history.

The production regularly explodes into self-conscious moments of theatricality, such as martial arts sequences, lampoons of Chinese opera arias, and song-and-dance numbers. These moments eschew the academic authority of the production's historical content and refuse the linear tendencies of dominant historiography. This strategy is employed early in the play as *Chinoiserie* dramatizes the attempts of a British envoy to negotiate a proposed treaty with the Qianlong emperor. Here, the production spectacularly emphasizes the ways in which history— as that which is used to legitimize national identity—is a performative construction whose production is akin to Chong's own, self-conscious dramaturgical strategies. Ambassador Macartney (played by Oquita) introduces himself by singing a bombastic ballad of self-praise, after which Liang Kentang—his diplomatic Chinese counterpart—demands a similar interlude. Music reminiscent of Chinese opera explodes from the orchestra, and Kentang (as represented by both Chen, a classically trained Chinese opera artist, and later Keane) performs a stylized ledger of his accomplishments, setting off a competition between the two diplomats who are vying for center stage (both dramatically and in terms of the theater of global politics).

When Macartney begs Kentang to hurry it along—anachronistically asking, "Remember what happened to Frank Sinatra on the Grammys?"—the Chinese diplomat responds in kind: "I would never blow my own horn this way, but this is how characters are introduced in the Chinese opera."[21] As we encounter two sovereignties locked in a contested exchange, the scene provides a miniature portrait of the ways in which both China and the United States have assumed a chauvinistic position of superiority with regard to the other. Asserting competing claims to universality and exceptionalism, Liang states, "We are the center of the civilized world," to which Macartney replies, "And we are the most powerful nation on earth."[22] *Chinoiserie* stages the dispute between the competing sovereignties represented by Kentang and Macartney as a geopolitically tense, physical pas de deux. This playful dramatization of history reveals the divergent ways in which *both* nations assert incommensurable claims of competing sovereignty. Rich with sequences like this, *Chinoiserie* demonstrates how the term *Pacific theater* might be more than just a metaphor, staging geopolitics as a dramatic encounter.

These first few moments of the play also blast apart traditional narratives of US constitution by reframing the historical moment that is popularly understood as an iconic event in the birth of US independence: the Boston Tea Party. Instead of beginning this story in Boston, *Chinoiserie* starts with a tale about the Bodhidharma (a fifth-century monk who is credited with bringing Buddhism to China). Hayes recounts a myth whereby the discarded eyelids of the Bodhidharma spring to life, giving birth to the first tea plants. After describing the importance of tea to the Chinese emperor, the actors sing and dance their way through the introduction of the commodity to European trade markets in the early seventeenth century. Here lies the root of an early conflict, for as the actors note, the "English addiction to *tea* becomes a severe drain on the royal treasury" because the emperor of China was unwilling to trade the commodity for anything less than sterling silver.[23]

Upon this revelation, Chen looks out over the audience and commandingly recites the emperor's declaration in Chinese. Chong, who has been otherwise silent since his opening monologue, assumes a similar posture and translates the statement: "Our celestial Empire possesses all things in prolific abundance and lacks no product within our borders. There is no need to import the manufactures of outside barbarians."[24] Chong's act of mediation allows those of us who do not speak Chinese to be privy to a part of the story of Western-Sino relations that is often discarded in Western narratives of the period: chiefly, that the Chinese

Empire was both uninterested in deeper engagement with European powers and sufficiently powerful enough to justify this disinterest. In translating this key phrase, Chong unseats the chauvinistic narrative of European and (by extension) US American superiority. By pointing to the fact that, from the very beginning, China expressed an ambivalence, if not outright resistance, to the incursion of Western traders, this tiny piece of information shatters the notion that it was the West that needed to resort to legislative and political maneuvers in order to exclude the invading forces of the East. This key exchange also sets up a reframing of the violent conflicts born from Western powers determined to force resistant Asian markets to open.

The tea sequence stages history as a performative construction that is used for the validation of political power and nationalist sentiment. Walter Benjamin reflected on the aesthetic or narrative valences of history when he argued that history is constructed in support of political regimes in order to justify the exercise of power in the present.[25] He called on historical materialists to refuse the self-valorizing deployment of history by the politically powerful in order to "brush history against the grain."[26] *Chinoiserie* does just this by staging history as a "constellation" (in Benjamin's words) of often competing, fragmented and fragmenting events, piecing these events together into a narrative whole in order to repair the elided history of Chinese America to the time line of global history.[27] As the tea sequence continues, the Boston Tea Party is introduced as a surprising member of this constellation.

Hayes delivers the following speech, raising her right hand into the air, extending it out toward the audience, and pulling it back to her body: "On December 16, 1773, a group of men including silversmith Paul Revere, disguised themselves as Mohawk Indians, boarded English ships and threw three hundred and forty-two chests of tea into Boston Harbor."[28] Keane emphasizes the differential narratives of history by responding, "This is commonly referred to as the Boston *Tea* Party in US American history books. For many years British history books referred to this as a terrorist act against the Crown."[29] Importantly, all the actors say the word "Tea" along with Keane, as if noting that the tea is the unifying factor in all of this, despite the divergent narratives of the history to follow. Centralizing "tea" as the lynchpin displaces the tradition of the European interstate order that focuses on states and charismatic leaders as the engines of history, showing how modern history is more likely explained as the product of empire, capital, and the circulation of commodities.

In this way, the Boston Tea Party—a story that is commonly used to articulate a narrative of US American exceptionalism—is removed from a familiar, US-centric proscenium frame that contains only the conflict between Britain and its American colonies. *Chinoiserie* restores the event to the broader global theater of European and later US imperialism. The production infers that the tea carried by the ship (owned by the East India Company) was likely Chinese tea, traded to the British by Chinese merchants for either silver or illicit opium grown in India (a fine point that *Chinoiserie* later makes explicit). Furthermore, Hayes's emphasis on the fact that the activists "disguised themselves as Mohawk Indians" draws attention to the emergent forms of settler colonialism concurrent with the US American Revolution. As Joseph Roach observes, Boston Tea Party activists took on the costume of Native Americans to "signify reckless defiance in the face of oppression and tyranny," a performance that was additionally aided by the ways in which indigenous persons also signify as "holders of legitimate [or native] entitlement to either repatriation or revenge."[30] Situated thus, *Chinoiserie* reminds the audience that the birth of the nation (which was, from the beginning, a global empire) required the performance of such a legitimate entitlement, which was accompanied by practices of displacement and depopulation on the domestic front.

The Boston Tea Party is regularly mobilized within nativist histories of the United States to exemplify the injustices that resulted in and framed the purportedly unprecedented nature of the united colonies' declaration that they were "and by right ought to be Free and Independent States."[31] The tea sequence takes the Boston Tea Party—an event that has been isolated by parochial, nationalist histories—and restores it to the larger, global framework from which it was drawn. Repairing this fragmented history, *Chinoiserie* shows how rather than being a singular occurrence that exemplifies the ipseity of the US Revolution, the Boston Tea Party and US independence are simply smaller components of a larger, interrelated web of events that gave shape to early global modernity and US empire. It reminds us that the colonial claims to native legitimacy articulated in the Declaration of Independence were primarily achieved through largely successful attempts to destroy or disenfranchise indigenous populations. Additionally, this sequence sets up one of *Chinoiserie's* key observations: that the dominant nineteenth-century articulation of Chinese immigrants as unwelcome and uninvited invaders occludes the fact that interaction with the Chinese was the result of forced entry into China (and, as noted in the previous chapter, other parts of Asia and the

Pacific) by Euro-American imperial powers. Reminding us of *Chinoise-rie*'s contention that history is more the product of narrative than ratio-nal fact, Oquita concludes the tea sequence with the question "Whose history is this anyway?"[32] Chong and other actors repeat this question at different points throughout the rest of the performance. Using perfor-mance to open up the analysis of history beyond the limited rationalist ends to which it is traditionally reserved, *Chinoiserie* reminds us that history is as much an aesthetic object, structured by narrative conven-tions as is a play. This provides a new perspective from which we might perceive and value otherwise excluded fragments of Chinese American history in order to repair them to the whole of history.

## The Chinese Must Go: The Scene of Exclusion

Turning to one of the most important moments in the legal history of Asians in America, the Chinese Exclusion Act, *Chinoiserie* begins by demonstrating the previous chapter's contention that popular cultural production functions as an ideological state apparatus and juridical unconscious of the dominant culture. It does so by setting up the legisla-tive history of Asian exclusion with a deconstruction of a popular theater piece of the era, Henry Grimm's 1879 play *The Chinese Must Go: A Farce in Four Acts*. The dialogue is drawn verbatim from the opening scene of Grimm's play and is performed with a metatheatrically self-conscious formalism. The alienating effect of this formalism frames the racial stereotypes dancing before the audience as social constructions with a political and legal impact on the persons they are meant to represent.

Chong's stage directions call for an "exaggerated, melodramatic [acting] style" that presents the characters as "racist stereotypes with broad accents and large gestures."[33] The exaggerated acting, itself a gesture to and jab at nineteenth-century melodramatic theatrical conventions, is fused with a sonic landscape that pushes the scene to the limits of comic inversion: gongs stand in for footsteps, slide whistles ape a puff on an opium pipe, and shattering cymbals signify the sounds of dishes being washed. Against this clamorous background emerges Grimm's portrait of the Chinese as eco-nomically cunning and dangerously ambitious. Here I revert to Grimm's original text, left primarily intact by Chong. Two stock Chinese laborers stand in a kitchen, discussing their plans to accumulate wealth in California:

AH COY: Chinaman plenty work, plenty money, plenty to eat. White
man no work, no money, die—sabee?

SAM GIN: Me heep sabee.

AH COY:   White man damn fools; keep wife and children—cost plenty
          money; Chinaman no wife, no children, save plenty money.
          By and by, no more white working man in California; all
          Chinaman—sabee?[34]

The scene builds on yellow-peril fears of Chinese overpopulation by
suggesting that Chinese American domination of California, and by
extension the United States, is not only already occurring but occurring as a result of carefully honed strategies deployed by the Chinese
underclass. Grimm's Chinese characters serve a function similar to
what Sean Metzger observes in the roles of popular nineteenth-century
yellowface performer Charles Parlsoe, who "animates the Chinaman
as a fetish that substitutes for and conceals dominant anxieties about
Chinese immigrants among the white majority in the late 1800s."[35]
Representations such as those in *The Chinese Must Go* helped to consolidate and disseminate fears about Chinese difference and economic
immigrant ascension, factors that culminated in the passage of exclusion legislation.

   A few moments into the scene, Chong assumes control of Grimm's
text with a critical injection that frames the ways in which performances
in pieces such as *The Chinese Must Go* shaped, and continue to shape,
dominant perceptions of Chinese-immigrant and Chinese American
difference. In this section, we encounter Lizzie, a white woman who is
being victimized by Ah Coy, a Chinese opium dealer whom she refers to
as stock minstrel character John (Chinaman). I revert to Chong's script
but underline the sections of the text that he inserts into Grimm's original script:

LIZZIE:   Has my brother been here, John?
          (*She repeats this line over and over.*)

SAM GIN: Your brother dam hoodlum, he pullee my tail all the time.

LIZZIE:   They are trying to pull you back to China, John. Oh, how ner-
          vous I am this morning.

AH COY:   You like smoke opium?

LIZZIE:   Yes, please.
          Did you see Broken Blossom, John? Did you see Shanghai Ex-
          press? No? How about the Foo Fighters? Know them? John?

AH COY:   Drinkee too much coffee; no good, makee too muchee shak-
          ing?—sabee?[36]

Breaking apart and then repairing Grimm's text with references to twen-tieth-century popular culture, *Chinoiserie* draws attention to the citation and replication of racist stereotypes in contemporary popular culture. Interrupting these repetitions with Lizzie's new lines, the spectator is thrown outside of Grimm's play, shattering the continuity of Grimm's citational reproduction of dominant racial tropes. At the same time, by referencing racialized figurations of Chinese difference in twentieth-century popular culture (such as the film *Shanghai Express* and the rock band The Foo Fighters), the scene emphasizes the direct connection between the types of popular representations of Chinese immigrants in the nineteenth century and those that occur in the present. Working reparatively with the traditions of yellowface performance, *Chinoiserie* exemplifies a historical tradition of Asian American activists and artists who, in the words of Krystyn Moon, use "*yellowface* as a means of revela-tion, illuminating past and present stereotypes that have mystified Asian and Asian American realities."[37] Breaking up the pieces of *The Chinese Must Go*, Ping Chong and Company put them back together in order to reorient them toward a critique of the violence of racialization, rather than a simple replication of it.

If Chong stages the racializing effects of pop-culture representations of Chineseness, the scene also reveals one of the blind spots of *Chinoi-serie*: the elided histories of Chinese-immigrant and Chinese American women. With the important and notable exception of Lily Chin, *Chi-noiserie* is predominantly organized around male bodies. Hayes is the only woman acting in the production, and other than Lizzie and Mrs. Chin, she exclusively portrays male characters. Similarly, the male actors never perform female roles. As such, the bodies of Chinese women in the seventeenth through nineteenth centuries are largely excluded from *Chinoiserie*. Chinese female difference is certainly incorporated into *Chinoiserie*'s narrative, most importantly in the form of Lily Chin. Indeed, the piece itself is dedicated to Betty Chong, Chong's mother.[38] But women are located inside *Chinoiserie* only through the figuration of the maternal (Lily Chin and Betty Chong). Furthermore, they exist only within the contemporary moment, without a place in history. *Chi-noiserie*'s overwhelming exclusion of women from its reconstruction of nineteenth-century Chinese American history thus reproduces a patri-archal tradition which genders the subject of history as male.

In dominant historiography, populations of Chinese women enter-ing the country in the nineteenth century have often been accounted for as being either the wives of laborers or prostitutes, although many were themselves domestic or agricultural laborers. The subjection of Chinese-immigrant women in the United States has been affected by the racialization of citizenship as white, a subject position that was produced in conjunction with the gendering of citizenship as male. As became clear in Reconstruction-era debates over suffrage, enfranchisement for recently liberated men of color was regularly articulated in opposition to suffrage for white women, with women of color subordinated and placed under complete erasure in the debates.[39] Chinese women were similarly subject to exclusion and subordination in the early history of Chinese America. Whereas naturalization codes made it difficult for Chinese men to immigrate to the United States, early forms of law made it nearly impossible for Chinese women.

In 1875, Congress enacted the Page Act, a law that George Peffer argues was meant to "comprise the legislative tool needed to stop the flow of the 'yellow peril' to American shores."[40] The Page Act had two imperatives: first, to ban the importation of "coolie" labor under the auspices of emancipation ideals and, second, to ban the importation of Asian women for the purpose of prostitution. The first provision of the law was relatively inefficient (requiring later enactment of the Chinese Exclusion Act), but application of the Page Act was remarkably successful in altogether halting the immigration of Chinese women. Through broad and rapid enforcement, the antiprostitution provisions were used to exclude nearly all Asian women from coming to the United States. As such, the law not only achieved the exclusion of most Chinese women from 1875 forward, but it did so in a way that always already defined Asian women in the United States as prostitutes or sexual deviants.

Figured thus, Chinese women came to constitute a category of person against whom the ideal national subjects could be defined as white and male. Laura Hyun Yi Kang has described this process as comprising "a jumble of legislative acts, judicial decisions, bureaucratic procedures, and popular cultural representations that have figured specific ethnic, national, class, and sexual configurations of Asian women as distinctly *un*-American."[41] The production of *The Chinese Must Go* in 1879 and the nearly concurrent enactment of the Page Act in 1875 evidence one such moment in the production of Chinese and, by extension, Asian American women as delinked from US citizenship and foreclosed from incorporation within the normative order of the US nation despite their presence within its boundaries.

In the previously cited scene from Grimm's play, reproduced in *Chinoiserie*, Chinese women are literally outside the United States, as Chinese men have "no wife, no children, save plenty money." This exclusion of Chinese women is not understood as the result of legislative bars to their immigration. Rather, Grimm suggests that the absence of Chinese women is part of an economic calculus enacted by Chinese men who conceive of Chinese women as an economic drain rather than uncompensated domestic labor. By Grimm's logic, this allows the men to accumulate wealth at a faster rate than their married white counterparts. Somehow this logic culminates in the threat of Chinese domination because, sans the economic drain of "wife and children," Chinese men will be able to accumulate capital and inexplicably repopulate at a rapid rate so that, "by and by, no more white working man in California; all Chinaman."

The anxiety over the absence of Chinese women was equally indicative of a fear of miscegenation. Theatrical representations of predatory Chinese masculinity, as in the scene with Lizzie, were mobilized to transform antimiscegenation fears into codified law through the passage of legislation that would strip US citizenship from any woman (white, Chinese American, or otherwise) who married a Chinese man.[42] So between the ban on immigration for Chinese women and antimiscegenation codes, most forms of marriage or sexual relations attempted by Chinese immigrants were subject to legal prosecution. But on Grimm's stage, Chinese women are no longer necessary because Chinese men have somehow discovered a means for taking control of not only the economic mode of production in California but also biological modes of reproduction, allowing a population of California by Chinese men without women.

If *Chinoiserie* does not stage the foreclosure and exclusion of women from the United States, it is not from lack of source material in Grimm's play. In a schizophrenic turn, the conclusion to Grimm's play makes a plot point out of the importation of a Chinese woman, but in keeping with the state's administration of the Page Act, she is a prostitute. In fact, she does not even exist. Sam Gin attempts to buy a Chinese woman for the high fee of $200, embodying all the vile and deviant desires of a sexual predator. As one white character explains it, Sam is looking for "a fine piece of meat." Unbeknown to Sam, his purchase is not a woman at all, however, but Lizzie's brother, Frank Blaine, "dressed as a China-woman."[43] After the money has exchanged hands, Frank runs away, leaving the villainous Sam destitute and heartbroken.

The conclusion of *The Chinese Must Go* affirms the popularly held idea that Chinese men are deviant and incompatible with US American norms. In turn, women are represented as people who do not in reality exist unless they are brought to life as part of a drag act enacted by white men. Earlier in the play, it is implied that Frank is shiftless and aimless due to chronic unemployment. Unsurprisingly, this is blamed on Chinese immigrants. As his father complains, "Isn't every factory and every store crammed with those cursed Chinamen?"[44] That Frank plays the role of the "Chinawoman" during the finale literalizes this trope by showing how the presence of the Chinese in the United States has turned otherwise promising US American youth into effeminate, sexual deviants. In Grimm's spectral menace of a United States overrun by Chinese immigrants, white men cede their dominance to listless effeminacy, Chinese women and children cease to exist, and young white women like Lizzie are left to be the victims of predatory Chinese masculinity. The only possible solution: *the Chinese must go.*

As Hayes takes on the role of Lizzie, her character is deployed in a way that critically demonstrates how the anxiety over miscegenation at the heart of a text such as *The Chinese Must Go* produced anti-Chinese sentiment in defense of a fragile, white femininity that would be corrupted by Chinese masculinity. This representational trope is further complicated by the choice to cast Hayes (a black performer) in the role of the drug-addled white victim. But whereas Lizzie's interjection of pop-culture references highlights the damaging effect that dominant representations of Chinese Americans have had throughout US history, the interjection also makes conspicuous *Chinoiserie*'s failure to indict the exclusion, foreclosure, subordination, and erasure of Chinese women. Indeed, the play reproduces this erasure. The history of Chinese women in the United States is literally and figuratively located offstage such that Chinese women are figured as a limit against which a recuperated Chinese American subjectivity becomes gendered and performed as male within *Chinoiserie.*

Shortly after the Grimm sequence, the cast performs a spirited rendition of an 1890 "John Chinaman" minstrel song named "Willy the Weeper." Directly linking performance practices such as the Grimm play and yellowface song to forms of legislative exclusion, the cast then launches into an abbreviated time line of the legislative debates leading to the Chinese Exclusion Act, from behind their music stands:

PING:     [Scene] 20.
ALL:      1848.
SHI-ZHENG: (*In Chinese*) Gold is discovered in California.

PING: (*Translating*) Gold is discovered in California.

MICHAEL: The Chinese become 49ers.

ALETA: The Chinese are the first Asian immigrants.

ALL: 1852.

ALETA: The Governor of California:

MICHAEL: "Let us encourage a further immigration and settlement of *The Chinese*—they are peculiar but who isn't?"

ALL: 1852.

SHI-ZHENG: The Governor of California four months later:

MICHAEL: "*The Chinese* are cunning and deceitful, they can never become like us and they are not of a race or native character which will ever elevate the social conditions of California."

ALL: 1869.

ALETA: Meanwhile down in the Mississippi. M-I-S-S-I-S-S-I-P-P-I.

RIC: "Emancipation has spoiled the Negro and carried him away from his place in the fields of agriculture. We therefore say let the coolies come, let them pick our cotton, let them work our fields, but they must become Christians, of course."

ALL: Of course, of course, of course.

MICHAEL: We did not let the Indian stand in the way of civilization, so why let the Chinese barbarian? I suggest we do to them as we have done to the Indian—

SHI-ZHENG: Put them on reservations.

ALL: 1882.

RIC: The Chinese Exclusion Act—the first immigrant law to exclude on the basis of race:

MICHAEL: "Hereafter, no state court or court of the United States shall admit Chinese to citizenship."[45]

This scene also reproduces the foreclosure and erasure of Chinese women from both national history and the specific history of Chinese exclusion. Although the citations in this section utilize predominantly gender-neutral language, they rely on a historical tradition that assumes that laboring bodies are always already male. Without acknowledging the targeted exclusion of Chinese women (the 1875 Page Act would have fit nicely between the 1869 and 1882 dates), "*The Chinese*" are once again gendered by *Chinoiserie* as male. I have focused so much attention on the exclusion of women from *Chinoiserie*'s accounting of the Chinese-exclusion era not to devalue the importance of the play so much as to point out that a reparative project is always incomplete, requiring further amendments and acts of restoration to realize its potential for justice. But if the difference represented by women is absented from the exclusion time line scene, the sequence is wonderfully successful in emphasizing the racial difference of the performers in order to show how exclusion occurred within a complicated matrix of comparative racial formations.

This scene paints a portrait of normative whiteness as it is produced through the hierarchical subordination of different racial minority groups as they shuttle inside ("Let us encourage a further immigration and settlement of *The Chinese*") and outside ("the first immigrant law to exclude on the basis of race") national and juridical belonging. Oquita's first speech is delivered with an elongated southern drawl, as he conjures and embodies the economically privileged subject position of a white, southern plantation owner. His statements stage the logic of racial slavery as it is disrupted by emancipation and projected onto the Chinese laborer, or "coolie," as part of an attempt to replace the vacuum of wholly exploitable racialized labor in the weak postbellum economy. Here we see how the coolie is performed into being within the popular imaginary. As Moon-Ho Jung argues, "Coolies were never a people or a legal category. Rather, coolies were a conglomeration of racial imaginings that emerged worldwide in the era of slave emancipation, a product of the imaginers rather than the imagined."[46] As a play such as *The Chinese Must Go* demonstrates, once imagined, popular performance forms were mobilized to give this imaginary figure a verifiable, flesh-and-blood presence. In the exclusion time line sequence, the "coolie" is revealed to be a performative construct, forged through comparatively racialized labor formations and popular representational tropes.

Whereas analyses of the Chinese-exclusion period run the risk of isolating the Chinese Exclusion Act (in the same way that dominant historiographies isolate the Boston Tea Party), *Chinoiserie* restores this moment in history to the continuum of comparative racialization, settler colonialism, and US empire. Oquita's dramatic delivery embodies this process as his character (an implied white plantation owner) imagines "the coolie" into being against the similarly imagined "spoiled" Negro, who has been carried "away from his place in the fields of agriculture." Oquita's bodily difference from the character he is portraying, as a Latino man, might also conjure implications for a spectator keen to the contemporary racial ordering of labor, wherein Latino migrant laborers are often associated with agricultural labor. At this moment, Hayes is injected into the sequence following Oquita's reference to liberated African Americans, drawing attention to her own racial difference. Her rapid performance of "M-I-S-S-I-S-S-I-P-P-I" highlights the overlapping racial narratives that were producing (and continue to produce) racialized labor in the US American agriculture industry.

In this concise scene, *Chinoiserie* emphasizes the continuity involved in overlapping mechanisms of comparative, analogical racial formation in US labor practice and immigration policy. Furthermore, because all the actors embodying these characters are in fact people of color, we see how the constitutive fiction of legal whiteness (signified variously by Oquita's, Chen's, and Keane's characters in this scene) is produced vis-à-vis the exclusion, subordination, and/or exploitation of different racialized bodies. Onstage the performers are simultaneously actors of color and the white politicians/legislators whom they are portraying. Their embodiment of the white characters disrupts the stability of the ideal white national subject that the actors signify, revealing this ideality to be a contingent and impossible fiction that is produced in part through the racialization of nonwhite subjects.

In the sequence's conclusion, Chinese exclusion is properly contextualized as a technology of more than just sovereignty (as the *Chae Chan Ping* court defined it) but of empire. Keane and Chen "suggest we do to them [the Chinese immigrants] as we have done to the Indian. . . . Put them on reservations," illustrating the expansion of imperial technologies used to colonize and contain Native Americans to racialized immigrants who were imported to meet the expanding labor needs of the United States. This link between Native American reservations and Chinese exclusion also subtly references the twentieth-century lovechild of these racist state policies: namely, the incarceration of Japanese Americans on concentration camps throughout the nation's interior during World War Two.[47] Although *Chinoiserie* was originally staged in 1995, for a twenty-first-century audience, this suggestion might also evoke the ongoing practices of indefinite detention and suspension of habeas corpus in the global war on terror. The scene thus links the ground-level effects of US imperialism on racialized subjects from the nineteenth century to the present.

## Restoring the Fragments

Restoration, reparation, and the repudiation of color-blindness come together onstage when Chong announces, "I am trying to find the famous image of the meeting of the Central Pacific and Union Pacific railroads at Promontory Point in Utah. The place where East met West, if only in a geographic sense."[48] He then describes the photograph, which is projected at the back of the stage: "Ten thousand Chinese pioneers or ninety percent of the workforce of the Central Pacific Railroad were not represented in the photograph."[49] The image begins to shift, as indicated by the stage directions: "*Gradually, the picture changes as a few Chinese workers are digitally added in color. Then more and more and more are added.*"[50] As "the Chinese workers are restored to the photo" from which they were erased, Chong refuses color-blindness by restoring color to their images, against the black-and-white of the historical document. In this simple gesture, *Chinoiserie* insists that it is possible to repair history, even if such a practice must always be, of necessity, incomplete. This latter observation is made clear in a subsequent projection: "20,000 pounds of Chinese railroad workers' bones were shipped back to China for burial. Some of the bones are still in storage and remain unclaimed to this day."[51] These unclaimed bones remaining in storage suggest that the excavation and reparation of the past does not complete and correct the violence of history. But it does offer us a pathway toward justice that remains otherwise foreclosed to us. Doing so, the play opens its dramaturgy up to criticism of its own omissions (including the elision of Chinese women's histories). It also signals the practice of reparative justice as an always incomplete process, one in which the shattered fragments wrought by the history of racial injustice might be pieced together to create better conditions for future generations who might "claim" these bones and give them a final resting place.

The Promontory Point photograph is not placed under erasure by *Chinoiserie*. Rather, the production absorbs and works with this photograph, using it to repair the damage done by the elision of Chinese workers from official histories of the nation. From this point on, the reparation of past injustices becomes the central theme of *Chinoiserie*. Directly after the conclusion of the Chinese Exclusion Act scene, the lights shift. The musicians begin to play quick, wandering arpeggios as two bright spotlights focus on Chong and Chen, with the other performers fading into a dark-blue light. Chong and Chen speak in turn, Chong in English and Chen translating into Chinese. Chong uses a retracted fan to gesture to the screen as a fragment of an image appears, featuring a vintage photograph of a white man seated on the ground in a hat. "This is a man," he says, and Chen echoes him in Chinese.[52] The photograph fades to another fragment, this time of a Chinese man, also seated on the ground in a different-style hat. Chong and Chen advance their exchange, describing different facets of the two men: "This is a man sitting beside another man." They continue on like this, the fragmented images shifting from one to the other. Eventually, their descriptions coalesce, and the image is fully restored: the men are seated on the ground, eating next to each other. A projection appears underneath the image, "Walter Scott and Wong Kee eating together." The music stops. Chong states, "Nevada, 1908. Walter Scott and Wong Kee tried to have lunch together. No one would serve Wong Kee. Walter Scott and Wong Kee sat in the sun and ate together."[53] In this sequence, Ping Chong and Company illustrate the ways in which structural racism rends through life on the ground level. Putting Kee and Scott's story back together in front of the audience, *Chinoiserie* revives a story otherwise lost to history. It subtly concludes the Chinese-exclusion section of the performance not with loss and immobilizing fragmentation but with Kee and Scott as a model of the ways in which the smallest of actions can be used to reject the insistent forces of racial injustice through practices that might otherwise be described as love. This ultimately reparative gesture is given a visual form in the final instance as the previously fragmented picture of the two men is revealed to us in its entirety.

## "Justice for My Son"

*Chinoiserie's* final segment focuses on the murder of Vincent Chin. While the production highlights fragments of the event surrounding the Vincent Chin murder throughout its earlier sections, these fragments are brought into "something like a whole" in the final moments of the play. The events of the murder and its subsequent trial, *United States v. Ebens*, occurred during a time of extreme anti-Asian sentiment in a period of economic decline following the ascension of the Japanese auto industry in the 1980s.[54] On the night before Vincent Chin's wedding, the twenty-three-year-old joined friends at the Fancy Pants strip club in Detroit, Michigan. At one point in the evening, white autoworkers Ronald Ebens and his stepson Michael Nitz took offense at Chin's touching an African American dancer, named "Starlene." In their objections, Ebens and Nitz attempted to regulate the sexuality of an Asian American man during a moment in which all three men engaged in the sexual objectification of a black woman. A fight erupted, and Ebens began to call Chin racist epithets, mistaking him for Japanese, before commenting, "It's because of you little motherfuckers that we're out of work."[55] The dispute spilled into the streets, and Ebens and Nitz chased Chin to a McDonald's parking lot. Ebens removed a baseball bat from his car and, in plain sight of multiple witnesses, struck Chin three times on the back of the head until Chin fell to the ground. Just before Chin slipped into a coma, he purportedly remarked to a friend, "It isn't fair."[56] Four days later, he was pronounced dead as a result of the injuries sustained in the attack.

At the jury trial, Ebens and Nitz were merely convicted of manslaughter, charged a fee of $3,870 and set free. A federal court later convicted Ebens of second-degree murder, but on appeal, Judge Albert J. Engel of the Sixth Circuit Appeals Court ruled that evidence of prior racist statements attributed to Ebens were inadmissible on the grounds that such offensive language would too highly prejudice the jury. Despite the fact that Ebens was on trial for a *racially motivated crime*, Engel determined that he had not received a fair trial because evidence of prior racist statements would too greatly prejudice a jury: "We need not know the racial composition of the jury, for nearly all citizens find themselves repelled by such blatantly racist remarks and resentful of the person claimed to have uttered them."[57] Engel also suggested that Ebens's extreme aggression was understandable in light of the loss of his job as a result of the US auto industry's inability to compete with Japan's. Additionally, Engel argued that the Detroit media's attention to Lily Chin's grief-stricken calls for justice made a fair trial impossible in Michigan. As a result, the trial was moved to Cincinnati, Ohio. Without the evidence of Ebens's statements to establish *mens rea* (state of mind), on retrial, the defense successfully argued that the death was the simple result of a bar brawl gone wrong and the fault of all parties involved. The event seemed an eerie manifestation of the *Ching Ling* court's 1888 determination that, "in cases of homicide among these Chinamen, it is almost impossible to ascertain who the guilty parties are."[58] The Cincinnati jury cleared Ebens of all charges in 1987.

As with the rest of the play, *Chinoiserie* restores these events to the broader frame of global history. The actors describe the buildup of British interests in China following the encounter between Macartney and the emperor, erupting into the Opium Wars and the annexation of Hong Kong. Throughout this sequence, we hear the phrase "boom boom boom," which has been repeated throughout the play. Within this context, the three words evoke the sound of cannon fire during the war. Three actors are then revealed onstage, bathed in a blue light, in a triangular formation. They deliver rapid-pace deconstructed, overlapping lines drawn from the testimony of various witnesses to Chin's murder. This testimony is delivered with linear choreography that frames the physical nature of the crime. The actors perform a visceral linguistic picture of the racist spectacle of Chin's brutal murder. I quote the scene at length:

| | |
|---|---|
| MICHAEL: | I heard Ebens *say,* |
| RIC: | "It's because of you little |
| | Japanese motherfuckers |
| | THAT we're out of work with GM!" |
| MICHAEL: | I'm not a little Japanese *motherfucker* . . . |
| CAST: | *Boom boom boom!* |
| MICHAEL: | *They jumped out from behind the truck* |
| RIC: | They attempted to grab and corner *Vincent* |
| MICHAEL: | *Nitz* |
| RIC: | *Ebens* |
| MICHAEL: | *Two big white guys* |
| RIC: | One with a *mustache* |
| MICHAEL: | Two big white *guys* |
| RIC: | One holding a *bat* |
| MICHAEL: | A bear hug from *behind* |
| RIC: | *A full swing to the head* |
| MICHAEL: | He held the bat with both *hands* |
| RIC: | A full swing to the *head* |
| MICHAEL: | *Again* |
| RIC: | *Again* |
| SHI-ZHENG: | *Again* |
| CAST: | *Boom boom boom* |
| MICHAEL: | *All I heard was* |
| CAST: | Boom boom boom |
| MICHAEL: | Doubles, triples and *home runs* |
| CAST: | Boom boom boom |
| MICHAEL: | His skull was *crushed* |
| RIC: | Pieces of brain bleed into *tar* |
| MICHAEL: | The body released turns and *falls* |
| RIC: | He was wearing white *socks* |
| MICHAEL: | The body released turns and *falls* |
| RIC: | Not a speck of blood on white *socks* |
| MICHAEL: | *A black man standing on the corner says*: |
| PING: | Ebens swung the bat as if a baseball player was swinging for a home run, full contact, full swing.[59] |

In previous versions of this chapter, I resisted quoting this scene, which is a reconstruction of the direct testimony describing Chin's brutal murder. This is not simply because they are painful words to write and to read but because I have a critical concern about the spectacularization of Chin's murder for consumption. As Fred Moten might argue, however, this attempt would likely fail insofar as the violence of his death would be "reproduced in [my] reference to and refusal of it."[60] Indeed, as Moten demonstrates, it is the "*conjunction* of reproduction and disappearance [that is] is performance's condition of possibility, its ontology and its mode of production."[61] It is precisely these conditions of possibility that allow Ping Chong and Company to access and stage a form of reparative justice, reproducing the testimony as a rejoinder to Judge Engel's erasure of the brutal violence done to Chin.

This sequence is a prime example of the way in which *Chinoiserie* works with the fragments wrought by racist *and* legal violence in order to repair Vincent Chin's story into something like a whole. The inability of Judge Engel to conceive of Asian American as a protected category under the hate crime statue, let alone to understand Chin as subject to the law's protection at all, resulted in complete impunity for Chin's murderers. In turn, Engel's negation of testimony that could have potentially illuminated the plaintiff's previous expressions of racial animus reduced Chin's murder to little more than a "home run" for the onlookers who watched Chin's murder as if it were a spectator sport. Restoring the facts of Chin's murder to the public record, *Chinoiserie* clearly repairs to Chin's death what Engel's application of the law labored to disappear: that it was a racially motivated murder. Putting the testimony sequence after the Opium Wars sequence also repairs Chin's murder to the broader context of racial and national conflict between Britain, the United States, and China. As the three men recount the gruesome murder, we again find the repetition of the phrase "boom boom boom," this time standing in for the baseball bat as it hits the back of Chin's head three times. This repetition quickly links (but does not simply reduce) the violence done to Chin's body to the international violence played out in the Opium Wars.

Staging Vincent Chin's murder trial, *Chinoiserie* demonstrates the utility of performance to rehearse and enact new avenues toward justice. The play forces Chin's murder back into the representational economy of reproduction that Engel removed it from, reminding the audiences that some acts of violence must be recalled and reproduced/restaged if we are to repair the damage done through their official erasure. By drawing its material from legal records, *Chinoiserie* works with the law to extract sustenance from the legal discourse of a culture that has worked to exclude Asian American presence and life from the United States. These fragments are reassembled to Ping Chong and Company's specifications so as to honor Chin's death for what it was: a senseless loss as a result of a brutal hate crime.

Immediately following this scene, the theme of justice is again given center stage. Hayes is revealed, standing at the middle of the stage in all black clothing. A projection identifies her as "Mrs. Chin." Whereas Chinese women have been excluded from the majority of *Chinoiserie*'s narrative, Lily Chin is the central figure in this latter part of the play. Her presence gestures to the many losses that have been suffered by Chinese women in America but also foregrounds her as a figure of political action. If her voice was so dangerous to the normative juridical order that it forced Judge Engel to enact her foreclosure by moving the case from Detroit to Cincinnati, *Chinoiserie* restores the primacy of this voice as a source of mourning and the type of political mobilization that aims to respond to her call for justice.

She speaks calmly and deliberately, employing a restrained, abstract gestural vocabulary to emphasize the emotional intensity of her speech. The text is drawn verbatim from an interview with Lily Chin:

> I want
> jjjjjjustice for my son
> a good boy
> a Chinese boy and an American boy
> you kkkkill him! You kkkkill him!!!
> Like some wild beast!
> Let me ask you
> if Vincent were white and not Chinese
> would you have been such savages?!
> You kkkkill him!! You kkkkill him!!!
> You . . .
> And I
> I want
> I
> wwwant
> I wwwant
> jjjjjjustice for mmmmmy son[62]

Hayes's performance is clear and angry, and she avoids any of the performed markers of stereotypical Asian ethnic difference, as exemplified by the accents and gestures in the Grimm sequence. As Karen Shimakawa observes, this moment "calls on audiences to self-consciously map

Chinese Americanness onto Hayes and requires that they shift their (realist) expectations of what a 'Mrs. Chin' might look, sound, or act like—*and* what the mother of the victim of a (virtually unpunished) hate crime might look like."[63] Casting Hayes in the role of Lily Chin draws a line of continuity between the type of racialized and gendered violence enacted against black bodies and those of other minority subjects. As Chong later described it, with this casting choice, he sought to define a relationship between differently racialized subjects, "to continue the linkage of the history of racism."[64]

Indeed, the vision of a black woman mourning the loss of her son onstage carries the trace of a historical antecedent: the public performance of mourning by Mamie Till after the brutal, racially motivated murder of her fourteen-year-old black son, Emmett Till, in Mississippi in 1955. (We might be thrown back, in this instant, to the exclusion time line, where Hayes spells out the name of that very state.) And might a viewer in the twenty-first century also look back to *Chinoiserie* and see in this scene a prequel to performances of parental mourning to come: the stoic sadness of Judy and Dennis Shepard, publicly mourning the loss of their white, gay son, Matthew, who was chained to a Wyoming fence, pistol-whipped, and left for dead in 1998; the haunting vision of Toni Gunn retracing the steps of her black, transgendered child, Sakia Gunn, on the Christopher Street Pier after Sakia's murder at the age of fifteen in 2003; the tearful pleas for justice by Su Zhen Chen; or the sound of marching feet as Sybrina Fulton and Tracy Martin walked with protesters through New York City, days after the public murder of their black son, Trayvon Martin, was painfully underinvestigated by local Florida police? Here, then, Hayes's delivery of the pronoun "you" is an indictment of all of us who foster the racist, sexist, and homophobic conditions that allowed the murders of Chin, Till, Shepard, Gunn, Chen, Martin, and countless others to occur in the first place and for some of those murders to go unpunished in the second. If Judge Engel foreclosed this articulation of grief from retrial by moving the case to Cincinnati, *Chinoiserie* restores this fragment of Lily Chin's lament to history and allows the audience to finally hear her call for justice.

## Into the Twenty-First Century . . .

The final moments of the production return the audience to the confrontation between Macartney and the Qianlong emperor. For the first time in the production, actors enter the stage in ornate costume.

FIGURE 2.2. Ping Chong in *Chinoise-rie*. Photo by Glenn Halvorson. Courtesy of Walker Art Center.

Introducing elaborate theatricality into a production that has been relatively minimalist from a design perspective once more emphasizes national and racial difference as performative productions, reified through various forms of social and political theater. The treaty is delivered to Macartney. Though in China, Macartney refuses to honor a Chinese custom requiring visitors to perform nine kowtows before the Chinese sovereign. The stage slips into darkness as we hear the sounds of cannonballs, evoking the violent clash between China and Britain during the Opium Wars. In the last instance, we are told that Hong Kong, Britain's prize from the wars, reverts to China in 1997. Forging genealogical links between the violence done to Chin, the Opium Wars, and the initial moment of sovereign competition during the Macartney envoy, the open-ended conclusion of the performance suggests that the question of justice for the future is hardly settled.

The very last moment of *Chinoiserie* charges us with this cause, as Chong gives up his place at the margins of the stage, moving to the carpet's center to join the other actors in an act of critical solidarity. Facing forward, he signs to the audience in American Sign Language against the sound of chirping crickets. A projection above him translates, "You believe in the goodness of mankind."[65] The lights fade before the actors join him, fully illuminated, for their bow. In this last sequence, Ping Chong and Company pass the responsibility for performing reparative justice onto the audience. As the audience leaves the theater, one final projection appears onstage: "To be continued in the 21st century."[66] This final image is both a threat (given the violent history that Chong has laid out for us) and a utopian promise. It is characterized by what José Esteban Muñoz, drawing from the work of Ernst Bloch, describes as the "anticipatory illumination" of aesthetics, which "cuts through the fragmenting darkness and allow[s] us to see the politically enabling whole."[67]

Justice will never come for Vincent Chin or Danny Chen: it does not come for the dead. If it is worth anything, justice is a project for the future that is built by those who fall heir to the injustice of the past. In *Chinoiserie*, Ping Chong and Company work with the fragments of a painful history, drawing on the most vicious treatments of Chinese Americans in both law (the Chinese Exclusion Act and the Vincent Chin murder trial) and performance (*The Chinese Must Go*) in order to piece together something like a politically enabling whole with which the audience can imagine and begin to build a just and loving future. In this way, the production responds to Su Zhen Chen's and Lily Chin's calls for justice by using the stage to imagine the kinds of collective, social acts that are required in order to make reparative justice possible. This occurs through an excavation, confrontation, and reconciliation with the past. Using the imaginative space of the stage, *Chinoiserie* models a reparative practice to create conditions of possibility in which justice might finally make itself known.

## 3 / Pledge of Allegiance: Performing Patriotism in the Japanese American Concentration Camps

The US flag is a central motif in Denise Uyehara's 2003 multimedia solo performance *Big Head*, an exploration of the relationship between the World War Two targeting and incarceration of Japanese Americans and contemporary racism experienced by Arab Americans and Muslim Americans in the post-9/11 era.[1] In a chilling sequence, Uyehara stands in front of a white screen as we watch scenes from an event at a mosque. First, a Japanese American activist organization is honored, before we view clips of men and women praying at the mosque, followed by an exterior shot in which a massive US flag is draped over the mosque's wall. Uyehara is dressed entirely in white, and these images are projected onto her body. She does not so much disappear into the footage as she blends with it. Her body becomes the connective tissue between the targeting of Arab Americans and Muslim Americans in the present moment and Japanese Americans over half a century before. As she stands in front of the footage through much of the performance, the audience is given a concise portrait of what occurs when the nation projects its fears and anxieties onto the racialized body. Watching the footage of a flag hanging over the mosque's wall, we also see what happens when a community attempts to diffuse this imposition with a bold performance of patriotism.

For those who are familiar with the history of the Japanese American concentration camps, the footage of the mosque in *Big Head* is unnervingly reminiscent of Dorothea Lange's wartime picture of a Japanese American–owned storefront with a large, defiant sign hanging in the

FIGURE 3.1. Dorothea Lange, Wanto Grocery, 1942. Courtesy of the National Archives.

window declaring, "I Am An American." Down the vacant street, an American flag flickers helplessly in the background. This and similar acts of patriotism and national identification were a surprisingly common occurrence in the Nikkei (Japanese American) life-worlds of World War Two. Many of these performances were sincere displays of patriotic zeal for the ideals of the nation, while resistant to the racist acts of the government. Others have been read as defensive, compulsory acts meant to protect the Japanese American subject from the racist violence of the state. This latter position is described by Michael Omi and Howard Winant as the "perverse hyperpatriotism of the 'relocation camps.'"[2] The significance of this paradox, performing national identification from the very space that negates one's position in the body politic, has been oft remarked on but rarely deeply interrogated.

In this chapter, I analyze the performances of patriotism that characterized everyday life in the camps. Focusing on the juridical and political technologies that encouraged Nikkei to perform patriotism during the incarceration process, I suggest that these performances may be one of the most significant, commonly overlooked aspects of this dark period in US history. The Japanese American incarceration process (often described as "internment") is a core site of analysis for Asian American studies.[3] The camps evidence the violent history of Asian American racialization by the state, a history that is often denied or at least elided by a pervasive national amnesia. As Caroline Chung Simpson states, the Japanese American concentration camps are overwhelmingly understood by many scholars in Asian American studies as "an unparalleled act in the history of the nation."[4] This is also a position that is resonant with the narration of the camps in contemporary political theory. Giorgio Agamben, for instance, gestures to the Japanese American concentration camps as exemplary of the state of exception's centrality to modern governance, after theorizing the concentration camp as "a biopolitical paradigm of the modern."[5] Including the Japanese American camps in his (highly selective) history of the state of exception, he describes them as "the most spectacular violation of civil rights (all the more serious because of its solely racial motivation)."[6]

While I believe it is important that we continue to insist that the lacerating violence of the camps be acknowledged in accounts of Asian American racialization *and* US history, I am wary of the articulation of the camps as an "unparalleled" or even paradigmatically "spectacular" event. In the long, comparative history of race and racialization in the United States, the Japanese American camps are neither "unparalleled" nor quantifiable as the "most spectacular" violation of civil rights with a "solely racial motivation." Both statements inadvertently elide related and structurally similar histories of subordination, relocation, concentration, and simultaneous exclusion/incorporation for racialized populations. Evidence of this claim is abundant, from the slave plantations of the transatlantic slave trade to the prison industrial complex, or the relocation and concentration of Native American peoples in reservations to the termination policies of the Bureau of Indian Affairs. Placed within this historical continuum, the incarceration of Japanese Americans must be understood as spectacular only insofar as it is one link in a chain of similarly "spectacular" practices that, taken as a whole, become all too banal in their unjustifiable regularity. So if not spectacular singularity, what is uniquely significant about the Japanese American concentration camps?

The importance of this period in history is not merely *that* the camps were productive of a state of exception for Japanese America. Rather, it is that the camps were significant of the deployment of new juridical and social technologies of racialization that sought to produce Japanese

American subjects as willing to accept and perform the simultaneity of citizenship and the suspension of its attendant protections. As I will show, it did so by investing in and adopting new methods that encouraged Japanese America to display, exhibit, and paradoxically legitimate their subjection through daily performances of patriotic national identification. Whereas the first two chapters of this book focused on theatrical or aesthetic forms of performance, I now shift my focus to the mode of quotidian performance that Erving Goffman understood as the "presentation of self in everyday life."[7] In shifting from the proscenium arch to the sphere of quotidian action, I do not mean to depart from analyses of the power of aesthetic performance practices. Rather, I demonstrate how even everyday acts of self-presentation have aesthetic and political dimensions that, at times, become quite theatrical in the constitution, exhibition, and potential disruption of racial subjectivity.

I begin this chapter by demonstrating how the state's legal and juridical speech acts during the war period sought to (and often succeeded in) compelling Japanese American subjects to present, display, and perform patriotism from the very space of civic negation. Then I turn to a group of performances executed by Japanese American schoolchildren that reified dominant racial ideology and paradoxically authorized and legitimized the concentration camps themselves. Finally I look to the activist and courtroom performances of one of the only organized resistance movements during the period, the Heart Mountain Fair Play Committee (HMFPC). Here, I demonstrate how HMFPC members deployed performances of patriotism to critically trouble both the state's claim to the Japanese American body and the legitimacy of the camps. I also show how the HMFPC strategically used such performances to create an archive of the actual violence of the concentration camps and to assert other possibilities for Japanese American subjectivity against the limited options proffered by the state.

## "Aliens and Non-Aliens": Japanese American Subjection in a Time of War

From the beginning, the incarceration process mobilized the performativity of the law to reshape Japanese American civic subjectivity. On February nineteenth, 1942, President Franklin D. Roosevelt signed Executive Order 9066, authorizing the War Department to form the War Relocation Authority (WRA). EO 9066 provided instruction to "all

Japanese persons, both alien and non-alien," living within US borders to prepare for evacuation and exclusion from the West Coast of the United States.[8] The executive order resulted in the legally mandated, forced removal and imprisonment of approximately 120,000 Japanese Americans, two-thirds of whom were natural-born citizens. Virtually all of the internees' Fifth and Sixth Amendment rights, including due process, were placed into a state of suspension as the Nikkei were rounded up without charge or trial and dumped into hastily manufactured concentration camps throughout the nation's interior.

The force of the order was bolstered by two centuries of preceding legislation and case law which included the bar to citizenship eligibility for Issei (first-generation Japanese American immigrants) defined in the Naturalization Act of 1790, restricting citizenship to "free white person[s]"; the *Racial Prerequisite Cases,* including *Ozawa v. United States* and *United States v. Thind,* fleshing out the contours of the bar to citizenship; the Chinese Exclusion Act and the subsequent *Chinese Exclusion Case;* the Gentleman's Agreement of 1907, an informal treaty with Japan that effectively ended Japanese immigration; the Johnson-Reed Act of 1924, establishing the quota system and barring almost all Asian immigration; and the prohibition on Issei land ownership prescribed by the Alien Land Laws.[9] This constellation of performatives consolidated the government's capacity to radically restructure the civic status of Japanese America with the issuance of EO 9066. With only six words ("all Japanese persons, both alien and non-alien"), citizenship was disarticulated from US-born persons of Japanese descent, who were transformed into "non-aliens." The order enacted a universal ascription of primordial Imperial Japanese identity to Japanese Americans, radically deterritorializing any previous national identification (to the United States, Japan, both, or elsewhere) they might have maintained before the order.

Performative acts of renaming and reclassification were central to the government's execution of the president's order. While the camps were being hastily constructed in remote sites throughout the nation's interior, Japanese American communities were swiftly rounded up and shipped to the only spaces big enough to hold large numbers of people. The overwhelming majority of these temporary sites were horse-racing tracks and their attached stables. Barely converted from their previous use, horse shit and hay still lined the stalls that evacuated families were forced to occupy. These spaces were named "Civilian Assembly Centers," a sterile term meant to belie the fact that they were places unfit for even short-term human habitation.

The term *concentration camp* was also performatively displaced with a different name. At its basic definition, a concentration camp is a space for the imprisonment and concentration of a group of people, often on ethnic or political grounds. The day before Roosevelt issued EO 9066, Congressman John Rankin (D-MS) took to the House floor to declare, "I'm for catching every Japanese in America, Alaska, and Hawaii now and putting him [*sic*] in concentration camps and shipping them back to Asia as soon as possible."[10] While upper-level administrators (including President Roosevelt) conceived of and confidentially referred to the camps as concentration camps, government officials determined that the term was dangerously evocative of the dark rumors emerging from Nazi Europe.[11] Thus, as the evacuees crossed through barbed-wire gates, flanked by guard towers with armed guardsmen, they found themselves welcomed into one of ten "War Relocation Centers." Among two of the largest camps were the Manzanar and the Heart Mountain Relocation Centers. Manzanar, located in the dusty abscesses of the Californian High Sierras, held 10,046 people at its peak, and Heart Mountain was built in the remote terrain of northern Wyoming, incarcerating around 10,767 Nikkei.[12] The official acts of euphemistic renaming not only obscured the reality of the camps as concentration camps at the time; it continues into the present, when the camps are commonly referred to with the less violent language of "internment."[13]

Although the performative shuffling of terms and names proved effective methods for controlling public perception of the camps, more was needed in order to pass the incarceration process off as legitimate and compatible with the constitutional values of US democracy. The government sought to narrate and represent the evacuation as voluntary, and the courts played a significant role in achieving success for this mandate. By renaming the concentration camps "relocation centers," or redefining the forced military evacuation as voluntary, these official speech acts were what J. L. Austin might call perlocutionary acts: "what we bring about or achieve *by* saying something, such as convincing, persuading, deterring, and even, say, surprising or misleading."[14] It was not just that the government described the incarceration process as voluntary or repeatedly insisted that the loyalty of the vast majority of Japanese Americans was not under question. By simply suggesting that a small minority of Japanese Americans might be disloyal, the vast majority of Nikkei were now compelled to prove that they were not within this minority. Performing a patriotic national identity could dispel charges of disloyalty while giving the forced relocation and concentration camps the look of a legitimate, voluntary evacuation.

Eve Sedgwick notes that Austinian performatives "can often be seen to do the work of Althusserian interpellation," and the incarceration process is exemplary of this observation.[15] The government's speech acts surrounding the incarceration process not only remade a forced, military relocation and concentration of a population into a voluntary evacuation; it achieved the perlocutionary effect of encouraging Japanese Americans to be interpellated into (and thus to perform and exhibit) a mode of patriotic civic subjectivity that paradoxically legitimized and authorized the negation of their civil rights. This paradox ultimately resulted in dominant narratives of the incarceration that describe Japanese Americans of the war era as "the quiet Americans."[16] Nikkei are regularly depicted as volunteering for and accepting the injustice of the incarceration as a means of demonstrating their loyalty to the US nation.

Official leadership in the Japanese American community colluded with the government to encourage Japanese Americans to cooperate with the government's mandates. This was nowhere more apparent than in the official position of the Mike Masaoka–led Japanese American Citizens League (JACL)—the largest Japanese American civil rights organization in the country. Masaoka reflected on the JACL position in his 1987 autobiography, explaining his logic thus: "In a time of great national crisis the government, rightly or wrongly, fairly or unfairly, had demanded a sacrifice. Could we as loyal citizens refuse to respond? The answer was obvious. We had to reason that to defy our government's orders was to confirm its doubts about our loyalty."[17] This rhetoric replicates the language that the Supreme Court ultimately used to justify the incarceration and to encourage Japanese Americans to willingly accept imprisonment as just another responsibility of loyal citizenship.

The JACL's ideal citizen-subject would put faith in the integrity of the nation and the Constitution, while marginalizing efforts to criticize and oppose the obvious injustice of the government's demands. Significantly, the JACL collaborated with the government to quell resistance among the Nikkei. In Masaoka's autobiography, for example, he sidelines those who dissented, minimizing the impact that their acts of disruption may have had in the history of the incarceration. The Manzanar riot (December 5–6, 1942) was a grassroots expression of public rage against the reinstated draft for segregated units (and the JACL's support for it). A hugely important event, it is afforded only a paragraph in Masaoka's autobiography, in which he dismissively attributes the uprising to the work of "dissidents."[18] My intention here is not to launch a condemnation

FIGURE 3.2. Dorothea Lange, Japanese Americans walking out of the Japanese American Citizens League San Francisco headquarters and into a bus headed for the camps, 1942. Courtesy of the National Archives.

of Masaoka and the JACL. Unquestionably, he was in a difficult position. But it is important to emphasize the fact that the JACL's rhetoric of citizenship dovetailed with the model proffered by concurrent legal performatives issued by the state.

In the final years of the camps, the WRA openly transitioned from justifying the camps as a military necessity to lauding them as spaces for training Japanese Americans to perform a controlled and assimilated national identity, despite the fact that many never considered themselves anything other than US American. On May thirtieth, 1944, Manzanar Camp director Ralph P. Merritt delivered an address to the incarcerated Nikkei titled "American in the War and American in the Peace." In the course of his lecture, Merritt clearly defined the camps' evolution from military structures into a civilian experiment in national subject formation. He argued that the camps, though "unjust," had served a positive effect in that they had essentially taught the "non-alien" Nisei (second-generation Nikkei) how to perform the role of modern US citizens:

> Young citizens of Japanese ancestry going out from Manzanar are now better trained, more stable, more deeply conscious of their rights of citizenship and their obligations as citizens than they would have been had evacuation not taken place. Therefore, I believe that in the long pull, in the terms of human values properly used, there may be enough good to offset the tragedy and financial loss and distress of the evacuation. Beyond the military necessity evacuation is justified by the rescue of the human values of our Japanese American Citizenship.[19]

Merritt paternalistically celebrates the "rescue of the human values" of a Japanese American citizenry that was apparently in danger of devolving into the moral sinkhole of being too Japanese. As a solution to the problem, the camps emerge as training grounds for the making of a patriotic, assimilated Japanese America.

Michel Foucault's description of the internalization and normalization of carceral, disciplinary logic into the political subject's body was manifest in the performances of patriotic political culture ubiquitously exhibited by the incarcerated Nikkei.[20] Through the internalization of US structures of control into the racialized body, and through the subsequent affirmation and display of these methods of control through performances both scripted and quotidian, the Japanese American subject began to perform a mode of controlled citizenship that would ultimately not require the disciplinary architecture of the camp for the state's claim to the Japanese American body to be affirmed. This shift could not occur as a result of the state's performative declarations alone but required the interplay of juridical, economic, and ideological forces that could compel Japanese Americans to perform in accordance with the government's speech acts. Merritt described the camps, in their capacity as laboratories for proper national subject production, as serving "a needed and necessary and demonstrated human service."[21] The success of this service was partially measured by the enthusiasm with which incarcerated Nikkei performed patriotic national identification, proudly demonstrating a claim to US citizenship in the very place that exemplified its negation. In the following pages, I turn to three different examples of such performances to consider the affirmative and disruptive role that they played in the making of this new, "rescued" mode of Japanese American citizenship.

## "We Didn't Have a Flag"

We begin in the classroom. Althusser recognizes the school as one of the central ideological state apparatuses responsible for the interpellation of the subject. "The school . . . teaches 'know-how,'" he writes, "but in forms which ensure *subjection to the ruling* ideology or the mastery of its 'practice.'"[22] But as interpellation occurs in and on the body, it is through embodied acts or performances that such "know-how" becomes corporeal. For Japanese American schoolchildren, many of these performances occurred in the everyday presentation of self under the watchful eye of the state, which was architecturally manifest in the form of guard towers. As I demonstrate in this chapter, whereas theatrical performance might reify, transmit, or contest racial knowledge (discussed in the previous chapters), the everyday presentation of self also has the capacity to confirm the dominant ideology. As Goffman wrote, in his discussion of quotidian acts of self-presentation, "when the individual presents himself before others, his performance will tend to incorporate and exemplify the officially accredited values of the society . . . as an expressive rejuvenation and reaffirmation of the moral values of the community."[23] To illustrate this process, I begin with a study of one of the most banal schoolroom rituals, the Pledge of Allegiance, which took on additional significance when performed in the camps.

After the photograph of the Wanto Grocery, discussed at the beginning of this chapter (see fig. 3.1), perhaps the second-most-popular image to come out of the Japanese American incarceration period is also from Dorothea Lange's visual archive. The photograph was taken at the Raphael Weill Public School in the days leading up to the roundup. In the image, two Japanese American girls stand proudly at the center of the frame. Each one holds a brown lunch sack in her left hand, with her right hand across her heart. A chorus of schoolgirls of different races frames them; many are visibly of Asian descent, but there are also white and African American girls in the group. One of the two girls looks directly into the camera's lens, while the other has her eyes trained above her, presumably on the flag. Significantly, this image is often misapprehended as a photograph of children taken within the camps, and the viewer would not be entirely incorrect in making this assumption. The Pledge of Allegiance was a daily ritual in nearly all the schoolrooms throughout the camps. Perhaps more ominously, the performance of the Pledge of Allegiance is itself a means exhibiting the disciplinary nature of the camps as they are drawn into the incarcerated Nikkei body.

FIGURE 3.3. Dorothea Lange, *Pledge of Allegiance*, April 20, 1942. Copyright the Dorothea Lange Collection. Courtesy of the Oakland Museum of California, City of Oakland. Gift of Paul S. Taylor.

The particular performance that I am about to discuss found its way to me by accident. While conducting research in the archives of the Japanese American National Museum (JANM) in Los Angeles, California, I found myself wandering the galleries one afternoon in need of a break from the stillness of the reading room. Near the exit of a temporary exhibition, a group of museum visitors gathered to watch a short documentary about Manzanar. I happened upon a moment in the film when a former elementary school teacher from the camps describes a rich performance by a group of her students. During her testimony, we never see her face but instead see images of incarcerated Manzanar schoolchildren. We may assume she is not Nikkei, based on the context in which she is speaking, as she explains that her desire to teach in Manzanar was inspired by what she perceived as the injustice of the camps. In a voice marked by a mixture of sadness and marvel, she reflects on her students' perseverant patriotism and ingenuity: "We didn't have a flag. So we would used to salute to an empty corner. And finally one of the boys said, 'Why don't we draw a flag?'"[24]

The documentary *Remembering Manzanar* is a twenty-two-minute film commissioned by the National Parks Service as an educational supplement for display at the Manzanar National Historic Site (MNHS). Produced in 2004, the documentary weaves together official footage from WRA archives, home video footage taken by the incarcerated, photographs, and oral histories gathered through interviews with former internees. Directed by Eric Owens and produced by Signature Communications, a firm that makes educational and industrial visual and audio programming, the film was originally displayed at the MNHS. It has subsequently toured various international film festivals and is commonly featured at museum sites. The DVD is also distributed for individual purchase and used in classrooms across the country. While the film is unremarkable as a work of documentary cinema, it is a useful resource insofar as it not only draws together archival footage and interviewee experiences of Manzanar but is in fact the official, visual medium by which the US government has chosen to tell the story of the incarceration to contemporary audiences. It would not be difficult to find different versions of this story (children saluting the flag from within one of the concentration camps), but there is one detail in the teacher's story that is of particular interest to us: the drawing of a flag and the salute to an invisible corner. In order to understand the importance of this detail, I must first explain the history of the ritual, including the role that the judiciary played in congressional attempts to make the pledge compulsory.

Nationalist ritual plays an important role in the production of any state. In Carl Schmitt's 1928 treatise on the Weimar Constitution, he described the ideal form of the state as being composed of a unity between the laws and the will of the people that authorize and embody the state's being: "The state does not *have* a constitution. . . . The state *is* constitution, in other words, an actually present condition, a *status* of unity and order. The state would cease to exist if this constitution, more specifically, this unity and order, ceased to exist."[25] The unity of law and will is primarily demonstrated through embodied, expressive practices, patriotic and legal habitus otherwise described as nationalist performance. Thus, for Schmitt, as Gopal Balakrishnan observes, "Demonstrations, gigantic rallies and general strikes are events which keep people alive, and in motion, the original constituent power of the people."[26] Performance and political theater is thus not a distraction from the realm of politics but one of its constitutive elements.

The Pledge of Allegiance is one of the strongest forms of ritualized, performed ideological interpellation in the United States. Each morning, masses of schoolchildren stand to face the flag, body erect, hand across the heart. They chant in unison so as to mold each of their individual bodies into the unity and order of "We the People" that is the constitutive source of the nation's power. Originally written by Francis Bellamy, a Christian socialist, Baptist minister, the pledge was meant to promote national unity and mark the four hundredth anniversary of Columbus's "discovery" of the Americas.[27] Bellamy's original 1892 pledge was significantly more succinct and secular than the ritual chant that survives today. It read, "I pledge allegiance to my Flag and the Republic for which it stands: one Nation indivisible, with Liberty and Justice for all." Significantly, in this version, the nation was not external to the citizen-subject, as one pledged to "*my* flag" rather than "*the* flag." The revision from "my flag" to "the flag" occurred between 1923 and 1924 when the National Flag Conference changed the words to "the flag of the United States of America," reasoning that the specification would indicate, for immigrants, to *which* nation the pledge refers.[28] In so doing, the revision externalized both flag and nation from the speaking subject. This revision coincided with the enactment of comprehensive immigration reform with the Johnson-Reed Act of 1924, which instituted the quota system with the specific intent of engineering a largely western European national population by discouraging (if not prohibiting) eastern European, Asian, and African immigration.[29] Finally in 1954, after vigorous lobbying by the Knights of Columbus, President Lyndon B. Johnson authorized the addition of the words "under God." This Cold War revision shifted the authority of the nation's power even further beyond the body of the speaking subject, or even the *demos*, and into the realm of Christian divinity.[30]

The ritual performance of the pledge sutures over what Jacques Derrida defines as the "indispensable confusion" of performative versus constative authority in the US Constitution.[31] It is not clear whether the signature on the Declaration of Independence creates "We the People" or whether it is "We the People" who authorize the Declaration and the Declaration's signing. (Derrida was not the first to observe this confusion of authority, as it was US Revolutionary War figure and the state of Virginia's first governor, Patrick Henry, who complained in 1788, during Virginia's debates over constitutional ratification, "What right had they to say, We, the people? My political curiosity, exclusive of my anxious solicitude for the public welfare, leads me to ask, Who authorized them to speak the language of, *We, the people*, instead of, *We, the states?*")[32] Even if "We the People" are paradoxically constituted by the inscription of the founding documents, while simultaneously presupposed by this inscription as the constitutive power that authorizes the documents to be signed in the first place, in the present day, it is the performance of patriotic national identification *as* We the People that continues to assure the legitimacy of the nation that was mythically invented by the Declaration. By the middle part of the twentieth century, the US government struggled with how to ensure this coconstitutive relationship between state and citizen and, specifically, how to inspire national subjects to perform and embody the unity and order of the people, the law, and the state. The Supreme Court entered the fray, not incidentally, in a series of cases concerned with compulsory flag rituals.

In the Court's short-lived 1940 ruling *Minersville School District v. Gobitis*, the justices promoted compulsory citizen-state relationships when the majority decreed that forcing school students to perform the Pledge of Allegiance was a legitimate exercise of Congress's power. Writing for the majority, Justice Felix Frankfurter affirmed the legislative authority to compel acts of patriotism in the populace, stating, "National unity is the basis of national security."[33] By this logic, the Court ruled that coerced performances of patriotism were a proper means of protecting national security and shared patriotic identity, while discouraging previous national allegiance: "'We live by symbols.' The flag is the symbol of our national unity, *transcending all internal differences*, however large, within the framework of the Constitution."[34] Thus, the Court affirmed the performativity of the post-1924 pledge, which excises the immigrant's primordial bonds to a country of origin and reorients his or her body within the unity and order of a US body politic that gathers under the symbol of the national flag. With an investment in the realm of the symbolic as a domain productive of national unity, *Minersville* demonstrates the ways in which embodied practices and aesthetic forms are central to the very constitution and legitimation of the national order.

Only three years later (with the incarceration well under way), the Court reversed course. Concerned with the advancement of fascism and, in particular, the state-based coercion of patriotism displayed prominently by the enemy Axis states, the Court overturned its *Minersville* ruling in a nearly identical case, *West Virginia Board of Education v. Barnette* (*WVBOE*). Writing for a new majority, Justice Robert H. Jackson poetically declared, "If there is any fixed star in our constitutional constellation, it is that no official, high or petty, can prescribe what shall be orthodox in politics, nationalism, religion, and other matters of opinion or force citizens to confess by word or act their faith therein. If there are any circumstances which permit an exception, they do not now occur to us."[35] Both *Minersville* and *WVBOE*, despite their divergent conclusions, demonstrate the state's anxiety about the production of national unity, national power, and national security through forms of patriotic performance. In the concurrent incarceration, this anxiety was being played out on Japanese American bodies.

The incarcerated Nikkei (from the elderly to schoolchildren) understood that a *lack* of patriotic display would confirm the fear that Japanese Americans were the enemy and a threat to national security. Returning to the teacher's story in *Remembering Manzanar*, the children turn each morning to confirm their status as part of "We the People" by pledging allegiance to the flag of the United States of America. In doing so, they not only bolster the nation (as that which is constituted by "We the People") but also inadvertently reveal the horrifying nature of the camps as a place where the law exists only in a state of suspension. This is made literal in the teacher's story because the students turn to salute a flag that *is not there.*

In spite of the simplicity of the Pledge of Allegiance, it is more than just an oath: it is an embodied ritual structured by a uniform choreography. One stands at attention, body erect with the hand across the heart. The gesture of the right arm draws the body inward while the gaze is cast outward, toward the symbol of national unity. The posture invokes a militant strength and preparedness, while the inward-drawn hand renders the most vulnerable part of the body (the gut) exposed. The choreography of the pledge is an embodiment of the subject's implicit trust for and surrender to the nation. This simple daily dance is significant of André Lepecki's description of choreography as a "haunting machine, a body snatcher."[36] The standing subject, pledging allegiance, is haunted or possessed by the national spirit. The collective realization of the pledge's choreography demonstrates each individual's incorporation into the symbolic unity that is produced by and productive of the national body politic.

Performing allegiance to the state from within the zone of the law's suspension, the student described by the teacher in *Remember Manzanar* signified both his inescapable desire to belong to the national order and his paradoxical exclusion from it. As reflected in the words of one former internee, "It must have been difficult for a teacher to talk about democracy when we were put into a place like that."[37] But if the very fact of the camps posed a threat to the ideals and assurances of US democracy, performances of patriotism (such as the scene of the pledge, just described) could be mobilized to defuse this threat. In a curious fashion, the performance of patriotism within the camps literally stages the Japanese American population as part of the unified "We the People" in whose defense the camps have been erected. This fact is painfully illustrated in the teacher's story, as the student literally produces the symbol of national unity when he draws the absent flag with his own hands. This was precisely what the government was encouraging Japanese Americans to do.

The government's attempt to produce a population that would perform patriotism from the scene of its own negation is most explicit in a Supreme Court ruling upholding the constitutionality of the military order. *Korematsu v. United States* continued the government's practice of issuing speech acts that obscured and rewrote the reality of the camps. In *Korematsu*, Justice Hugo Black writes,

> It is said that we are dealing here with the case of imprisonment of a citizen in a concentration camp solely because of his ancestry, without evidence or inquiry concerning his loyalty and good disposition towards the United States. Our task would be simple, our duty clear, were this a case involving the imprisonment of a loyal citizen in a concentration camp because of racial prejudice. Regardless of the true nature of the assembly and relocation centers—and we deem it unjustifiable to call them concentration camps with all the ugly connotations that term implies—we are dealing specifically with nothing but an exclusion order.[38]

There could be no more accurate a description of the incarceration process than "the imprisonment of a loyal citizen in a concentration camp because of racial prejudice." Within a single paragraph, however, Black utilizes the Court's performative power to rewrite reality by revising the vocabulary of the process, erasing "ugly" words such as "concentration camps."

Black facetiously pretends to focus only on a military order, shrugging off the constitutional questions of racial discrimination:

> To cast this case into outlines of racial prejudice, without reference to the real military dangers which were presented, merely confuses the issue. Korematsu was not excluded from the Military Area because of hostility to him or his race. He was excluded because we are at war with the Japanese Empire, because the properly constituted military authorities feared an invasion of our West Coast and . . . decided that the military urgency of the situation demanded that all citizens of Japanese ancestry be segregated from the West Coast temporarily.[39]

Despite the disavowal of "racial prejudice," the passage is itself centrally productive of racial knowledge about the Nikkei body. Whereas Black assures the reader that "Korematsu was not excluded . . . because of . . . his race," he goes on to link Korematsu's ethnic status as a person of Japanese descent with the military's fears of an invasion by Japan. Black's ruling thus evidences what Kandice Chuh succinctly describes as the "transnationalization of Japaneseness" through the performative production of Nikkei racial difference as always already oriented toward the Japanese empire.[40]

One of the astounding perlocutionary effects of this passage is that if loyalty might not have been in question at the beginning of the case, it most certainly was by the time Black put his pen down. Repeatedly, the Court raises suspicions about Japanese American disloyalty, only to disavow them. In the second sentence of *Korematsu*, Black writes, "No question was raised as to petitioner's loyalty to the United States."[41] Later, he personalizes the Court's insistence on the loyalty of the majority of Japanese Americans: "most of whom we have no doubt were loyal to this country."[42] But if the Court affirms the loyalty of "most" Japanese Americans, the very notion of a small minority that is not loyal at once legitimizes the existence of the camps and calls on Japanese Americans to prove that they are not among this minority. The implications of the Court's ruling are clear: in disavowing charges of disloyalty, the Court raises the possibility of disloyalty, which Japanese Americans can now dissipate only by accepting incarceration without trial as a means of exhibiting and displaying their loyalty to the state.

The Court remarks that despite upholding the exclusion order, "we are not unmindful of the hardships imposed by it upon a large group of American citizens."[43] It is here that the perlocutionary intentions behind the Court's affirmation of Japanese American loyalty are fully realized: "But hardships are part of war, and war is an aggregation of hardships. All citizens alike, both in and out of uniform, feel the impact of war in greater or lesser measure. Citizenship has its responsibilities as well as its privileges, and in time of war the burden is always heavier."[44] In this passage, the Court moves from affirming the constitutionality of the military's incarceration of Japanese Americans to officially suggesting that Japanese Americans must accept the incarceration as a "responsibility" of citizenship. In other words, the Court sets out to recruit Japanese Americans in the camps to the cause of their own subjection. That Masaoka's description of the process is almost identical to Black's is only one small measure of the Court's success in this endeavor.

By articulating the suspension of liberty and civic protections experienced by the Nikkei as just another "hardship of war," Black necessarily compels the Nikkei subject to perform his or her ban *from* the national body as the only means to affirm allegiance *to* this national body. As Althusser reminds us, interpellation does not happen *to* the subject but with the subject's complicity: "Ideology 'acts' or 'functions' in such a way that it 'recruits' subjects among the individuals (it recruits them all), or 'transforms' the individuals into subjects (it transforms them all)."[45] The camps are thus transformed from prisons into stages where Japanese Americans may prove their loyalty. They do so by exhibiting their patriotic acceptance of the suspension of their rights and the negation of their freedom. So if there is any problem with Omi and Winant's discussion of the "perverse hyperpatriotism of the camps," it is that the performance of patriotism is not so much a perverse aberration in the process of national subject formation as it is the foundational ritual that structures the constitutive relationship between the racialized subject and the state.

## Declarations of Independence

It was not merely patriotic ritual that allowed Japanese American internees to exhibit their loyalty through the display of all-American activity. Theater and dance were central components of the school experience for Nikkei youth. They were key sites for training Japanese Americans to embody and affirm the typical US identity desired by the state. Unsurprisingly, they were also zones in which Japanese Americans could attempt to gain access to the dominant culture by aligning themselves with this culture's racist ideology. On the one hand, Nikkei youth were trained to perform whiteness as the ideal means of being a proper national subject. On the other, they engaged in popular practices of racial mimicry that reified the downward stratification of other racialized subjects while confirming the ascendant aspirations of many Japanese Americans.

The 1944 Manzanar High yearbook dedicates a page to the drama activities of Manzanar's youth. The top third of the page features a photograph of sixteen young actors, awkwardly lining the edge of a poorly constructed performance space. Their costumes are typical of the clothing of the period, with young women in debutante gowns and casual day wear. Many of the women have flowers pinned in their hair, designed in the Victory Rolls hairstyle popular in the midforties. The boys are mostly dressed in suits with bowties, with the exception of one young man at the center of the stage in a police officer's costume. On the right side of the frame, at the edge of the stage, is a young woman in a maid's uniform.

The play, *Growing Pains* by Aurania Rouverol, is a mostly forgettable domestic drama by an author who made her career as the screenwriter of the Andy Hardy franchise for Mickey Rooney and Judy Garland. The original Broadway production was a flop, running for barely twenty-nine performances in 1933. More than just an exercise in dramatic expression, however, the internees emphasized *Growing Pains* as an opportunity to embody normal (i.e., non–Japanese American, not incarcerated) US American roles. As the yearbook states, "This Senior Play tells the story of a typical American home, in this case that of the McIntyres."[46] In an inversion of yellowface traditions, the Manzanar seniors use the play as a vehicle to take on the roles of the ideal, white family. As "McIntyre" is a name generally associated with families of Scottish descent, the play allowed students to embody a form of successful, ethnic-immigrant ascension to privileged white normalcy. From the extraordinarily abnormal site of the concentration camps, the production of *Growing Pains* gave students the opportunity to experience "the normal awkward growing up stage" of the teenage protagonists.[47] In *Growing Pains*, Manzanar seniors could play at being "typical [white] Americans" and otherwise experience teenage life that was interrupted by the incarceration process. From unhappy circumstances, the students used the stage to enact a world in which "many things happen to them, but the end is [ultimately] bright and promising."[48]

The Manzanar High production of *Growing Pains* exhibits Japanese American pretentions at assimilation through a seamless, nontheatrical representation of the white characters. That is, the students *simply are* the McIntyres and their white neighbors, without the aid of makeup or other hyperbolic costume: whiteness is represented as a neutral and natural state. But a character that stands at the threshold of the scene intensifies this performance of whiteness. The young woman in the maid costume, identified as Yoshiko Kusunoki, is visible only as silhouette. Her features are unidentifiable save that her arms, legs, and face have been darkened: she is in blackface.

Blackface traditions were no strangers to the camps. In a study of Japanese American performance in the concentration camps, Emily Roxworthy analyzes the incorporation of blackface minstrelsy by the Nuthouse Gang, a troop of Nisei performers incarcerated in Tule Lake, Utah. As Roxworthy observes, the performance of blackface minstrelsy

FIGURE 3.4. Manzanar High School drama production of Auriana Rouverol's *Growing Pains*. "Our World, 1943–1944," Manzanar High School yearbook. Courtesy of UCLA Special Collections, Charles E. Young Research Library.

aimed at garnishing approval from the camp's white administration and displaying "hidden internee talent": "the Gang's donning of black face . . . suggest[s] an ambivalent identification with the oppression and spectacularization delivered upon African Americans but also a theft of racist black tropes in order to elevate the internees' own hidden talents."[49] In the case of *Growing Pains*, Roxworthy's suggestion of "an ambivalent identification with the oppression of African Americans" is too generous a read. If anything, Sophie the maid's presence on stage serves only to affirm the rest of the cast's attainment of an assimilated, ideal national subject position *against* the subordinated figure of a black domestic laborer.

Whereas the rest of the cast simply inhabits whiteness onstage without the adoption of makeup (suggesting that Japanese Americans were inherently capable of *becoming* and *being white*), the play radically distances the racial difference of Sophie the maid from the Japanese American actress by blacking up Kusunoki (making it clear that she is only *playing black*). Adding significance to Sophie's portrayal in blackface is the fact that Rouverol's script never identifies Sophie's race, nor are there even hints of it in Sophie's few scraps of dialogue (which signifies, mostly, as vaguely working class). Certainly, popular theater and film during this period stereotypically represented domestic workers as black women. Indeed, Pauline Meyers, the actress that originated the role of Sophie on Broadway, was African American. But neither does Rouverol identify Sophie's race, nor is it in any way relevant to the plot of the play. This would have made it that much easier for the students to represent Sophie as white (like the other characters) or otherwise unmarked by race. As such, it would not be unreasonable to perceive the choice to present Sophie in blackface as an attempt to re-create the popular performance forms, and tropes, of Broadway or Hollywood, with their racism intact.

Sophie's representation *as* black (and this choice may have emerged either from the white theater teacher who directed the play, Louis Frizzel, or the students themselves) signifies as an attempt to appropriate and replicate dominant performance forms *and* racial hierarchies that consolidated white privilege vis-à-vis the representational yoking of black women's bodies to domestic labor. Representing Sophie as black, and portraying her by blacking up Kusunoki, gave students another means of consolidating their pretentions at ethnic ascendancy to whiteness (i.e., Americanness). As Michael Rogin observes in his study of minstrel performance in Hollywood cinema, "blacking up and then wiping off burnt cork [was] . . . a rite of passage from immigrant to American."[50] Playing the McIntyres and the other white friends, the Japanese American students were able to claim and exhibit the symbolic trappings of national, racial, and class ascendance by aligning themselves with and embodying bourgeois, white ideality. In doing so, they reproduced and affirmed the racial hierarchy of a white-supremacist United States through the blackface figure of Sophie. After all, how better to show that one is aligned with and loyal to US ideals than to adopt, replicate, exhibit, and perform the racist ideology of the nation's white ruling class?

*Remembering Manzanar* also features Japanese American students executing a performance of white American ideality that is consolidated in the figure of an ethnic other. In footage of a school pageant performed by primary school students, we see home video footage of ten small Nikkei children. They are dressed in luxuriant US independence-era costumes and hold up the large colonial flag between them. As is common with elementary school theatrical productions, the performers look more uncomfortable than anything else. They are rigidly facing forward, exhibiting the uneasy stares of self-conscious children. The flag is suspended between the students, prominently displaying the circle of thirteen stars and stripes of the original colonies, but they are standing

FIGURES 3.5 and 3.6. Screen still of Manzanar pageant in *Remembering Manzanar*. Produced by Signature Communications for the National Parks Service, 2004.

outside in a scene that is saturated with light and, no doubt, the punishing desert sun. The viewer is reminded that this scene is not occurring in one of the original colonies but in the expansive terrain of the US West. There is hardly an appeal to verisimilitude as the children don silly, powdered colonial wigs styled in grand bouffant style, comedically too large for their heads and teetering awkwardly atop their tiny frames. The extravagantly lacy costumes look uncomfortable and irritating.

In this scene, the ten incarcerated children perform the hyperideal of US liberty from within a concentration camp established by the US government for its own citizens. But in other footage from the same pageant, we see a different picture of the United States. Here, a group of school-children dressed in stereotypical "Indian" costume are dancing in a circle. They wear dark leather clothing with oversized, colorful beads. Feathers adorn their hair, and there are smiles on their faces as they perform the problematic yet quintessential pastoral of the western frontier. Ridiculously large feathers flop around at the back of felt headbands as the circle of children enthusiastically perform the commonly embodied signifier of the "Indian," hand popping across the open mouth in a "war whoop."

If the children in colonial clothing signify the birth of national independence, it is all too telling that the myth of the birth of the nation is figured in dialectical relationship to indigenous bodies. The Declaration of Independence's power and authority is drawn from a claim to an original, inalienable, natural right that was at once prior to the power of the former state (Britain) and constitutive of the new one (the future United States). This right became fully established with the "dissolve" of previous "political bands" that introduced the new figure of the US subject/citizen. But as Gayatri Chakravorty Spivak argues, "Euramerican origins and foundations are [partially] secured by the places where an 'origin' is violently instituted."[51] Thus, the rights entailed by the new bands produced in the authorization of the Constitution by "We the People" of these not-yet-then United States required the violent destruction of indigenous populations *and* their political orders so as to secure the origin narrative on which US independence was constructed.

While it is not clear that the colonial pageant happened at the same time as the Indian dance, this is a safe assumption. The makeshift stage's light-blue plank background at least makes it clear that they were performed on the same stage. In these pageants, the students represent an ideal national identity, not merely through the embodiment of patriotic figures and symbols (the colonial pageant) but through the adoption of the dominant culture's practice of "playing Indian." Philip J. Deloria convincingly argues that during periods in which national identity comes into crisis, white people in the United States, from the colonial period to the present, engage the practice of "playing Indian" as a means of exploring, affirming, and rearticulating US national identity. For the dominant culture, Native Americans at once symbolize an inherently US American subjectivity and a rebellious spirit of transformation. Thus, the assumption of the costume of indigenous peoples, as we saw in the discussion of the Boston Tea Party in chapter 2, gave whites in the United States the opportunity to occupy an "unchanging, essential Americanness and the equally American liberty to make oneself into something new."[52] The appropriation and performance of Native Americanness allows members of the dominant culture to justify the genocidal cleansing of Native peoples (by reifying their figuration as violent rebels), to refuse to acknowledge the ongoing sovereignty struggles of Native Nations (by representing them as a lost or "vanished" people), and to resolve the guilt inspired by this violence by casting white citizens as the inheritors of Indian customs and lands. As the footage from Manzanar makes clear, this was not a tradition wholly reserved for white US Americans.

It is completely without irony that two of the WRA relocation centers (Poston and Gila River) were constructed on land that was "leased," or reappropriated, from Native American reservations. Representing colonial patriots alongside the specter of indigenous peoples, the pageants reproduce the national narrative that reveals the imperial nature of the US project, linking the founding of US liberty with the dispossession and genocidal destruction of indigenous peoples. As Cedric Robinson argues, the "founding myths" that constitute the authorizing "origin" narrative for the nation "were substituted for history, providing the appearance of historical narrative to what was in actuality part fact and part class-serving rationales."[53] These authorizing nationalist myths were inextricably linked to the production of the "Savage" and "Negro" through the fragmentation, subordination, extermination, and subjection of nonwhite populations in order to consolidate a concurrent nationalist narrative of white supremacy.[54] From the "Savage" to the "Negro," nonwhite ethnics were established as the threshold against which ideal national subjects and ideal nationalist narratives could be formed. Performance and, in particular, the practice of racial mimicry (blacking, browning, or yellowing up to play the part of African Americans, Native Americans, and Asian Americans) played a central role in this process. Appropriating these practices, the children in the camps accessed and embodied a patriotic, ideal national subjectivity, but they did so only through the reification of the dominant racial hierarchy that presupposed their incarceration.

## The Heart Mountain Fair Play Committee

If Nikkei performances of patriotism aligned with the perlocutionary intentions of the government's legal performatives, some Japanese Americans mobilized patriotic performance to stage an intervention into this very process. Frank Chin, among others, argues that many of the suppressed performances of resistance that occurred within the camps greatly complicate the assumption that Japanese America simply accepted the burdens of the incarceration.[55] The Heart Mountain Fair Play Committee (HMFPC) is exemplary of this tradition as one of the largest sustained, organized resistance movements in the ten WRA camps.

Initially Japanese Americans were barred from joining the armed services. As the need for enlistment grew and as a partial result of heavy lobbying by Masaoka and the JACL, in early 1944, Congress amended the Selective Training and Service Act of 1940 (STASA) to allow Japanese Americans to serve in segregated units. A draft was instituted, and although some Nisei saw the chance to serve in the military as another opportunity to prove loyalty to the nation, for many incarcerated Nisei the draft was perceived as the ultimate insult. Having been stripped of one's constitutional rights through the incarceration, the Nisei were now being forced to serve and defend the nation that had unjustly imprisoned them. Following the amendment to STASA, at a Heart Mountain community meeting where internees gathered to debate the recently reinstated draft, an elderly Issei named Kiyoshi Okamoto stood in defiance of the draft and declared himself the "Fair Play Committee of one."[56] Inspired by Okamoto, young Nisei quickly began to organize the draft-resistance movement. By late 1944, sixty-three Heart Mountain draft resisters were tried and convicted of violating STASA, with many receiving a prison sentence with a minimum of three years.[57]

One of the leaders in the HMFPC, Frank Seishi Emi, was born in Los Angeles on September twenty-third, 1916, nine months after his middle-class parents emigrated from Japan to California.[58] Unable to find work in the United States, the Emi family started a farm and opened a produce store.[59] A practitioner of judo from the age of fourteen, Emi attended Los Angeles City College, studying to become a pharmacist, before leaving school to take over his family's produce business. He married in 1940, and his wife, Amy, gave birth to a daughter in 1941. On September tenth, 1942, the entire Emi family (including Frank, Amy, their daughter, Frank's parents, and his siblings) was sent to Heart Mountain after four months in the Pomona Assembly Center (a converted racetrack). Like many Nikkei business owners, the Emi family was forced to sell their business at a substandard rate when removed to the camps.

Emi's involvement in the resistance initially developed as a response to the "loyalty questionnaire" delivered to all the incarcerated Nikkei in early 1943. The ill-composed questionnaire featured the now-infamous twenty-seventh and twenty-eighth questions:

27: Are you willing to serve in the armed forces of the United States wherever ordered?

28: Will you swear unqualified allegiance to the United States of America and faithfully defend the U.S. from any and all attacks by foreign or domestic forces, and forswear any form of allegiances or obedience to the Japanese Emperor, or any other foreign government power or organization?[60]

Ironically, the Supreme Court delivered its *WVBOE* ruling around the same time that the questionnaire was distributed to internees. If the Supreme Court reasoned in *WVBOE* that attempts to force compulsory declarations of patriotism were an illegitimate exercise of state power, the questionnaire was a direct affront to the Court's logic. A highly performative document, the questionnaire reinforced the state's claim to the subjectivity of the incarcerated Nikkei, as demonstrated by EO 9066, rewriting their allegiances and identifications within a national script that cast the Nikkei body as always already oriented toward the Japanese empire.

As has been much observed, the paradox of question twenty-eight was that a yes answer would render Issei alien to a claim of national allegiance, subjecting them to the whims of US law without the protection of Japanese national status. Although the affirmative answer would not suspend citizenship for Nisei, it would indicate a formerly existing allegiance to Japan that many Nisei never felt in the first place. It also disallowed the complicated, ambivalent, and textured forms of affective and political identification *across* both the United States and Japan that characterized life in the diaspora for many Nikkei.[61] For Nisei to answer in the affirmative to the twenty-seventh question also volunteered them for a military draft while still imprisoned as potential enemies of the state. Additionally, an affirmative answer to the twenty-eighth question accepted the undeserved "guilt" of an implied bond to the Japanese empire, retroactively legitimizing the imprisonment. The questionnaire was also complicated by the fact that, for Nisei, the affirmative answer would further widen a generational rift between the youth and their Issei parents because of their different national status.

Initially, Guy Robertson, the civilian WRA director of Heart Mountain, allowed the HMFPC's meetings to continue as part of the "democratic" structure of the camps. However, as camp administration became aware of the subversive nature of the meetings, "permits" were revoked—although the meetings continued to occur in the open.[62] Internal dissent as to the proper means of responding to the draft was vigorous. Extant minutes kept by the HMFPC list only the topics discussed and not the nature of the meetings. However, in a surviving diary entry by Stanley Hayami, a teenager incarcerated at Heart Mountain (who later died in Italy while serving in one of the segregated military units), Hayami describes a meeting in which internees discuss the draft reinstatement. Whether or not this meeting was organized by the HMFPC, Hayami's entry provides valuable insight into the environment that characterized meetings of this nature. Furthermore, his description sheds light on the internal divisions within the incarcerated population:

> The Niseis wanted to join provided that they got certain guarantees: such as citizenship, land owning and such. However the kibeis [second-generation Japanese Americans who had been sent to Japan for education] . . . opposed this, they said, "why bother? We want to go back to Japan after the war anyway." Well all they did was argue and no solution was found for a united action, because the Niseis brought up with American ideas just naturally opposed the kibeis brought up with Japanese ideals each thought the other dumb and grew more hate between themselves.[63]

Hayami's description evokes much of the hierarchical, generational divisions that characterized Nikkei life during the period. In a divide-and-conquer strategy reminiscent of the ethnic divisiveness of European colonial regimes, those in opposition to Nikkei resistance (the JACL, the US government, and the civilian administrators of the WRA, in particular) exacerbated differences between Issei, Nisei, and Kibei as a means of sewing dissent and mistrust, thus discouraging unified organization among the incarcerated.

Following the questionnaire and the reinstatement of the draft, Emi and his brother Arthur began to employ activist performances as way of testing the state's control over Nikkei bodies within the camp. Many young men defiantly answered no to both questions; these men became known as the "No-No boys," who are famously depicted in John Okada's stunning postwar novel *No-No Boy*.[64] After Frank Emi's death in 2010, the *New York Times*'s obituary incorrectly described Emi as a No-No boy.[65] What is interesting about the Emi brothers' performance, however, is not their outright defiance. Rather than affirm or deny the two questions, the Emi brothers sidestepped their interpellative imperatives altogether by issuing a Bartlebean alternative.[66] They wrote, "under the present conditions and circumstances, I am unable to answer these questions."[67]

One of the challenges posed by an Althusserian notion of ideological interpellation is that given the near totality of ideology, which exists without a clear exterior, one is hard-pressed to enact any resistant strategy that does not simply confirm the source of domination against which one struggles. Direct counterperformatives (or the refusal of an authoritative power's legitimacy) are likely to fail given that they do not have the force to achieve felicity. For Japanese Americans, even the resistant act of answering no to both questions fell flat from a legal perspective. But this is not to say that they were without a potentially productive effect.

The Emi brothers' response opens up an unexpected terrain of possible, critical resistance. This is the domain of what Sedgwick calls the periperformative. Periperformatives, she explains, are utterances "signifying that, though not themselves performatives, they are *about* performatives, and more properly, that they cluster *around* performatives."[68] So whereas "I forswear any form of allegiances or obedience to the Japanese Emperor" is an explicit performative, "under the present conditions I am neither able to swear nor to foreswear" is periperformative in that it does not, itself, swear or foreswear. Instead, it gestures to the conditions under which one cannot enact the performative. This unleashes a range of possibilities that might not be otherwise possible within the interpellating sphere of pure performativity.

Though periperformative utterances may seem weak in that they do not achieve the same force as an Austinian performative, they can be strategically useful in challenging the force of the explicit performative precisely because they undermine its anticipated outcome. They are particularly effective when used to disrupt the interpellative hail of the law, which Sedgwick demonstrates when she turns to the law to explore the periperformative:

> Suppose (to imagine a different legal situation) a judge demands that I plead guilty or not guilty, in a case where either of those pleas would be a legitimate performative act; but either of them would equally reinscribe the law's legitimacy in regulating behavior. . . . I *could* also respond explicitly that in such functions I am not properly a subject of the law, and hence can't be either guilty *or* innocent of "the crime," which I don't acknowledge to be one. But such an utterance, like any other expression of opinions or

feelings, . . . would have zero proper performative force, which is
to say in this context legal force. Its gravity from that point of view
would be confined to the periperformative realm.[69]

Whereas we might conceive of the sidestepping of the compulsion to
plead either guilty or not guilt as failure by virtue of the fact that it has
"zero performative force," the concept of the periperformative allows us
to see the profound political potentiality that such an action might have.
It can both criticize the ideology of the dominant culture and unleash
other possibilities previously limited by the interpellative performativity
of the law.

Periperformativity has an already existent relationship to performance. Austin famously excluded performatives issued "by an actor on
a stage" as "fall[ing] under the doctrine of the *etiolations* of language."[70]
Sedgwick shows us how to fold such utterances into a broader theory of
the performative by way of the periperformative and, in so doing, points
us to the (politically) disruptive potentiality included within the articulation of periperformatives as they appear in a theatrical context. Certainly, such speech acts may have an "etiolating" effect on language, but
this might be exactly what one *wants to* achieve if attempting to disrupt
the interpellative performativity of the law's hail. That is, if to etiolate is
to weaken, then the periperformative enunciation (whether uttered by
an actor or an activist) has the capacity to weaken the interpellative force
of the law. In this way, it is useful to conceive of the Emi brothers' questionnaire response, and subsequent HMFPC actions, as something other
than an attempt to negotiate and win within the existing structures of
US law. Such an attempt was bound to fail anyway, given that they had
already been convicted and imprisoned before being charged or asked
to plea. Instead, the political power of the HMFPC's actions was their
disruptive, periperformative theatricality.

After the Emi brothers answered their own questionnaires, they
took their performance to the streets by producing mass copies of their
answers and posting them around the camp, encouraging others to do
the same. In the period that followed, members of the Fair Play Committee pursued "tests" regarding their exceptional civic status within the
camps. Emi utilized activist performance again on the twenty-ninth of
March 1944 when he and two other leaders of the Fair Play Committee,
Minoru Tamesa and Sam Horino, attempted to leave the campgrounds
without permission. The three HMFPC leaders took advantage of the
state's constant surveillance of their bodies by walking across the line

of surveillance (the boundary of the camp). Fully aware of what would happen (their detention and charges of violating camp regulations), the act was done as a form of political theater, or what Rebecca Schneider identifies as the ability for performance to render bodies explicit and thus "make apparent the ways in which bodies are stages for social theatrics."[71] Nikkei bodies were placed under constant surveillance by the state and forced to perform in an orderly and disciplinary fashion in order to avoid charges of subversion. By engaging in this nonviolent, open act of resistance, Emi and his conspirators forced the state to *watch* as they refused the "body snatching" choreography of the state. As expected, the three men were stopped by a guard at the camp's boundary and denied exit. Emi later recalled, "The MP stopped us and said if we kept walking, he would shoot us."[72] Taken into custody, the conspirators found themselves thrust onto another stage, this time a juridical one.

The three men were apprehended, and Emi and Tamesa were held for three days, before Robertson began hearings against a host of the HMFPC conspirators. Shortly after the action, Okamoto and Horino were brought before the camp director under the pretense of a "leave hearing," which, as Eric Muller points out, was a blatant miscarriage of justice insofar as neither man had applied for leave: "Robertson nonetheless denied them the leave clearance for which they had not applied and ordered them shipped off for indefinite segregation with the 'disloyals' at Tule Lake."[73] Emi, Tamesa, and fellow HMFPC member Niro Abe were brought before Robertson for two separate hearings, the first on March thirty-first and then a rehearing on April fourth.

As demonstrated by Robertson's treatment of Okamoto and Horino, Emi and his collaborators had very few illusions about the likelihood of actually receiving procedural justice. As such, the HMFPC leaders used the hearings to stage rhetorical performances for an audience that was much broader than the administrators in the room. At the end of the hearing on the thirty-first, for example, Emi asked, "There is one last request I would like to make. Could I have a copy of this hearing?"[74] Robertson responded, "I wasn't even going to have it transcribed but you may have a copy if you want it."[75] Robertson seemingly conceives of the hearings as just another bureaucratic duty to be lost to history. With an understanding that, in A. Naomi Paik's words, "testimony is not only a form of evidence but also a form of representation," Emi's request suggests a self-conscious strategy to take control of the representation of his body for history through his performance before the camp's administration.[76] This is a theory borne out by Emi's later publication of the transcripts.[77] Emi and his cohort, recognizing that their performances would have little legal impact on Robertson's ruling, use the theatricality of courtroom examination to force the administration to at least lay bare the true nature of the camps and to do so on the historical record.

During the April fourth exchange with Robertson, Emi made his goals somewhat explicit: his performances were meant to disrupt the performativity of the incarceration process and to clarify (or at least to reveal) the confused status of his citizenship:

EMI:   In my position, I do not know just what my status is as a citizen. I do not know whether I am a full fledged citizen, they say I am, but actual factors are a little bit different, and I don't know whether I am in the same status as the Indians, aren't they wards of the government, Mr. Carroll [a relocation officer]?

CARROLL: I don't know that they are, they are on reservations.

ROBERTSON: They are considered wards of the government, but they are free Indians.[78]

Tellingly, Emi's statement did not rely on an assertion of the ipseity of the camps but, instead, linked the practices in the camps with the subordination of Native Americans. By pointing to the familiar resemblance between the legal status of Native Americans and the incarcerated Nikkei, Emi invites Robertson to admit that incarcerated Japanese Americans, like Native Americans, inhabit the impossible subject position of a ward that is free. Furthermore, Emi gets Carroll to gesture to the reservation system, which is revealed as the institutional precedent for the concentration camps. From here, Emi and his collaborators use every opportunity to challenge the legitimacy of the hearing, of the camps, and of Camp Director Robertson's authority to detain them.

In the opening moments of the March thirty-first hearing, Robertson assumes the role of the judge and asks, "Do you want to enter a plea of guilty or not guilty?"[79] At first, rather than plea, Emi asks for a definition of the hearing: "Is this a hearing or a trial?"[80] Robertson equivocates, defining the matter as a "hearing," but insists that Emi must submit a plea. To this Emi responds that it is, therefore, "more or less a trial." Again, Emi deploys the periperformative to sidestep a guilty plea by arguing that there can be no guilt ascribed to his departure from the camp because, as a US citizen, he is constitutionally provided freedom from detention without trial: "I thought that as long as I am an American citizen I had the right to go where I pleased."[81] Stated thus, Emi stages a challenge to the camp (and state) authority to suspend the civil rights of the incarcerated Nikkei.

This forces Robertson to admit the suspension of Emi's rights, once more for the record:

EMI: . . . As far as guilty or not guilty goes, I personally believe I am not guilty because I am an American citizen and I wanted to find out how far my rights went. I wanted to find out how long I could be detained here against my will.

ROBERTSON: I understand that. You are supposed to obtain a pass before you can go through the gate. Lt. Kellogg is supposed to apprehend anyone who goes through without a pass. *As to your rights in the matter, that will be taken care of later.* If I can prove that you violated a Project regulation, it is up to me to assess a penalty *regardless of your rights in the matter.*[82]

Twice, Robertson articulates the deferral necessary for the suspension of Nikkei rights ("that will be taken care of later," "regardless of your rights in the matter"). Despite Emi's US citizenship, Robertson circumvents Emi's query ("to find out how long I can be detained here against my will") by affirming a new legal logic wherein all rights and petitions of grievance associated with them can be brushed off without attention.

As a result, Emi presses the point further, inaugurating a testy exchange:

EMI: In other words, Mr. Robertson, you imply that you have more power than is set forth in the Constitutional Bill of Rights?

ROBERTSON: No, Frank. I have power to do what I am doing.

EMI: Then I contend what you are doing is against the rights I have as a citizen of this country.[83]

Robertson admits what the official performatives of the government labored to obscure, that the juridical rule has been suspended in order for him to establish and claim authority over Emi, "regardless" of Emi's rights. This admission raises a critical question: if the law is suspended, from where does Robertson derive the authority to "assess a penalty" on Emi?

In this exchange, we begin to see how the confusion attached to the concentration camps was not the observation of the government's racism, as Justice Black facetiously asserts ("To cast this case into outlines of racial prejudice . . . merely confuses the issue"), but rather the constitutional crisis posed by the camps themselves. For as Emi observes, the procedural world of the camps was "not very American. It does not conform to the democratic principles of the nation."[84] Without the legitimacy of democratic power drawn from the "We the People," Robertson must accept his position as the emperor with no clothes. This becomes clear as Robertson himself cannot articulate the constituent source of this power, which increasingly seems to derive from nowhere at all, save his own assertions: "I have the power to do what I am doing."

As Robertson continually trips over the status of his own authority, he turns to the camp's attorney, Donald T. Horn, who refers to (but does not name) EO 9066 as the authorizing source of Robertson's power to detain and try Emi. Horn tautologically elucidates the authorization of sovereign power over the Nikkei by stating, "you can't administer a project like this without necessary rules and regulations."[85] But Robertson interrupts and negates him: "Just a minute. You haven't explained that quite right. I don't make the rules. This is not one of my orders he has violated."[86] Incapable of articulating the source of this power, save to tautologically assert that he has it because he has it, Robertson paradoxically absorbs the sovereign authority to execute and decide the law while denying that he is the source of this power ("I don't make the rules").

The HMFPC's courtroom performances draw the constitutional crisis posed by the camps out into the open. They do so, in part, through disidentificatory assertions of patriotic loyalty. Near the end of one of the hearings, Emi clarifies his position: "One thing I would like to have clear in your mind, Mr. Robertson. Any action that I have taken, it is not with the intent of disloyalty, it is purely from the standpoint that I consider myself a loyal American citizen."[87] The risk involved in this strategy is clear, however, as Emi testifies that he will submit to the exclusion order if it is determined constitutional by the Supreme Court: "I will abide by anything the Supreme Court says or by what the Supreme Court says because that is the *law of the land*."[88] Emi bolsters his performance of patriotic national identification by quoting the Supremacy Clause of the Constitution's Article IV, which establishes the Constitution as the "supreme law of the land." But whereas Emi's performance initially draws its authority from the Constitution, he quickly displaces the source of this authority into the governmental branch that has been developed to interpret the document. Doing so, Emi abdicates his own claim to constitutional authority, relinquishing it to the Court, and thus exposes himself to the future (in *Korematsu*) when the Supreme Court in fact ruled that the power exercised by agents of the state, such as Robertson, was legitimate.

In many ways, Emi's move presages the dominant strategy for achieving social justice in the postwar period. Since passage of the Reconstruction Amendments and later the Civil Rights Act of 1965, civil rights are understood as the primary protections from discrimination afforded racial minorities. But as the state is the keeper of these rights, racialized populations are compelled to turn to the law (confirming the state's legitimacy) while being recognizable *as* minority subjects in order to petition for justice before the law. As Chuh argues, "Only by claiming position as, or identity with, the legal norm can one achieve this version of justice."[89] As I have argued throughout this book, this positional claim most often happens through acts of performance or self-presentation, evidenced in the camps by performances of patriotism. But while the performance of normative subjectivity has the potential to result in forms of procedural justice, when the law is the source of *injustice*, such a performance ultimately strengthens the state while locking the subject into the forms of racialized identity projected onto him or her by the law. Time and again, our strategies of liberation transform into the technologies of our subjection.

Negotiating this paradox, Emi's accomplice Niro Abe builds on Emi's performance of critical citizenship but does so with a nuanced difference. Abe firmly articulates his identification with the Constitution and the rights that it *should* provide him. More than Emi, however, Abe internalizes sovereign right rather than placing it in the juridical body outside his own. In his testimony, Abe challenges Robertson's understanding of the Constitution and opinion of the constitutionality of the incarceration. Robertson replies, succinctly, "I don't have a right to say."[90] Rather than accept this answer, Abe draws on the constitutive power of "the people" and claims this power as his own.

Abe argues that the power to interpret the Constitution is not only a capacity of the citizen but also the citizen's right and duty:

ABE: If my citizenship is for the United States I think I should *have a right to speak when it is right and when it is wrong.* Doesn't your conscience ever hurt you? I am not for anyone like the WRA or JACL. I was brought up to respect the Constitution of the United States and the Bill of Rights and I was taught that if the United States calls for me to protect the Constitution of the United States I think I should go. I even have a wife and I am

having a kid coming up. I think I should go. I am not kicking
or anything. I am not fighting for the United States President
or Secretary but I am fighting for the Constitutional rights. We
are not bargaining with anyone. We are just fighting for our
rights. You know just as well as I do. Doesn't your conscience
ever bother you?[91]

Abe conceives of sovereignty as retained by the people, rather than existing in the official organs of the state ("the United States President or
Secretary"). By challenging Robertson's "conscience," Abe also charges
Robertson with both moral failure and a failure of citizenship. Robertson has failed to be an active citizen because of his disavowal and exter-
nalization of the law. He executes the law without identifying himself
with it, unlike Abe, who sees it as his strict duty to internalize, interpret,
and fight for the Constitution and the Bill of Rights. Abe's performance
frames Robertson's disavowal ("I don't make the rules") as a disavowal
of the Constitution and, thus, his duties as a citizen. This rhetorical position suggests that if the people are the constitutive power of the Constitution, they cannot assert, as Robertson boasts, that they "don't make
the rules." For Abe, the rules exist only because the people have made,
legitimated, and continued to authorize them through their collective
performances of citizenship. As such, if an enacted rule is unjust, it is
the democratic right and duty of "the people" to critique, challenge, and
deauthorize this rule.

Robertson is backed into a corner where he can only continue to cite
"rules," remaining completely incapable of providing sufficient authority for those "rules" and their eclipse of the constitutional rights of the
incarcerated:

ROBERTSON: My conscience doesn't hurt me a bit when I enforce a law
that is in effect. I am not the judge. We have nine judges . . . that are supposed to be the highest tribunal in the
land. They do not allow me to say whether it is constitutional for you to say so. It is up to that tribunal. They may
nullify that law but until such a time comes that they say it
is not a law, it is a law and every officer of the United States
is to enforce it.[92]

In response, Abe refuses the performative authority of the law as existing in and of itself: "If you got a letter from Washington giving you an
order would you enforce that rule and perform your duty regardless of

whether you thought it right or wrong?"[93] With powerful prescience, Abe rejects the Nuremburg defense two years before it was established (and rejected) in the aftermath of the war. His rhetoric suggests that the Constitution is under attack because the people have come to execute the law without internalizing it as their own. Abe firmly disestablishes the force of law from agents of the state such as the president (and potentially the Supreme Court). Instead he internalizes and performs sovereign right by affirming the law's power as that which should be squarely manifest within the bodies of "We the People."

## "A Willingness to Do That"

In a curious moment near the beginning of the April fourth hearing, Emi asserts his belief that he should answer his country's call to sacrifice himself on the field of battle. Robertson responds thus: "I think your thoughts are a little bit wrong. It may be a fact that the Japanese government exacts that [a sacrifice] from all its people. I believe you will find that the United States government exacts only a willingness to do that."[94] This was precisely the novelty of the camps: they signified a shift from technologies that would force submission from racialized subjects to those that would exact from such subjects a "willingness" to perform and exhibit their own subjection. To be clear, both systems are violent, but the difference between them needs to be accounted for if we are to understand the ways in which contemporary power works *through* the very subjects who are subordinated by it. The performances of patriotism that occurred in the concentration camps are evidence of Foucault's assessment that individual subjects "are not only [power's] inert or consenting target; they are always also the elements of its articulation."[95] The legal performatives that structured the Japanese American concentration camps tried to obscure the constitutional crisis posed by the racially motivated relocation and incarceration of US citizens without trial or charge. As I have shown, the success of this experiment was measured by the ability to compel Japanese Americans to cooperate with the government, granting legitimacy to the process by getting them to willingly exhibit and perform patriotic national identification from the site of the negation of their citizenship.

The results of these performances were multiple and even potentially subversive (as in the case of the HMFPC). As Austin argues, "when the speaker intends to produce an effect it may nevertheless not occur, and . . . when he does not intend to produce it or intends not to produce it may nevertheless occur."[96] The HMFPC activists must have been well aware that their performances in the hearings would have "zero proper performative force" as a matter of law. However, if we conceive of their performances as a self-conscious and even theatrical intervention into the interpellative, performative process that structured the incarceration of Japanese Americans on the whole, we start to see the disruptive political power of such performances. The government effectively offered two limiting subject positions to Japanese Americans: the loyal, self-subjecting, patriotic American or the disloyal subject of the Japanese empire. Both positions legitimated the incarceration process. Deploying a periperformative performance of patriotism, the HMFPC unleashed a range of other possibilities. Like Uyehara in *Big Head*, their bodies became a screen for the projection of national anxieties about racial difference. And as in *Big Head*, it was through performance that these bodies became an archive of the strategic practices deployed by Japanese Americans to stage and disrupt the racially interpellative projections of the state. As we shall see in the next chapter, it is precisely the unpredictability of such performances that imbue them with a powerful political performativity.

# 4 / The Nail That Stands Out: The Political Performativity of the Moriyuki Shimada Scrapbook

It could be a picture of any field. In the foreground are a few scraps of wood. Cutting through the middle of the photographs is a beam riddled with rusted nails. Wild grass arches up and over the refuse of a wood structure long since collapsed or dismantled, and in the background, a smattering of blurred, barren trees reach up into a cloudy sky. The image was taken by Cincinnati-based photographer Emily Hanako Momohara in 2002 on what used to be the Tule Lake concentration camp, a segregated camp for Nikkei whom the government thought to be dissident or potentially disloyal. Tule Lake was the depository for draft resisters and no-no boys, a fact that is subtly referenced by the subject of the painting—a board with nails sticking out of it—and Momohara's title, "The Nail That Stands the Tallest, Gets Hit the Hardest." This Japanese proverb—*deru kui wa utareru*—has long been associated with the camps. It is often used to explain Japanese American cooperation with the government during the war period and postwar denunciations of those who resisted. Momohara's photograph reminds us of the ways in which Japanese Americans "stood out" during the war years and how those who resisted were hammered hardest by being transferred to Tule Lake. It insists that even if most people in the United States do not know about or understand the significance of Tule Lake, the ruins of this place continue to haunt the country. The visual documents of the past contained in Momohara's series, titled *The Camps*, stand as a warning against the new forms of racial hysteria and encampment (such as Guantánamo) taking root in the early twenty-first century.[1]

FIGURE 4.1. Emily Hanako Momohara, "The Nail That Stands the Tallest, Gets Hit the Hardest, 2002, Tule Lake." Courtesy of the artist.

The proverb from which Momohara borrows her title is usually interpreted to support popularly held ideas about Japanese cultural homogeneity. In this sense, the proverb is understood as an imperative to conform, which would explain its popular association with narratives of Japanese American assimilation. I have always had an unorthodox understanding of its significance, however, one that I attribute to my shin-Issei mother. I was a particularly effeminate child. Being queer and mixed race in the largely white, often-homophobic landscape near the Colorado and Wyoming border led to more than a few nights crying out the taunts of the day. In a successful attempt to comfort me, my mother uttered the proverb. Her intention was not to encourage me to try and act like the other children. Both she and I knew that this was impossible.

Instead, she gave it to me as a form of sage advice for surviving a hostile environment. Some of us do not have the capacity to "blend in," but armed with the knowledge of the hammer's impending fall, we can at least develop oppositional strategies to dull, escape, or combat the effects of its blunt force.

Translated into a photograph, Momohara's image allows the spectator to access the implicit visuality of the proverb. In order to stand out, a nail must be visible, which is what makes it vulnerable to the hammer's blow. Japanese Americans during the war, whether they wanted to or not, "stood out." They stood out because they looked different from the desired white body of the ideal national subject and looked too much like the enemy. Because of this visual dissonance, Japanese Americans were treated like a threat to the unity of the nation, which the state used to justify their incarceration during the war. Unsurprisingly, visual culture and visual rhetoric played a central role in the definition of Japanese American racial difference during the prewar years. They were also central technologies of the government's attempts to sell a portrait of the camps as voluntary wartime communities, rather than racist prisons. In this chapter, I trace the visual construction of Japanese American difference before and during the war, before turning to a study of the ways in which Nikkei deployed photography to stage a performative interruption in the state's visual subjection of Japanese America.

Initially the government banned Japanese Americans from taking photographs of the camps entirely. At the same time, visual media (including photography and film) were used for propaganda purposes as the WRA employed white photographers and filmmakers to document the relocation efforts and camp life. In order to assure that the images people saw were of a voluntary process, the government banned all photographers from documenting the camps' military elements, including guards, weapons, guard towers, and barbed wire. In the early days of the war, many Japanese Americans sneaked contraband imaging equipment into the camps. Eventually, Japanese Americans were allowed to take photographs, but the ban on photographing any of the military installations remained in effect throughout the war. This chapter largely focuses on the photographs of Moriyuki Shimada, a young man detained with the rest of his family in Heart Mountain, Wyoming, when he was twenty-two years old.

Beyond serving as a remarkable record of the vibrant life-worlds that Japanese Americans created in the camps, Shimada's scrapbook contains a number of photographs that evidence the photographer's defiance

FIGURE 4.2. Moriyuki Shimada, the Moriyuki Shimada scrapbook. Gift of Mori Shimada (91.10.2). Courtesy of the Japanese American National Museum.

against the ban on photographing the camp's military installations. Shimada staged photographs in which subjects performed scenes that are bursting with assimilated national conformity, gender normativity, and ideality: shots of young men playing baseball, crowds lining up to go to the movies, or young women posing as if they were a Broadway chorus line. Were they not framed by the architecture of a concentration camp, they would seem much more at home in a Norman Rockwell painting. I suggest that by taking portraits that did not necessarily "stick out," Shimada was able to camouflage his efforts to document the regulatory technologies of military surveillance and containment that the government wanted to render invisible. As such, Shimada's photographs function as performatives that interrupt both the subjection of Japanese Americans through visuals means and the government's attempt to erase any images of the true, military nature of the camps.

By focusing on visual objects, this chapter issues a different interrogation of the legal nature of performance aesthetics and the aesthetics of the legal performative than in the previous chapters. As such, it has a slightly different rhetorical and methodological approach. My analysis of Shimada's photographs *as performatives* is allied with D. Soyini Madison's description of "the performative not as an utterance that refers to an extra-linguistic reality but as a heightened or symbolic act that makes something happen, disturbs, re-invents or creates—large or small—a consequence. In other words, a performative serves as a distinct moment, a punctum or rupture, from the ordinary and familiar that results in a specific causal effect."[2] Because of the official limits and controls that the state placed on the imaging of life in the camps, Shimada's photographs are performative acts that "disturb" the state's visual representation of the camps as voluntary and "rupture" the law's figuration of Japanese Americans as homogeneous national security threats. In using the term "punctum," Madison gestures to Roland Barthes's *Camera Lucida*, a work that also provides a methodological framework for my approach to the Shimada scrapbook.[3] Working with Barthes, I argue that Shimada's photographs are scenes of encounter, whereby the photograph *performs for* the spectator, creating an affective relationship with the spectator that invites him or her to *perform in response* to the photograph. Using a performance studies approach to visual culture, I argue that the images in the Shimada scrapbook are (a) political performatives, (b) objects that perform for a spectator, and (c) documents of the strategic performances enacted by Shimada and his subjects in order to defy the government's ban on photographing military installations within the camps. Reading these three components together, I show how Shimada's scrapbook makes visible and in many ways disrupts the visual subjection of Nikkei during the war.

## The Visual Racialization of Japanese America

Before turning to the Shimada scrapbook, it is important to foreground the ways in which the guard towers and surveillance apparatuses of the concentration camps were the logical extensions and architectural manifestations of prewar legal technologies for managing Asian racial difference. These practices utilized visual perceptions of phenotypical difference to racialize Asian immigrants and Asian Americans as permanently located outside the law and thus the national body politic. In courtrooms, Asian immigrants were subject to the scrutiny of the state's disciplinary optic, which in turn produced Asian racial difference as undifferentiated, a homogeneous mass or "yellow horde" that could be rendered exceptional to the protections of citizenship eligibility. Among other effects, this resulted in the incarceration process, whereby the Japanese American body was placed on spectacular display for the state. Nikkei were subject to the state's ever-present eye, which was manifest in the forms of guards and guard towers, as well as the imaging equipment of officially commissioned WRA photographers.

The field of the visual is central to the process constituting the imagined community of the nation. It also plays a central role in the production of ideal national subjects along racialized lines. Throughout US history, the subjection of racialized bodies to surveillance, exhibition, and display has played an important role in the racialization of different ethnic groups as excluded from the normative limits of national belonging. This history overlaps with, among many other examples, the scenes of subjection characterizing slavery, the ethnographic spectacles that accompanied modern raciology, and the compulsory performances of racial stereotype in popular entertainment forms (such as *The Chinese Must Go*).[4] Visual technologies of racialization are often amplified during periods of war, economic decline, or social upheaval. As Elena Tajima Creef argues, "In times of national crisis we take refuge in the visual construction of citizenship in order to imagine ourselves as part of a larger, cohesive, national American community."[5] Thus, the (dis)articulation of race and citizenship is often impossible to disentangle from the politicized vision and performance of both.

Franz Fanon understood the process of racialization as occurring within a circuit of visual assessment, performance, and consumption, which he described as the ethnic subject's self-consciousness of being "taken by a racial epidermal schema."[6] For Fanon, the racial epidermal schema lays claim to ethnic subjects as they come to see themselves through the eyes of the dominant white culture and to perform within the coordinates demanded by the dominant spectator. Thus, for Fanon, it is not only being viewed that makes him a racialized subject (encapsulated in his famous description of a child responding to his visage with the statement "Look, a Negro!") as it is the process of (re)constituting his body to be viewed and consumed as such.[7] The embodied practice of performing the self for the other's visual consumption becomes a means of negotiating the dialectical tension between his concept of self and the status of his (black) body as it is subject to (white) vision:

> And then the occasion arose when I had to meet the white man's eyes. An unfamiliar weight burdened me. The real world challenged my claims. In the white world the man of color encounters diffi- culties in the development of his bodily schema. Consciousness of the body is solely a negating activity. It is a third-person conscious- ness. The body is surrounded by an atmosphere of certain uncer- tainty. . . . [All of my] movements are made not out of habit but out of implicit knowledge. A slow composition of my *self* as a body in the middle of a spatial and temporal world—such seems to be the schema. It does not impose itself on me; it is, rather, a definitive structuring of the self and of the world—definitive because it cre- ates a real dialectic between my body and the world.[8]

Describing "consciousness of the body" as "solely a negating activity," Fanon gestures to the ways in which self-presentation, or the perfor- mance of everyday life, subjects the racialized body to the spectatorship of "the white man's eyes." This gaze defines and negates the racialized subject's will to exist beyond a bodily schema. The self is locked within a series of coordinates produced by social, spatial, and racial knowledge that shape the racialized body as he or she performs a self for the world, effectively becoming a subject through this performance.

In US law, ethnic subjects are claimed by a racial epidermal schema as they perform themselves for the regulating eye of the law, as politicians, legislators, judges, and law enforcement officials "watch" racialized pop- ulations, writing law and other legal performatives in response to the visual difference of their bodies, shaping racial knowledge and coordi- nating the crisis of difference management within the state. Racializa- tion in the United States was thus bolstered by the collusion of visual and legal technologies. The legal history of Asian American racial forma- tion epitomizes this process. In the Naturalization Act of 1790, the first Congress established a uniform rule that limited citizenship eligibility to any "alien, being a free white person, who shall have resided within the limits and under the jurisdiction of the United States for the term of two years."[9] Despite subsequent revisions to the naturalization code, the racial prerequisite remained intact until it was rescinded in 1952 with passage of the McCarran-Walter Act. In the *Racial Prerequisite Cases*, petitioners struggled with courts to determine exactly what was meant by the term "white person." Asian petitioners in particular placed their bodies before the optic of the state in the hopes of receiving a judgment that would expand the definition of whiteness to the Asian body.

For the courts, *being* white became synonymous with *looking* white. Advocates argued that the lightness of a petitioner's skin, his or her capacity for cultural assimilation, and/or his or her scientific descent from the Caucasus and Aryan races qualified Asian-immigrant petitioners for categorical "whiteness" and, thus, for naturalization.[10] Calling on a range of rationales for rejecting the petitions, courts commonly proffered "commonsense" justifications that utilized visual assessment of the plaintiff (the pallor of skin, shape and color of eyes, hair texture, etc.) to determine citizenship eligibility. The collusion of visual and legal technology in the production of race is present in *In re Ah Yup*, the first prerequisite case, in which the 1878 California circuit court denied a Chinese petitioner's eligibility for citizenship.[11] Judge Lorenzo Sawyer's opinion used a visual terminology of physical characteristics to define commonsense understandings of the phrase "white person."[12] Later, in *In re Camille*, an 1880 Oregon circuit court case dealing with a Native American petitioner, Judge Matthew P. Deady declared, "In all classifications of mankind hitherto, color has been a controlling circumstance."[13] The formal vocabulary of the *Prerequisite Cases* reveals an interesting symptom of the visual obsession at the heart of these cases. Whereas judicial opinions are generally written in the language of authority, the *Prerequisite Cases* are instead full of the sensory language of speculative vision. Namely, the word *appear* is ubiquitous: "It does not *appear* to the satisfaction of the court . . ." (*In re Kanaka Nian*) and "it *appears* the words 'white person' do not . . . include the red race of America" (*In re Camille*) are just a few examples of many.[14] Indeed, in a Utah decision, *United States v. Dolla*, the court went so far as to have an Indian petitioner "pull up the sleeves of his coat and shirt" to show his skin, as "the presiding judge closely scrutinized his appearance" to determine his racial classification.[15]

It took forty-five years for the Supreme Court to settle the prerequisite debate in two cases, *Ozawa v. United States* and *United States v. Thind*, both cases in which the petitioners were Asian immigrants—the former Japanese and the latter Indian.[16] The crisis reached an apex for the Court in *Ozawa*, as Justice George Sutherland—himself an immigrant of English descent—frantically cobbled together every possible justification to exclude the light-skinned and culturally assimilated Japanese petitioner. Takao Ozawa wrote his own brief in the case and emphasized the performance of everyday life as evidence of his suitability for citizenship: "I am sending my children to an American church and American school in place of a Japanese one. . . . Most of the time I use the American (English) language at home, so that my children cannot speak the Japanese language."[17] Sutherland acknowledged the heartfelt conviction of Ozawa's performances, conceding that he "was well qualified by character and education for citizenship."[18] But ultimately the Court denied his petition. Sutherland bent over backward to produce a ruling that can best be summarized by paraphrasing Justice Potter Stewart's famous dissent in *Jacobellis v. Ohio*: *I shall not today attempt further to define what a white man is; and perhaps I could never succeed in intelligibly doing so. But I know one when I see one, and the petitioner involved in this case is not that.*[19] Put simply, when standing in the company of white citizens, Takao Ozawa stood out.

Sutherland's opinion anguishes over the permissibility of visual evidence to determine race:

> Manifestly, the test afforded by the mere color of the skin of each individual is impracticable as that differs greatly among persons of the same race, even among Anglo-Saxons, ranging by imperceptible gradations from the fair blond to the swarthy brunette, the latter being darker than many of the lighter hued persons of the brown or yellow races. Hence to adopt the color test alone would result in a confused overlapping of races and a gradual merging of one into the other, without any practical line of separation.[20]

He inadvertently demonstrates the indeterminacy that structures the spectatorial relationship as he worries that visual assessment of racial difference might result in a conceptual miscegenation of the races, rather than a "practical line of separation" between them. Sutherland thus admits an argument staged by contemporary theorists and artists, such as Adrian Piper and Kip Fulbeck, who show how the line between the visual assessment of the body and the extraction/projection of racial meaning from/onto it is always already a fraught process.[21]

Despite the fact that Sutherland describes the visual test as "manifestly . . . impracticable" for determining and affixing racial meaning, he remains unwilling to relinquish it entirely. Instead, the Court allowed visual determinations so long as they occurred alongside other justifications (legal precedent, congressional intent, common knowledge, and scientific evidence) and confirmed the desired outcome of reifying whiteness as a stable and exclusive racial category.[22] Sutherland's opinion in *Ozawa* produces a racial double bind. The "test afforded by the mere color of the skin of each individual" is permissible when it will assist agents of the state in excluding visibly brown and otherwise perceptibly racially nonwhite subjects from citizenship. But it was to be discarded when a racially ambiguous subject troubled the "practical line of separation" that maintains "white" as a stable category equivalent with US citizenship.

Legal routes were not the only means for defining the image of the US body politic as consisting only of visually "white" bodies.[23] The visual exclusion of Asian bodies from the historical record of the United States played a similarly determinate role, as in the case of the Promontory Point photograph discussed in chapter 2. But at the same time that Asians in America were rendered invisible within official visual records of US history, the technologies of anthropology and ethnography accompanied imperial and colonial expansion into the Asian theater in order to consolidate a portrait of Asian difference as incompatible with Euro-American civilization. As Fatimah Tobing Rony has argued, ethnographic cinema (but also photography) was and continues to be "a primary means through which race and gender are visualized as natural categories . . . [and] has been the site of intersection between anthropology, popular culture, and the constructions of nation and empire."[24] Whether through the visual exclusion of Asians in America or the visual spectacle of Asians in Asia, the Asian body has been manifestly located outside the nation.

After the attacks on Pearl Harbor, the nation became obsessed with identifying the Japanese body in particular as a visual threat to national security. "Unlike the imposed invisibility of Chinese American male laborers at Promontory Summit," writes David Eng, "popular rhetoric advocating the mass incarceration of persons of Japanese ancestry during World War II turned precisely on a question of visibility."[25] Waves of propaganda characterized the Japanese as round-faced, bucktoothed, short, and evil aliens. In 1942, *Life* magazine issued an infamous visual editorial on "how to tell Japs from the Chinese." Displaying the face of Chungking's minister of economic affairs (Ong Wen-hao) above Japan's premier and general (Hideki Tojo), the article sought to "dispel" confusion between the two, adducing "a rule-of-thumb from the anthropometric confirmations that distinguish friendly Chinese from enemy alien Japs."[26] Ong was flatteringly characterized as resembling refined architecture: "his complexion is parchment yellow, his face long and delicately boned, his nose more finely bridged."[27] Tojo, in turn, was characterized as brutal and animalistic, betraying "aboriginal antecedents in a squat, long-torsoed build, a broader, more massively boned head and face, flat, often pug, nose, yellow-ocher skin and heavier beard."[28] Tojo was thus defined as an enemy by falling back on the frontier trope of the "aboriginal" or indigenous subject as the ultimate, internal national security threat. So just as frontiersman had done in the outposts of the Old West, US citizens during the war were being trained to *watch* for the racial Other and then *see* him or her as the enemy.

The visual regulation of Japanese America was used as a correlative justification for legally establishing internal exclusion in the form of concentration camps where Japanese Americans could be put under constant surveillance by the state. As Lieutenant Commander Kenneth D. Ringle of the Office of Naval Intelligence wrote in 1942, in an internal memo criticizing the War Department's approach to the incarceration, "the entire 'Japanese Problem' has been magnified out of its true proportion, largely because of the physical characteristics of the people."[29] Fred Korematsu (whose case, *Korematsu v. United States*, was discussed in the previous chapter) affirmed Ringle's fears during federal district court testimony in a successful 1983 appeal to overturn his wartime conviction:

> According to the Supreme Court decisions regarding my case, being an American citizen was not enough. They say you have to *look like* one, otherwise they say you can't tell a difference between a loyal and a disloyal American. . . . As long as my record stands in federal court, any American citizen can be held in prison or concentration camps without a trial or hearing. That is if they *look like* the enemy of our country.[30]

Korematsu clearly perceives how dominant spectatorship of Japanese American visual/somatic difference apprehends and produces Japanese Americans as subject to the permanent possibility of a state of exception. One has to "look like" an American citizen (a "free white person") in order to receive the full rights and protections secured by citizenship. This is particularly poignant given an often overlooked detail of Korematsu's case in 1944: not only did he attempt to avoid the exclusion order, but he underwent plastic surgery so as *not* to look Japanese in order to do so.[31] Despite surgically altering his face in an extreme attempt to embody Ozawa's performance of and claim to whiteness, Korematsu's physical makeover ultimately failed him. Sutherland's visual double bind prevailed, and Korematsu stood out.

## The Political Performativity of Photographs from the Camps

Sutherland expressed ambivalence about the role that visuality should play in the legal determination of racial difference; the government was no less ambivalent about the role that visuality would play in the incarceration process. As Linda Gordon describes it, the government "wanted a record but not a public record" of the incarceration.[32] The WRA hired photographers, many of them former Farm Security Administration photographers (including Dorothea Lange) to document the process. A longtime San Francisco resident, Lange counted a number of Japanese Americans among her close friends and saw the job as an opportunity to document the injustice of the incarceration process. But Lange was thwarted at every turn, primarily by army officials, and her photographs were quickly impounded by the government.[33]

A year after Lange's experiences in the early stages of the incarceration process, her friend and fellow photographer Ansel Adams petitioned his Sierra Club acquaintance Ralph P. Merritt (the Manzanar director discussed early in the previous chapter) to spend a few weeks in Manzanar in order to take photographs of the Japanese Americans detained there. Merritt enthusiastically agreed. The famous nature pictorialist wrote to Lange for advice. Because Adams was working independently, and therefore free from government censorship, Lange saw it as an opportunity to publicize the injustice of the camps. Adams wanted to publish a book and mount a museum show, whereas Lange encouraged him to capitalize on the political performativity of the photographs by getting them immediately into newspapers. In a handwritten plea to Adams on November twelfth, 1943, Lange wrote the following:

> Those truths which you encounter at Manzanar should be put before the public as fast as possible. Now is the time. Not six months or a year from now. Because the situation is constantly shifting and I fear the intolerance and prejudice is constantly growing. We have a disease, its Jap-baiting and hatred. You have a job on your hand to make a dent in it—tho I don't know a more challenging nor more unpopular one. I went through an experience I'll never forget when I was working on it and learned a lot. Even if I accomplished nothing.[34]

Lange describes the political performativity of photography as that which disrupts the official "Jap-baiting and hatred" of the dominant culture. She also understands the power of aesthetics as that which might contribute to a cure for the "disease" of racism. Unfortunately, Adams disagreed, pursuing ultimately self-serving ends. He withheld his images from the press in order to publish *Born Free and Equal* in book form and then mounted a well-received show at the Museum of Modern Art in New York a year later.[35]

Performativity can be as much a tool for revolutionary transformation as for the reification and codification of dominant power structures. Whereas Lange understood visual images as imbued with a powerful performativity that is disruptive of the official racism that structured the incarceration, the government similarly harnessed the performative potential of visual media to bolster public support for the camps by creating a unified, coherent portrait of the incarceration. To do so, it deployed visual imagery that corroborated the government's narration of the camps as voluntary "wartime communities." In a 1944 WRA propaganda film titled *A Challenge to Democracy*, for example, one watches respectable, middle-class Japanese Americans passively disembarking from trains. This is accompanied by the paternal voice of a disembodied narrator. The narrator states, "They are not prisoners, they are not internees. They are merely dislocated people. The unwounded casualties of war."[36] Accompanying images show children playing in a garden and smiling, happy people going about their everyday business. The narration, aligned with the ideality depicted in the images, transforms the camps into "wartime communities" that were simply another hardship of war. The incarcerated Nikkei are callously visualized as "unwounded," devaluing the economic, psychological, and even physical wounds of imprisonment. Photographs of and by the incarcerated tell a different story.

Nikkei photographers shared Lange's understanding of the political performativity of aesthetic images. Toyo Miyatake was an Issei avant-garde photographer, active in the modernist art scene of Little Tokyo in the years leading up to the incarceration. Incarcerated at Manzanar with his family, Miyatake sneaked contraband film equipment into the camps to document life for this very purpose. His son Archie recalled, "One day [he] called me into the barrack [at Manzanar] and said, 'I have to tell you something. As a photographer I have a responsibility to record life here at this camp so this kind of thing will never happen again.' Speaking in Japanese, he told me that he had smuggled in a camera lens and ground glass. He showed me the lens and film holder."[37] This scene evidences Miyatake's strategic investment in the photographic medium as a way of intervening in the injustice occurring in the camps. From the use of Japanese, to maintain the secrecy of the mission from white camp workers who might overhear, to the makeshift nature of the camera, Miyatake's photographic act took on an insurgent quality. Archie Miyatake articulates his father's understanding of the historical status of the photograph as akin to Barthes's description of a photograph's documentary function: "in Photography I can never deny that *the thing has been there*. There is a superimposition here: of reality and of past."[38] The photograph can thus animate the past, which is of powerful political importance when this is a past, or even present, that exists behind a screen of official occlusion.

Despite Miyatake's hope, there is a disconnect between the documentary function of the photograph and the artist's political intention, that is, assuring that "this kind of thing will never happen again." As it turned out, photography of the camps (including Miyatake's) had a distinct political impact on the future, playing an instrumental role in achieving redress for many of the incarcerated by testifying to the stark experiences of Japanese Americans in the camps as part of the successful movement for reparations in the 1980s. But this is an impact that falls a great deal short of foreclosing the possibility of future acts *like* the incarceration. In noting this, I do not mean to demean Miyatake's sentiment— which was admirable, to say the least. Rather, I want to point us to his key insight that the photographs have a politically performative nature, which is to say that they were created to *do* something, to make something happen. I suggest that the nature of this political performativity might be less causal than Miyatake desired but that it is exactly this indeterminacy that makes the aesthetic experience of the photograph politically performative.

The legal and visual apparatuses of Asian American racialization were meant to help the dominant spectator to translate the Japanese American body's visual racial difference into an indicator of a national security threat. But the line between visual assessment and singularly determinative meaning is fraught, to say the least. So if Sutherland's anxiety that visual apparatuses might prove indeterminate in proffering a "practical line of separation" between the races proves true, this truth is wonderfully productive in ways that the justice could neither anticipate nor appreciate. It is because of the indeterminacy of the aesthetic, visual experience that the correlation between the body, a visual assessment of it, and the production of racial knowledge begins to break down.

Madison conceptualizes the performative as that which has the capacity to be disruptive; it can "disturb" established orders and "re-think" dominant logics. Images of the incarceration, whether taken by Nik-kei in defiance of government bans or by WRA photographers whose photographs were then impounded, were imbued with this very power. As such, I submit that it is the indeterminacy of the aesthetic encounter with the photograph—its capacity to disrupt the dominant narratives put forth by the state about the incarceration and the Japanese American body—that makes these images politically performative.

Here, I am drawing on the work of Rancière, who suggests that the political nature of aesthetic experience occurs in the the marriage between disruption and indeterminacy:

> Aesthetic experience has a political effect to the extent that the loss of destination it presupposes disrupts the way in which bodies fit their functions and destinations. What it produces is not rhetori-cal persuasion about what must be done. Nor is it the framing of a collective body. It is a multiplication of connections and discon-nections that reframe the relationship between bodies, the world they live in and the way in which they are "equipped" to adapt to it. It is a multiplicity of folds and gaps in the fabric of common expe-rience that change the cartography of the perceptible, the think-able and the feasible. As such, it allows for new modes of political construction of common objects and new possibilities of collective enunciation.[39]

So while the photographs might not be able to "produce the rhetorical persuasion of what is [not] to be done [again]," they are capable of dis-rupting the unity of the government's narratives about the incarceration. These photographs reframe the relationship between Japanese American bodies, the camps in which they lived, and the ways in which they nego-tiated and adapted to the state's claim to their bodies. In other words, despite the best performative attempts of the state to harness the causal effect of the visual and to use vision as a means of "rhetorical persua-sion," the indeterminacy of aesthetic experience rips apart this causal logic and unleashes "a multiplicity of folds and gaps" which expand the possibilities of racial subjectivity beyond what is "thinkable" and "fea-sible" for the dominant culture.

It is not only, as Sutherland suggested, that the line of racial separa-tion is blurred by the fact that race cannot be reduced to purely visual data. Part of what makes the aesthetic experience of visual spectator-ship so rich with indeterminacy is that there is an affective dimension that enlivens the relationship between the spectator and the thing that is seen. Here, Barthes's deeply affective methodology for analyzing the photograph is useful. For Barthes, it is not simply that one perceives and makes sense of an image, so much as one's encounter with the image is charged by a range of feelings and attachments that determine one's experience of it. This experience is characterized as a highly performative practice of animation. Barthes writes, "It animates me, and I animate it. So that is how I must name the attraction that makes it exist: an *animation*."[40] Barthes, Miyatake, and Rancière theorize the photograph as an event that animates the space between the spectator and the image, making it possible for *something* to happen. Given its documentary function, the photograph performs for the spectator to confirm the injustices that occurred within the camps. As an aesthetic object, the photograph's performance produces indeterminate effects, unleashing a multiplicity of meanings and possibilities with the potential to disrupt the racializing limits projected onto the Nikkei body. In order to explore this potential, I turn to a series of images from the Shimada scrapbook for the remainder of this chapter.

## The Moriyuki Shimada Scrapbook

It is unremarkable. At two and a half by three and a half inches, it is a simple image of a young couple seated on wooden steps leading up to a barrack door. She is wearing a white button-up dress that rides just beneath her knees, and her hand is placed heavily on her lap. Her feet are cropped from the image, and her hair is perfectly fashioned in the style of the era. Her counterpart looks like a Nisei Clark Kent. He wears glasses with perfectly coiffed hair, save a small, raven spit curl spiraling down onto his forehead. He is wearing dark slacks and a white sweater. His left hand is propped casually on the side of his chin as a pensive expression crosses something approaching a smile that reveals laugh lines at the sides of his mouth. There is an air of sadness to his expression, and he is leaning his frame just slightly away from hers. In turn, her smile curls into a semiamused near frown. Her body is parallel with his, leaning toward him, her head cocked slightly in his direction. Offsetting the slight distance between them, her left hand reaches behind his right arm into the space between his legs. His left hand, just delicately, curls into her right.

They touch. I do not read this as the romantic hand lock of two lovers desperate to hold on to each other. Instead, I encounter a portrait of casual and generous familiarity. I cannot help but see this image as a

FIGURE 4.3. "Sid and Mary," the Moriyuki Shimada scrapbook. Gift of Mori Shimada (91.10.2). Courtesy of the Japanese American National Museum.

humble document of the everyday acts of care that pass quietly between people of color in the often-hostile environment of this country. Subtle, easily missed performances such as these are largely absent from or over-looked in the popular and official records of life in the United States. But the brush of the woman's hand against the man's is irrefutable proof of the acts of tenderness that are shared between us despite the ways in which we may hurt or the terrible and violent historical conditions under which our relationships develop. I am, of course, projecting my own desires onto this image. Who knows what this couple actually felt for each other? And to be clear, by speaking of their tenderness and rela-tionality, I am not in any way projecting heterosexual romance (or even the couple form) onto them. What leaps out at me from this picture is a touch that can be powerful, tender, and life affirming whether shared by passing strangers or the oldest of friends.

The man and woman constitute themselves for Shimada's camera with a reserved self-consciousness, but this image is not cheapened by its status as a performance. Theatricality is the point. Barthes understood photography to be formally akin to the stage, "it is not (it seems to me) by Painting that Photography touches art, but by Theater."[41] The photograph uses the body to stage a scene and create a narrative. Its theatricality allows me, as a spectator of the photograph, to piece together its elements to tell a story as I view it: in this case a story of a touch, of connection and singularity beyond the violently reductive limits of the camps. Importantly—and we will return to this later—Barthes conceives of death as the intermediary between both the photograph and the theater. If the classical actor's mask mediates the presence of the dead by bringing it to life on stage before the living, the photograph is always an experience with death as "figuration of the motionless."[42] The photograph, then, like the barbed wire, is significant of a mode of containment, it has a flattening, constraining power. This is part of the peculiarity of the photograph, as that which at once mediates stasis while allowing for an "animated" encounter.

Even though the photograph is a "figuration of the motionless," it is also a referent (and documentary proof) of what "has been there." The photographic encounter "animates" and performs for and with the spectator. It shows me how people in the past have lived and loved despite the seeming impossibility of both. "It allows me to accede to an infraknowledge," writes Barthes, "it supplies me with a collection of partial objects and can flatter a certain fetishism of mine: for this 'me' which likes knowledge, which nourishes a kind of amorous preference for it."[43] It does not matter that the scene performed by the couple in the photograph may not be indicative of an actually existing relationship, because the affective response that it inspires gleans from the photograph its own life force. Here, in this moment, in this photograph, despite the camps and the many sadnesses that followed after the war, this is what they are doing: they touch, ever so gently, one hand to the other. This moment of care reaches beyond the constraints of the barbed wire, opening out into what Rancière describes as the "new possibilities of collective enunciation." This collectivity is not only the couple, or Shimada, but the Nikkei who experienced the hardship of the camps and those of us who have inherited their legacy. The enunciation is nothing less than the politically performative refusal to accept the racializing technologies of the state.

Barthes's methodology was developed to unlock the secret of the photograph's ontology. But photographs are not the only things that keep secrets. The structure of the scrapbook is inherently intimate: it withholds its secrets from the general public. Scrapbooks are usually produced only for the eyes of loved ones and their descendants as a means of revisiting moments from the private past. By rendering the scrapbook public, in the archive of a museum, the photographs hover somewhere

FIGURE 4.4. "Sid M.," the Moriyuki Shimada scrapbook. Gift of Mori Shimada (91.10.2). Courtesy of the Japanese American National Museum.

between personal, affective mementos and public documentation that inspires different, public feelings. Indeed, the Shimada scrapbook was so worn that it has been deconstructed by the archivists, each photograph saved individually, removed from its original context and offered up to the public as a deconstructed scrap of a life rent apart by history. But even in these scraps are clues to the secrets held within.

Although the two people in the photograph are not identified, two independent portraits in the scrapbook reveal their names. In one portrait, the man stands at the top of the steps of the same barrack (designated F-E by a sign hanging above his head). The ground is covered in snow, and he poses, studiously, in a black sweater with a white collar framing his neck. He holds a book in his hand and looks into the camera

To Mori,

Always,
Mary

FIGURE 4.5: "Mary," the Moriyuki Shimada scrapbook. Gift of Mori Shimada (91.10.2). Courtesy of the Japanese American National Museum.

with a studious gaze. Written across the photo in ink that must have been smudged at the time of his inscription are the words, "To Mori / My best wishes / Sid M . . . / 10, 1943." Sid's last name has been obscured by a combination of penmanship and the smudged ink. In another portrait, the young woman stands alone. In the background are a barrack and a figure so greatly out of focus as to be indistinguishable. She is wearing a white button-up blouse with a heart pin fastened near the lapel, an etching of Heart Mountain riding across the top of the pin and the number 225 just beneath it. Her shining, white teeth are glimmering and perfectly straight. Unlike the contemplative, candid frown captured in the photograph with Sid, her expression is marked by the kind of reserved, tedious pleasantness common to the official portrait pose. Written across the photo in impeccable script are the words, "To Mori, / Always, / Mary."

In Sid and Mary's double portrait, the two are framed by a short pine banister on either side, reaching from the edge of the stairs on which they are seated to an open door leading into the barrack behind them. Over the right banister is some kind of rug or blanket, and on either side of the banisters extends the dark exterior wall of the shoddy building with dusty earth at its base. The texture and cracks in the inflammable structure exemplify the cheap and dangerous material conditions inflicted on the incarcerated Nikkei. Twice in the scrapbook this documentary element comes into full fruition with photographs of a fire raging out of control in one of the pine barracks. In the photo of Sid and Mary, however, it is their sad and subtle performance of the touch that overwhelms me.

Barthes defines the affective signature that surges up every time I view this photograph as a highly subjective *puncture* or *prick*—what he calls "the punctum."[44] Barthes opposes the punctum to the "studium," defined as the subject matter of the photograph. In turn, the punctum is different for every viewer, and it is innately tied to the irreducible domain of *feeling*. The punctum is the performative element of the photograph par excellence. In the photograph of Sid and Mary, the studium—as I noted—is unremarkable: two young people seated and holding hands on the steps of their barrack. It is the punctum that "will disturb the *studium* . . . for *punctum* is also: sting, speck, cut, little hole—and also a cast of the dice. A photograph's *punctum* is that accident which pricks me (but also bruises me, is poignant to me)."[45] The punctum is what makes way for the performative encounter with the image. Having been pricked, the spectator develops a unique, indeterminate affective relationship with the image and its subjects. Indeed, by creating a life that

FIGURE 4.6. "Out of control," barrack fires, 1944–1945, the Moriyuki Shimada scrapbook. Gift of Mori Shimada (91.10.2). Courtesy of the Japanese American National Museum.

exceeds the photograph, "the *punctum*, then, is a kind of subtle *beyond*."[46] The photograph is significant of a mode of containment: a moment frozen in time, a scenario that cannot be changed. But the punctum allows us to reconcile the seeming limits of this containment with a possibility of a beyond. In the case of the photograph of Sid and Mary, this gentle touch gives me access to a world beyond the limits of racialization, or their barbed-wire corollary at the camp's edge. As such, the photograph becomes the stage for the enunciation of multiple and alternative modes of understanding the Nikkei incarcerated in the camps beyond the limits of the barbed wire.

In the photograph of the couple, for me, the punctum is the gentle brush of the skin of his hands against hers, his foot leaning against the back of her leg. Taking in these minor caresses, I encounter Sid and Mary in their affective particularity. There is an aura circling this couple that blurs the barrack behind them. The tunnel focus evokes a forward movement, propelling the couple from the center of the photograph out, toward the viewer. What comes into relief are the two, seated next to each other, his hand touching hers, the back of his foot brushed lightly against the back of her leg. The familiarity between the two is touching. The pose and its frame do not exhibit a couple touching each other *in spite of* the incarceration but *within it.* They express attachment through their touch, which pushes back against the constriction of the barbed wire and reroutes the interpellative, racializing gaze of the law. This touch extends beyond the two subjects to the photographer, and even to me as I am drawn into a collective community of spectators. The sadness in their smiles reminds us that not all wounds come at the end of a gun but sometimes through an act of law or the indifference of a nation. And still, there is the simple and everyday beauty of one person brushing up against another, loving the other, holding his or her hand, even in a place structured by exclusion, grief, isolation, and erasure.

## Staging the Pose: Placing the Body before the Eyes of the State

How are we to reconcile the seemingly political dimensions of what I have described as the photograph's documentary function and the politically performative indeterminacy that I have thus far discussed? That is, if it is indeterminacy that makes the photograph political because it undermines causality, what do we do with the photograph that attempts to document an injustice with the seeming intention of achieving specific political ends (as in the example of Miyatake, discussed earlier). I now turn to this question to proffer a critical interrogation of Shimada's strategic defiance of the ban on photographing the military architecture of the camps.

A similar and shocking detail is shared across five of the photographs in the scrapbook. It is a distant subject that lingers and haunts each shot: a guard tower. Capitalizing on the ordinariness of the scenes captured in these photographs, the photographer uses the inconspicuous nature of the candid pose as a means of documenting the disciplinary legal and military apparatuses of the camps. That is, by taking photographs of subjects performing a national ideality that blends in, rather than standing out, Shimada and his subjects camouflage their efforts to make a record of the parts of the camps the government wanted to hide from public sight. At the same time, these images demonstrate how self-presentation for visual recognition on the part of the subject mirrors the state's requirement that the subject submit him- or herself to the state's visual optic. What emerges, then, is a document of not simply the regulative nature of the camps—which the government sought to hide from public view—but also the performances of self-subjection that were ambivalently executed by the incarcerated Nikkei.

The pose is the core component of the camouflage in these images. Here, posing is not accidental but an articulated act of self-presentation and performance. "Now, once I feel myself observed by the lens," writes Barthes, describing the sensation of posing, "everything changes: I constitute myself in a process of 'posing,' I instantaneously make another body for myself, I transform myself in advance into an image."[47] The act of constituting one's body for visual consumption is also akin to the process of racial subjection within the "racial epidermal schema" that is described by Fanon. In the racial epidermal schema, the racialized subject enacts a "slow composition of [one's] *self* as a body in the middle of a spatial and temporal world" that is structured by the logic of dominant spectatorship (or what Fanon describes as "white eyes"). This composition is thus not unlike the theatrical pose of the photograph, in which one makes "another body" by "transform[ing] [one]self in advance into an image."

Significantly, in *Camera Lucida*, Barthes discusses a series of photographs of and by racialized subjects, most notably a 1926 photograph by James Van Der Zee of a black family.[48] But Barthes admits no explicit interest in the racialization of the photographed subjects as such. While there is a suspect side to Barthes's refusal to engage with a discussion of race in his analysis, I want to hold on to a potentiality in this methodology insofar as Barthes also offers a way for reading the subject of the photograph in a fashion that does not require a quick reduction to a racial epidermal schema. Discussing a Richard Avedon portrait of black labor leader A. Philip Randolph, Barthes defines his interest in the photograph as "the air" of the image: "a kind of intractable supplement of identity, what is given as an act of grace, stripped of any 'importances': the air expresses the subject insofar as the subject assigns itself no importance."[49] The pose can allow the subject to inadvertently capture an air, to *supplement*, exceed, and disrupt the reduction of a subject's bodily difference to the parameters established by the racial epidermal schema. As a supplement (in the Derridean sense), the air of the subject allows for the viewer to ascribe alternative qualities to the subject without entirely reducing the subject to his or her body. As such, the pose has the capacity to take on a critical, political performativity by staging (a) the compulsion of the racialized subject to form the body to an image and (b) the supplemental air of the pose that unsettles the reductive nature of this compulsion. Performing the pose, then, is at once the way in which the

FIGURE 4.7. "L.A. girls," the Moriyuki Shimada scrapbook. Gift of Mori Shimada (91.10.2). Courtesy of the Japanese American National Museum.

visual optic of the state lays claim to the ethnic subject and the act that exceeds the limits of a racial epidermal schema and disrupts this claim.

In one image from the Shimada scrapbook, a group of five young women exemplify the power of the pose as a means of making another body for oneself, for an audience, and inadvertently for the state. They are all sideways, and each has her left foot extended in front of her, as if they were a line of chorus girls. Their arms are curved, with a hand placed lightly on the hips, and every single one has a smile on her face (with varying degrees of pleasure and dis-ease). The combined poses of the five young women produce a kind of chorus line that looks fabulous yet displaced. Removed from the more appropriate setting of a Broadway stage or even a high school auditorium, the citation of a chorus-line pose draws into relief the fact that the young women are locked away from the zones of popular entertainment that exist outside the camps. Configuring their bodies into this formation, however, they make themselves into something other than prisoners; they become performers and entertainers to be viewed.

The women's poses look frankly uncomfortable, as if each one of them is completely aware that she is not entirely the intended subject of the image. In the distance stands the tiny frame of a guard tower. In an inscription on the back, Shimada retrospectively acknowledges the guard tower as a central subject of the photograph: "L.A. girls. Had picture of their social club but I gave it away along with many others. One of the very few pictures that I have with the guard tower. I see Tets (with glasses) at Mt. View's bon odori. Didn't go this year.—Mori Shimada." Shimada's notes reveal some of the photographer's own affective attachments to the photograph. Identifying the guard tower as key to an interpretation of the image, the other figure of interest becomes the second woman from the right, wearing glasses. Spinning out of the camps and into his postincarceration present, Shimada's note links the image to the *obon* festival put on, after the war, by a Buddhist temple in the Mountain View suburb of San Francisco. Most Shin-Buddhist temples in the United States host this holiday. It is a three-day festival to honor and commemorate one's ancestors and is most famous for the *bon odori* dances. These are large collective dances that occur in circle formation. Incidentally, the uniformity of the movements in *bon odori* are evocative of the organized poses enacted by the "L.A. girls." In this way, Shimada's inscription superimposes itself over my reading of the pose, blurring the space between the Broadway chorus line and the Japanese diasporic custom of *bon odori* dances.

Captured in relation to the choreographed pose of the group, the guard tower and barbed wire fail to signify containment. In many ways, the tower and the fence seem facile, void of any life or force at all when viewed against the vivacious pose of the chorus line. But if the guard tower seems uninhabited in this image, then the photograph captures posing as a performance of self-regulation. That is, instead of running to exit the camp, they are playing chorus girls at the edge of its barriers. They compose their bodies in such a way that invites the viewers to look at them, just as their desire to be viewed is met by the omnipresent eye of the guard tower. A few bare car tracks are imprinted in the dried mud, and a motionless car rests in the distance just beside the shoulder of the woman on the far left. The scarcity of tracks punctures the image and suggests the absence of traffic on this island of cultural, juridical, and social isolation. The diamond-like peak of Heart Mountain that reaches up from behind the chorus line serves as a kind geographical barrier further emphasizing the isolation and containment of the camp. The massive expanse of dried mud, shaped with the imprints of the last car to enter or exit the camp, suggest that even if one of the incarcerated Nikkei wanted to go somewhere, there would be nowhere to go.

Earlier, I noted Barthes's observation that the photograph is a media-tion of a kind of death. *This* is an image of political death: the moment of civic suspension captured in time for all time. It is also a scene of containment, staging the logic of contemporary political discipline, or what Foucault describes as *panopticism*. For Foucault, the panopticon is a signifier of the constant surveillance of the state. Using the prison as the initial and paradigmatic form of panopticism, Foucault describes the heightened visibility of the modern prisoner as a mode of theatrical-ity (or performance) that transforms visibility itself into the prison. He writes, "They are like so many cages, so many *small theaters*, in which *each actor is alone*, perfectly individualized and constantly visible."[50] But the cage—which makes the inmate's body constantly visible to the regu-latory eye of the state—becomes superseded by this visibility itself. Thus, in the end, "Visibility is a trap."[51] It is precisely by being seen, constantly, by the state that the individuated subject is then subjected to the state's regulation of his or her body.

Internalizing this surveillance, the subject performs self-regulation regardless of whether he or she is actually being watched:

> Hence the major effect of the Panopticon: to induce in the inmate a state of conscious and permanent visibility that assures the auto-matic functioning of power. So to arrange things that the surveil-lance is permanent in its effects, even if it is discontinuous in its action; that the perfection of power should tend to render its actual exercise unnecessary; that this architectural apparatus should be a machine for creating and sustaining a power relation independent of the person who exercises it; in short, that the inmates should be caught up in a power situation of which they are themselves the bearers.[52]

It is in this capacity that the pose *can* become a reduction to an image; it is this way that one's performance in response to the self-conscious knowledge of one's own visibility makes visibility into a trap, or the body-on-display into a prison. This mode of discipline through inter-nalization is directly related to the kinds of legal, visual subjection dis-cussed earlier in this chapter (and in the preceding one) insofar as the Nikkei subject is asked to put his or her body on display for the optics of the state and, in doing so, becomes a subject of and for the state. If this chapter thus seems to have shifted away from more direct engagements with legal discourse, it is because I am attempting to demonstrate how the visual, legal regulation of the subject not only occurs in the pages of judicial opinions but starts to activate itself in the disciplinary optic of the state (clearly manifest in the form of the guard tower) as it comes to insinuate itself into the performance of everyday life.

The production of Japanese American racial subjectivity occurs as the subject began to internalize and then externalize (through performance) the image projected onto him or her by the state. We thus see a through line between Ozawa's attempt to meet the demands of the naturalization bar by performing assimilated whiteness before an immigration judge to the spectacular display of "L.A. girls'" bodies for the guard tower in Heart Mountain. Being subject to the panopticon's gaze and aware of what the state desires to see, as a carceral subject I do, in fact, "transform myself in advance into an image." Precisely in the moment that the "L.A. girls" become visible, they reveal visibility itself to be the logic of containment at play within the camps and, in a larger sense, in the process of racialization. As with the Manzanar students performing the Pledge of Allegiance, discussed in chapter 4, the "L.A. girls" image documents the prisoner's complicity and contribution to the structure of power relations through their pose. At the same time, this pose blends in insofar as it looks like any other image of US American youth at the time, thus allowing Shimada and the women to create a contraband image of the guard tower.

In another scene, the internalizing structure of the pose's complicity with the panopticon is rendered even clearer, especially when the photograph is contextualized by the history of the Arizona camp in which it was taken. A group of nine young women stand casually posed in front of a massive saguaro cactus. On the peak of a rising hill in the background, a good distance behind the women, is a guard tower. Overpowering both the tower and the women, the cactus looms above them, reaching at least eighteen feet into the wide-open and empty expanse of sky above. The ground is barren, save traces of sagebrush working their way up a hill rising in the distance. The women are milling around in a somewhat disorganized fashion, looking unfocused in various directions. One young woman stands a full body's distance from the others, looking confused and unprepared. Unlike the carefully articulated pose exhibited in the "L.A. girls" photo, this group cites a different photographic genre that demonstrates the desire to be viewed: the tourist photograph.

The intense Arizona heat is palpable, as the young women wear loose-fitting pants and blouses. Their hands are at their sides, and their scattered points of gaze suggest that the photographer may not have been the only person photographing the scene. Shimada was likely *not* to have

FIGURE 4.8. "Feb 20 1943 Gila R. Camp," the Moriyuki Shimada scrapbook. Gift of Mori Shimada (91.10.2). Courtesy of the Japanese American National Museum.

been the photographer, considering the distance between Heart Mountain and the Arizona setting of the image. Letters, potentially contraband photographs, and other ephemera circulated between camps as dispersed friends and family communicated throughout the war. The shot looks like a candid tourist snapshot or, rather, the moment of confusion just before a group of tourists congeal themselves into a cogent ensemble ready for the camera's flash. The monumental status of the saguaro behind them further reifies the sense of a tourist snapshot, mirroring the fashion in which phallic tourist monuments such as the Eiffel Tower, Taj Mahal, or Statue of Liberty traditionally loom over the photographed tourist. The compositional citation of the tourist candid is undermined, however, by the dusty, sagebrush-covered hill and guard tower behind them, reminding us that the genre of the photograph (a tourist image) is negated by the fact that the women are denied the mobility that makes recreational travel possible.

An inscription on the back of the photograph reads, "Feb 20 1943 Gila R. Camp." Like Poston, Gila River (which actually was made up of two divided camps: Butte and Canal) was built on a Native American reservation.[53] The Pima Native American tribe reluctantly approved the land grant for the US government to incarcerate the Nikkei on Pima territory *only after* thousands of Nikkei had already been relocated to the camp. For payment, when the incarceration was over, the government left the tribe the structures built by the WRA. In effect, the tribe was paid with a ready-made concentration camp. As opposed to Heart Mountain, which had a number of guard towers, Gila had only one, and this was torn down because of a staffing shortage a mere month after this snapshot was taken. The barbed-wire fence was also taken down around this time. Thus, whereas the guard tower in the chorus-line photograph *looks* empty, the guard tower in the Gila River photograph most likely was.

Evoking tourists desiring to be captured by the photographer's lens, the young women perform a similar type of self-subjection to and internalization of the visual apparatuses of the state exhibited in the "L.A. girls" photo. The tourist photograph is a fitting means of doing this insofar as the phallic statuary of sites such as those enumerated earlier are often objects charged with nationalist sentiment. As we pose before the Washington Monument or Eiffel Tower, we document our presence in a particular national context and, in some ways, place ourselves on view for the optic of that polity. The strategy of using everyday poses to mask the conscious documentation of contraband military architecture is more obvious in this photograph. The disorganized stance of the group does not arrest the viewer's focus in the same way that the chorus line can. As a result, the guard tower is more prominent here. However, one young woman quickly draws the eye. She is wearing glamorous, white movie-star sunglasses. The movie star's sunglasses often signify a disingenuous bid for privacy (the darkened frames of the glasses) married to a star's bottomless hunger to be seen as he or she flaunts him- or herself (incognito, behind the glasses) in public places. Adorned in the white sunglasses, the young woman in this photograph is staring directly at the photographer like a celebrity basking in the paparazzo flashbulb.

Again, the guard tower does not stand as an agent of containment for the women so much as it is woven into the fabric of discipline and surveillance that the camp residents internalize and then externalize through the pose. In the Foucauldian sense, they stage the fact of being "caught up" in a structure of power that exists independent of them. The subjects of the photograph, and the photograph itself, perform the banality that often characterizes the subjection of racialized bodies, wherein the surveillance technologies of the state are internalized to such a degree that the prisoners place themselves on display, movie-star glasses and all, to be captured by the regulative optic of both the guard tower *and* the photographer's lens.

In another photograph of Heart Mountain, Shimada captures a massive group of people waiting in a semiorderly line leading to one barrack, with another barrack on the right side of the frame. The line of people slices through the center of the frame, dividing the viewer from the barracks, and a broad rectangular shadow covers a large section of the empty ground beside the line. The rectangular shadow is parallel with the line of patiently waiting Nikkei. Above the scene are a few of the sparse, transparent, and well-dispersed clouds common to a finer day in the US West. Despite the fact that the image is black-and-white, the spectator can easily imagine the pure cerulean of the Wyoming sky suspended above the gray and brown world of the concentration camp. At first sight, the photograph recalls Shimada's images of incarcerated Nikkei waiting to board the trains that would take them to and from the camps. Contrary to a viewer's first assumption, however, this is not a scene of a crowd waiting to endure dislocation or even the bureaucratic tedium of waiting in line for administrative reasons. The crowd is actually in line awaiting entrance to one of the popular movie screenings regularly held at the camp's cantina.

Like the group shots discussed earlier, just out of focus and in the corner of the photograph looms a shadowy black guard tower. The clear

FIGURE 4.9. "Long line at the movies, May 1944," the Moriyuki Shimada scrapbook. Gift of Mori Shimada (91.10.2). Courtesy of the Japanese American National Museum.

light of the sky pours through the windows of the tower, making it look uninhabited and empty. Unlike the posed images discussed earlier, the majority of the people in this photograph may have no idea that they are being photographed. Their backs are to the camera, and they are looking toward the barrack to which they await entry. As in the "L.A. girls" photograph, the image references the state's technologies of vision and internalized surveillance, introducing the new medium of cinema as a dominant part of that logic in the twentieth century.

Cinema has long been a form of ideological interpellation, evidenced in no small part by the WRA propaganda that sought to idealize and justify the state of exception realized in and on the bodies of incarcerated Nikkei during the war. If Foucault observed the carceral presence of the guard tower, serving as the dominant eye for which the subject poses, cinema and other projective technologies have increasingly replaced the tower in this capacity. Fanon evidences this mode of racializing, cinematic interpellative subjection as he describes the experience of seeing himself as he is seen in (and as) an act of cinematic spectatorship: "I cannot go to a film without seeing myself. I wait for me. In the interval, just before the film starts, I wait for me. The people in the theater are watching me, examining me, waiting for me. A Negro groom is going to appear. My heart makes my head swim."[54] The declaration of Fanon's racial difference based on visual observation ("Look, a Negro!") once amused and later fractured him. But now, in the theater, it is internalized to such an extent that he identifies with it (albeit with a sense of irony) as he describes seeing himself on the screen in the form of the "Negro groom."

One does not necessarily need to identify with and as the racialized figure on the screen in order for the film to function as an ideological state apparatus. Cultural production can have as much of an impact on the subject as an act of law can. In a different version of the Fanonian movie theater, for example, critical race theory pioneer Mari Matsuda describes a similar instance: "I was sitting in a theater enjoying mindless entertainment when I was hit by a racist word or image that was about me. Suddenly, the movie stopped for me. I felt attacked, singled out, and degraded. Everyone else in the room went on watching as though nothing assaultive had happened. Following their cue, I, too, remained silent and calmed myself down."[55] The violent performativity of the hate speech within the film literally attacks her. But rather than standing out and voicing an objection, she follows the cue of the dominant spectator. As she later points out, by being lulled into this passive role, remaining silent and calming herself down, her actions as an audience member lend support to the racist ideology espoused within the film.[56]

This is the visual trap that produces (and simultaneously contains) racialized subjects out of (and in) the fragments left in the wake of seeing oneself as one is seen by the regulatory apparatuses of the US government (from the courts in the *Prerequisite Cases* to the guard towers in Heart Mountain) *and* in the ideological apparatus that is popular culture. In the camps, Japanese American subjects "compose" or "constitute" themselves in order to become something like a whole in the form of an image that is determined by the racial epidermal schema. They do so in order to be made visible for and then consumed by the dominant spectator. Even if they do not *become* this image, they are lulled into the kind of passive docility that allows for it to be projected across their bodies. In both instances, they are primed for the state to lay a claim to their subjectivity.

That the subject of the photograph is a movie audience is a reminder of the important role popular entertainment plays in the process of national and ethnic subjection. Rey Chow assesses the importance of cinema and spectatorship to forms of national subjection in the modern era by showing how self-consciousness of one's position as a subject (in her case study, a "third world," postcolonial subject in China) is shaped by the experience of identification with both the spectator and the object that is viewed: "National self-consciousness is thus not only a matter of watching 'China' being represented on the screen; it is, more precisely, watching oneself—as a film, as a spectacle, as something always already watched."[57] Audience members watch the projection of a national ideal on the screen. They identify with this image and internalize it, attempting to configure and perform the self in a fashion to match it. "They 'know' themselves not only as the subject, the audience," writes Chow elsewhere, "but as the object, the spectacle, the movie."[58] Film, like the panopticon, is internalized and then performed by the posing subject.

This scrapbook image brings into relief the ways in which viewing an image is related to being seen *as* an image. Similar to my earlier description of the internalization of the law's discipline and visual subjection of the ethnic body in the *Prerequisite Cases*, the internalization of cinematic imagery in the production of the racialized subject as spectacle is uniquely captured in this photograph. The Nikkei wait in line to watch a projected image that the subjects internalize as their own, while standing beside a guard tower that signifies the constantly watching state which has suspended their civic and juridical status as citizens. In this photograph, waiting to watch a film is linked to the exposure of the self to the spectral eye of the state, as encapsulated by the observant guard tower. The subjects no longer shape their bodies to fit the tower's gaze, or only the gaze of the camera. Now, they fit their bodies to please the gaze of an imaginary movie audience in their heads. Occurring in a concentration camp, the violent effects of this counterplay between seeing and being seen are brought into clear relief.

There are two more photographs in the scrapbook in which Shimada captures a guard tower, and in the final one is another indication that the presence of the tower in these five photographs was not an accident

FIGURE 4.10. "Chi Akizuki fence and guard tower," the Moriyuki Shimada scrapbook. Gift of Mori Shimada (91.10.2). Courtesy of the Japanese American National Museum.

FIGURE 4.11. "Meiji Kawakami," the Moriyuki Shimada scrapbook. Gift of Mori Shimada (91.10.2). Courtesy of the Japanese American National Museum.

of providence. These last two photographs are individual portraits of athletes, two players from one of the popular in-camp basketball teams. Signatures that cross the photographs at a diagonal identify the subjects: Chi Akizuki and Meiji Kawakami. However, the images look more like dystopic basketball trading cards than photographs of local sports heroes. The two athletes are wearing team uniforms marked with the name of their in-camp team, "San Jose," but in the background, in the perimeter of both photographs, one can see the barbed-wire fence and guard tower.

FIGURE 4.12. "San Jose Basketball Team," the Moriyuki Shimada scrapbook. Gift of Mori Shimada (91.10.2). Courtesy of the Japanese American National Museum.

Donning team uniforms with the names of places such as San Jose, team members performatively staged their affective affiliation with the "homes" from which they were excluded. Looking at the images of the San Jose team, one is reminded that *home* for many Nisei was not Japan, as the government assumed. Rather, for most of the youth in these photographs, home was in urban and suburban enclaves such as Seattle, Los Angeles, San Francisco, Bainbridge Island, San Jose, the Imperial Valley, San Gabriel, or Berkeley. This act thus fits within Madison's conception of the performative, which was articulated in a study of what happens when a subject wears geographically and culturally specific clothing "out-of-place."[59] Transposed from one site to another, "the dressed body . . . becomes a spectacular act that yields new meanings and possibilities and that yields a distinct action that creates, imagines, or disturbs a particular social phenomenon."[60] Wearing clothing from within the site of exclusion is a performative act that upsets the state's projection of suspect Japanese nationalist affiliation onto the incarcerated Nikkei body. It displays and thus reroutes the subject's affective ties toward homes on the urban and suburban West Coast. In the portraits of Akizuki and

Kawakami, this disruptive statement is all the more apparent because of the presence of a guard tower at the edge of each photograph.

Akizuki stands with his legs just slightly bent and the ball clasped tight between his hands. The ball pushes out in front of his body, like he is preparing to toss it to an imaginary team member just outside the shot. His muscles are tensed with anticipation, clear and distinguished. He is gazing forward, his eyes concentrated on an unseen point, and his hair is perfectly placed, save a wisp of black reaching forward and out in front of his face. Distinct from Akizuki's pose, Kawakami's is less offensive than defensive. His legs are barely bent and less shapely than Akizuki's. His back is curved as he crouches forward, his arms reaching beneath him, as if holding the ball away from another player. His gaze is less intent and more contemplative, as it just barely avoids meeting the eye of the viewer. His left ear is exposed, listening for a coach's instruction.

At the same time, the setting ruptures through the perfection with which the athletes perform their roles as players enacting a national pastime. Rather than posed on the sleek black asphalt on which the game is supposed to occur, Akizuki and Kawakami are posed in the middle of a rugged dust field. The gray expanse behind them extends without end, save the line at the horizon of each photograph where the camp's barbed-wire perimeter reaches from one side of the frame to the other. Whereas the land beyond this fence stretches into the infinitesimal horizon, the barbed-wire fence and twin images of the wooden guard tower clearly limit the space in which Akizuki and Kawakami perform. The performative identification with San Jose is thus framed by military installations that literally foreclose these identifications, making them impossible beyond the powerfully performative acts of imagination staged by the athletes.

The position of the guard tower in these shots should not be overlooked. In four of the five images, it haunts the very limits of the photographic frame. (The exception is the Gila River photograph, which, the reader is reminded, was likely not taken by Shimada.) The guard tower's seemingly accidental presence at the edge of these two photographs of the athletes indicates a kind of framing and conscious inclusion. Had Shimada wanted, of course, he could have easily shifted his camera just a few inches to one side or the other to crop the tower from the photograph. No doubt, the thought must have occurred to him, as he had surely been told, like Lange or Miyatake, that he was not to take photographs of the military installations. The composition evidences his defiance of such instructions, juxtaposing highly stylized performances of ideal national belonging against the stark, exceptional conditions of the camps and the architecture of military containment and surveillance. Indeed, both Akizuki and Kawakami stand in nearly the exact same spot, perfectly centered between the tower and the fence, indicating Shimada's conscious effort to capture all three in the photograph's frame. Furthermore, on the back of Akizuki's photograph, Shimada's handwriting identifies the tower, fence, *and* the athlete as official subjects of the portrait: "Chi Akizuki fence and guard tower."

Photographing subjects willing to perform idyllic and even cinematic scenes of US life from within a space characterized by the exceptional suspension of the law in the camps, Shimada and other incarcerated photographers (such as Miyatake) often exploited the seemingly benign nature of the photographic pose to mask the taking of contraband images. As such, Shimada and his subjects demonstrate the potentials for mobilizing mimetic performances of national ideality and everyday life in order to disrupt the government's neat and self-justifying portraits of camp life, unleashing a range of critical, politically performative possibilities from within a space of seeming foreclosure. Strategically performing in a way that would not stand out, these images create a powerful indictment of the criminal nature of the camps and the government that oversaw them.

## "A Kind of Subtle Beyond"

In this chapter, I have suggested that Japanese American images of the internment might not lead directly to calculated outcomes, such as the one that Miyatake valiantly articulated as a motivating factor in his defiance of the photographic ban in the camps. Instead, images of the incarceration are politically performative precisely because of the ways in which they disrupt the line between spectatorship, intended outcomes, meaning, and action. As Rancière reminds us, despite the fact that there is "no direct road from intellectual awareness to political action," the aesthetic encounter makes possible politically charged "processes of dissociation: a break in a relationship between sense and sense—between what is seen and what is thought, what is thought and what is felt."[61] Clearly something may well be "felt" by the spectator during the encounter with the image, but this affective relationship cannot be accurately plotted. Indeed, this "break" between sight, thinking, and feeling is part of what imbues the images in the Shimada scrapbook with a politically performative power. It disrupts the link between the visual apprehension of racial difference and the construction of racialized knowledge established by the racial epidermal schema at play in the camps.

I want to be clear, however, that I am not suggesting that the Shimada scrapbook should be received as a practice of outright liberation. If anything, Shimada's images demonstrate the difficult and contradictory problems posited by the interplay of visuality and entrapment vis-à-vis the process of racialization. If visibility is a trap, many of Shimada's photographs are an exercise in making visible, containing, and ultimately indicting the militarization of the camps, which the government wanted to render invisible from its official records. Strategically deploying benign performances of everyday life that would not otherwise stick out or attrack undue attention, Shimada and his subjects were capable of creating a visual record of the camp's military apparatuses and, by so doing, entrapping the trap. But to do so, they had to once more render the Nikkei body subject to a form of visiblity (for the photographer, viewer, or audience) that runs the risk of replicating the violence of containment and entrapment.

This is one of the ambivalent paradoxes posed by the technologies of the racial epidermal schema: if visuality is the trap by which racial meaning is projected onto the body of the racialized subject, visibility may also be the means through which the trap (or hammer) can be avoided or interrupted. But does such a practice merely produce new conditions of containment or entrapment? In an era in which the recourse to visibility and identity is often utilized as a means of combatting forms of institutionalized discrimination, do contemporary attempts to become visible (through political, legal, and aesthetic representational means) not, to some degree, merely extend the apparatuses of the camps into our daily lives? And if this is the case, what are the conditions necessary for us to dismantle the guard tower—both the one at the edge of the camp and, more importantly, the one that each one of us has internalized?

The Barthesian "kind of subtle *beyond*" is politically powerful insofar as it insists on the possibility of a space that exceeds the dominating apparatuses of the visibility trap. In one of the few scrapbook images without a human subject, two faded *koi-nobori* kites float at the top of a pole erected on one of the barracks, flickering in a dusty wind. The construction of the barrack is shoddy and weak; the flags are full bodied and full of wind. The earth and empty corridors between the barracks open up, and for a moment I can smell the clear, warm air with a slight trace of the dust in it. I hear the fabric of the flags whipping around and rubbing up against each other in the dry Wyoming wind. It is desolate and terrifying. I imagine the streets filled with Nikkei bringing this frozen world alive through their daily routines. I hear their voices talking

FIGURE 4.13. "Koi-Nobori," the Moriyuki Shimada scrapbook. Gift of Mori Shimada (91.10.2). Courtesy of the Japanese American National Museum.

to each other in English and hushed Japanese, gossiping, disclosing loves and losses, and telling stories under the shade of the *koi*. Here, in this prison, these floating fish are significant of a kind of subtle *beyond* to what is thinkable and feasible, floating upward, out of sight, and toward something that we have never actually known, a thing we might otherwise call freedom.

# 5 /    Illegal Immigrant Acts: Dengue Fever
and the Racialization of Cambodian America

During Dengue Fever's Echo Park concert to promote its 2008 album *Venus on Earth*, the Los Angeles–based indie-rock band makes its way through a boisterous set in its hometown, before a mixed crowd of Angelino hipsters and intergenerational Cambodian immigrants and Cambodian Americans. The band's five multiethnic, American, male instrumentalists perform their roles with playful abandon. Commanding the stage, twenty-something lead singer Chhom Nimol alternates between wailing and cooing, her voice leaping through sonic hoops in both Khmer and English. In the final moments, voice shaking and a few tears streaming down her cheeks, Chhom lights a candle onstage in commemoration of the victims of the Khmer Rouge. In this surprising setting, a war that most US Americans have forgotten, or simply ignore, slips into the room in the hands of a pop singer.

Formed in 2001, Dengue Fever performs covers of and music influenced by classic Cambodian rock songs from a musical subculture that flourished in Phnom Penh during the sixties and seventies. In 1975, life in Cambodia was radically altered by the advent of four years of tyrannical rule by the Communist Party of Kampuchea (CPK, a.k.a. the Khmer Rouge). The Khmer Rouge period, which occurred in part as a result of US military intervention in the region during the Vietnam War, not only inflicted countless tragedies on the people of Cambodia but resulted in the production of a significant Cambodian American refugee population in the United States in the period following the war. In recent decades, pre–Khmer Rouge music has experienced a significant revival within both Cambodia and its diaspora. Dengue Fever builds on the revival of this tradition for familiar audiences and introduces the music to new fans by performing in places in Asia, Europe, and North and South America.

Dengue Fever began to work together at the beginning of the global war on terror, the largest and longest period of US warfare since Vietnam. In many ways, the band performs a bridge across these two military conflicts, which have arguably had the greatest impact on Asian-immigrant and Asian American racialization since the immigration reforms of 1965. Following the events of September eleventh, 2001 (9/11), there has been intensification in the racialization of South, Southeast, and Central Asian immigrants as well as their Asian American descendants. This process contributes to the expansion of widespread anti-immigrant sentiments that are often speciously framed as interests in border security. Southeast Asian immigrants, many of them Vietnam War refugees, are thus suspended between a war that the United States wants to forget and an ongoing conflict that understands their racialized, immigrant presence as a national security risk.

This chapter traces the ways in which Dengue Fever centralizes the figure of the immigrant in its performance practice, reading the band within the historical and legal context responsible for the racialization of Cambodian immigrants and Cambodian Americans. As we have seen throughout this book, the Asian-immigrant body in the United States is often racialized as an "illegal" national security risk. Chhom's performance of Asian-immigrant subjectivity onstage complicates the racialization of the Cambodian-immigrant body as always already illegal and thus subject to the intrusive and often violent legal regulation of the state. Here, I deploy Junaid Rana's conception of "illegality" as "not only an actual state of legal status but also a condition of political subjectivity that places migrants outside the law."[1] As Mae Ngai similarly observes, "The legal racialization of [Asian] ethnic groups' national origin cast[s] them as permanently foreign and unassimilable to the nation. . . . [They are] 'alien citizens' . . . born in the United States with formal U.S. citizenship but who remain[] alien in the eyes of the nation."[2] The experiences of Cambodian Americans, as a small population, are rarely attended to, even within the field of Asian American studies.[3] But the racialization of Cambodian immigrants and Cambodian Americans in US law since the Vietnam War is a prime site for tracking the state's apprehension of the new Asian immigrant's body in the contemporary era. Including legislative imperatives regulating patterns of Cambodian migration in the post-Vietnam period, the subjection of neoliberal welfare policy to

FIGURE 5.1. Dengue Fever, 2011. Photo by Lauren Dukoff. Courtesy of Dengue Fever.

the Cambodian-immigrant body in the late eighties to midnineties, and the national security policies of the GWOT, US law ensures that Cambodian Americans shuttle between erasure and spectacular presence as always already "illegal" subjects. As we will see, Dengue Fever's staging of Chhom's experiences as an immigrant reflect these realities.

This chapter ties together the various arguments that I have made about both aesthetic and quotidian performance practices that intersect with the law in the making and complication of Asian American subjectivity. Situating Dengue Fever's performance practice within the legal and historical context from which it emerges, I argue that Dengue Fever often places Chhom's immigrant experiences at the core of its repertoire. Staging Lisa Lowe's contention that "immigrants retain precisely the memories of imperialism that the U.S. nation seeks to forget," the band uses the stage to restore these memories before its audiences.[4] It performs repurposed scraps of a forgotten past in order to refuse the politics of imperial amnesia that have shaped Cambodian American racialization from the post–Vietnam War era to the present. Then it centralizes the figure of the Cambodian immigrant and even emphasizes its figuration as "illegal" or "outside the law," thus inviting the audience to trouble the very concept of the "illegal immigrant." Dengue Fever's performances thus disrupt national amnesia about the United States' imperial past while unsettling the discursive link between illegality and the Asian immigrant's body.

## After Orientalist Nostalgia: Performing the Immigrant-as-Native-Informant

Singing in two languages, with an indie-rock, retro appeal, and influenced by genres ranging from US surfer and psychedelic rock to Cambodian folk traditions and Ethiopian jazz, Dengue Fever is at once significant of globalization's increasingly cross-cultural conditions of cultural production and indicative of historical practices of Orientalist appropriation. When a pair of Jewish American siblings, Ethan and Zac Holtzman, set out to form Dengue Fever, the search for a Cambodian front woman was synonymous with a search for an ethnic subject who would authenticate the band's appropriation of Cambodian pop music. On the one hand, this impulse initially reified the opposition of various socially produced and hierarchically stratified subject positions (East and West, Cambodian and American, male and female). On the other hand, once Chhom was a member of the band, her performances began to disrupt them.

During a millennial vacation to Cambodia, Ethan Holtzman was exposed to the vibrant pre–Khmer Rouge rock scene, which was populated by musicians such as legendary singers Sinn Sisamouth, Ros Sereysothea, Pan Ron, and Yol Aularong. On returning to the United States, Holtzman and his brother Zac set out to create a band that would reinvigorate the sound of classic Cambodian rock from the Echo Park neighborhood of Los Angeles, California. They named the band after the hemorrhagic fever that vanquishes large numbers of the working poor in Southeast Asia, a disease that Holtzman contracted during his trip.[5] With Ethan on keyboard and Zac on guitar, they recruited bassist Senon Williams, saxophonist David Ralicke, and drummer Paul Smith. At a loss for a lead singer, the group decided that they needed a Cambodian front-woman, holding auditions in Long Beach nightclubs with disappointing results until they encountered Chhom Nimol.

Chhom grew up in Battambang, a large city with a strong regional music legacy that is not far from the border of Thailand, before moving to the United States in 2000. She was something of a pop sensation in Cambodia before her arrival in the States. Her parents worked as wedding singers, and she followed their lead. The performance-based TV variety show rules in the domain of Cambodian popular entertainment, and as a teenager in the 1990s, Chhom began to win televised singing contests, propelling her to regional stardom. After receiving an invitation to perform at a Minneapolis wedding, she came to the United States at the age of twenty on a two-week tourist visa. She remained in the country and eventually relocated from one of the largest Cambodian American/ immigrant enclaves (Minneapolis) to another (Long Beach), to be closer to her sister. She began to perform in the local Cambodian-immigrant nightclub scene, eventually auditioning for Dengue Fever and becoming its lead singer. Between 2003 and 2012, the band released four studio albums, a documentary directed by John Pirozzi with an accompanying soundtrack in 2009, and a 2010 compilation of classic tracks from the pre-CPK-era music scene.[6] While the early albums relied heavily on covers of pre-CPK-era music, recent albums mostly feature original material composed collectively by the band.

Although the band began with impulses that replicate traditions of Orientalist representation and imperial appropriation, what actually emerged as the band developed is infinitely more complicated. From the earliest moments, Chhom performed as a figure moving between, across, in, and out of the geographical, cultural, and temporal coordinates accessed by the band. In a sense, she became a kind of native informant, lending the band Khmer authenticity while also performing in a fashion that would undermine this authenticity. I draw the term "native informant" from ethnographic protocols that designate a subject who stands between the Western ethnographer and the space of inquiry central to the ethnographer's research. Gayatri Spivak appropriates the term to argue that the speaking ethnic subject regularly occupies a foreclosed position on and against which the logic of Western rationalism and reason has been constructed: "I think of the 'native informant' as a name for that mark of expulsion from the name of Man—a mark crossing out the impossibility of the ethical relation. . . . He (and occasionally she) *is* a blank, though generative of a text of cultural identity that only the West (or a Western-model discipline) could inscribe."[7] For Spivak, the native informant serves as the exterior and limit point against which the proper Western subject (philosophical, literary, historical, cultural, and, I would add, legal) emerges. She is foreclosed from being a speaking subject precisely because she blurs the boundaries between discretely maintained temporal, cultural, national, and racial spaces. At the same time, this foreclosure is always already incomplete insofar as she is compelled to perform as a speaking subject, serving as translator, medium, and source of authenticating knowledge. She is at once foreclosed from speech while being compelled to perform as a speaking (translating) subject. But in the act of translation, she has a significant amount of latitude that allows her to perform as a disruptive presence. Taking on a role that is meant to move across the distinct cultural spaces that have been constructed by and in Western epistemology, she has the capacity to deconstruct them with her border-crossing presence.

In early performances, Chhom's body functioned as an index of authenticity. She provided what E. Patrick Johnson describes as the "notion of bodily presence as a sign of authenticity," which occurs when a predominantly white group appropriates a racialized performance tradition and then invites performers of color to perform with them.[8] Early on, for example, male band members insisted that Chhom wear "traditional" clothing, despite her desire to wear the signifiers of consumer pop culture (Guess jeans, etc.) that are popular in both the United States and the developing world.[9] Chhom was thus coerced into performing her role as a native informant, authenticating the other band members' appropriation of Cambodian rock traditions. This was made all the more fraught given the differences in gender, class, and citizenship status between Chhom and the men. While the band's success offered a bohemian livelihood for the male members, who were largely drawn from middle-class backgrounds, for Chhom, their enterprise was intimately tied up in forms of economic survival, indissoluble from a need to maintain economic independence to protect her immigration status once she became "properly" (or "legally") documented in 2002. In other words, in order to survive and maintain proper status within the United States, Chhom was compelled to perform within Orientalist representational coordinates that made her commercially viable for US audiences. As I have argued throughout this book, however, performance aesthetics routinely disrupt neat trajectories of intent and cause, and Chhom's assumption of the role of native informant is no exception to this rule.

The band's performance of pre–Khmer Rouge rock music cannot be entirely dismissed as neocolonial appropriation insofar as this musical scene was itself generated by a long history of empire and cross-pollination between Cambodian musicians and cultural/musical traditions reaching from France and Spain to the Philippines and Hong Kong to the American hemisphere. To be clear, I am not dismissing the ways in which Chhom is racialized through the band's performance practice or her often Orientalist reception in popular media. The authenticity *thing* never really goes away. But it is worth considering the alternative possibilities opened up by Chhom's work with Dengue Fever. If her presence in the band was initially intended to lend authenticity to the band, it is precisely because of her status as a figure moving between, through, and across different national, racial, and temporal coordinates that the concept of authenticity begins to break down. As Johnson writes, "the mutual border crossing of identities may be a productive cultural and social process that furthers a progressive politics of difference."[10] As Chhom centers her experiences as a Cambodian immigrant within Dengue Fever's repertoire, her voice and body index and give sound to the forgotten imperialist histories that account for Cambodian-immigrant and Cambodian American racialization. During these performances, the very concept of authenticity begins to break down, critically problematizing both the subjectification and subjection of Cambodian Americans.

By performing the role of the native informant, Chhom stages the Asian immigrant as a transnational figure who moves across boundaries, destabilizing them in the process. The efficacy of Dengue Fever's border-crossing musical performances is facilitated by what Josh Kun describes as the audiotopic nature of music:

> The audiotopia is a musical space of difference, where contradictions and conflicts do not cancel each other out but coexist and live through each other. Thus, in a sense, audiotopias can also be understood as identificatory "contact zones," in that they are both sonic and social spaces where disparate identity-formations, cultures, *and* geographies historically kept and mapped separately are allowed to interact with each other as well as enter into relationships whose consequences for cultural identification are never predetermined.[11]

As a space in which discrete, "disparate identity-formations, cultures, *and* geographies" not only interact with each other but coexist despite their seeming contradictions, music allows for the rethinking of various forms of social and cultural stratification. I thus theorize Chhom's performance of the immigrant-as-native-informant as the presence that guides us through the audiotopia, allowing us to rethink, respond to, resignify, and remember the separation of these spaces in politically productive ways.

In keeping with the hipster roots of indie rock, Chhom performs the native informant with a slightly ironic distance. The cover art to Dengue Fever's 2005 sophomore album, *Escape from Dragon House*, for example, deploys a visual image of the native informant with an ironic blend of do-it-yourself artistry and nostalgic ethnic pastiche. On the cover, Chhom stands in the gracious position of host, welcoming the listener to the sonic adventure promised by the album. Her smiling face takes up the left third of the image and has been digitally altered to give it a Technicolor sheen evoking a midcentury LP cover. Her hair is piled on her head in a tower of curls, and dangling gold earrings hang from each ear. The right two-thirds of the cover feature a psychedelic lime-green record with a yellow label printed with the title of the album. In the upper part of this label is a small hand drawing of a man cycling a woman in a bicycle rickshaw. At the top of the cover is the band's name written in an amateurish orange script. The inside photograph is a blurry image of a busy Phnom Penh street, packed with people riding on the ubiquitous motos that fill the rapidly developing thruways of urban Southeast Asia. These spaces are often depicted as zones that are exterior to Western modernity. But even as the cover displays a sense of ethnic, nostalgic pastiche, the inside image acknowledges the conditions of modernity that structure life in developing countries throughout the Global South. Between the nostalgic temporal signature of the rickshaw on the album's cover and the snapshot of global modernity inside the liner notes, the album itself evokes the shuttling in and out of temporal spaces with a knowing wink.

This ironic mode of temporal and cultural border crossing comes alive in Dengue Fever's onstage audiotopia, as during a March 2008 concert at Manhattan's Bowery Ballroom. The band takes the stage around ten p.m. in a small, crowded space in New York's Lower East Side. Drunk and drinking twenty- and thirty-somethings linger in a hazy darkness before Chhom's voice pierces the air, singing a haunting Khmer folk song without accompaniment. The boisterous crowd, seduced by her sonic prayer, grows quiet before the band breaks into a raucous set. Somewhere in the middle, with the audience sweaty from dancing and knocking up against each other, the band breaks out into a masterfully psychedelic track from *Dragon House*, "Sni Bong."

"Sni Bong" is something of a sonic mirror of the aesthetic deployment of the native informant on *Dragon House*'s cover. Musically, it sounds like the theme song for a James Bond spectacular from the late sixties. An original penned by the band, "Sni Bong" has an ominous, dangerous

FIGURE 5.2. Album cover art for Dengue Fever's *Escape from Dragon House*, 2005. Courtesy of Dengue Fever.

bass line, minor-key tonality, seedy saxophone runs, wild vocal acrobatics, and a magnetic riff near the end of the song in which Chhom delivers a purring spoken verse atop a fluttering flute and sweetly tapping drum. She performs most of the song in Khmer, with a chorus that combines her mournfully longing wail and the band's persistent grind, but concludes in the pleading English lyric, "Hold me close to you tonight, Oh Sni Bong."[12] As the band reaches the explosive denouement, Ethan Holtzman's organ, Williams's bass, and Ralicke's sax crescendo into the winding chain of minor-key notes that slide throughout the song, evocative of the Orientalist soundscapes that characterize the most famous (and most offensive) of Bond's Asian adventures. Dancing to the song, the audience seems to be as energized by the cheesy, cinematically derived licks as they are by the band's virtuosic musicality.

The cover to *Dragon House* and a track such as "Sni Bong" contain playful winks, as if to suggest to the listener or viewer that the band is well aware of the aural and visual stereotypes that they are playing off in evoking a potentially fictional "time before" and a "place elsewhere" that is consolidated in the body of Chhom's native informant. The cover's wild color combinations (the gaudy juxtaposition of Chhom's towering hair and the lime-green record) are so visually overstimulating that even if we wanted to believe that this was a record cover from 1969, the temporal authenticity of the image is not quite in order. Similarly, the citation of both the musical ingenuity of Cambodian musicians from the sixties and seventies, fused with the wildly stereotypical and Bond-like scoring that flows throughout "Sni Bong," suggest that the musical time and space that Dengue Fever is citing is perhaps one that never truly existed.

This is not to say that the past did not happen but that the nostalgia that regularly attaches itself to performances of the past has more to do with cultural fictions than the realties of the events that actually occurred. These seemingly contradictory temporal and cultural coordinates float together in the audiotopic space created by Dengue Fever and channeled through Chhom's native informant. Whereas her role as a native informant runs the risk of making the gendered ethnic body into a proxy for the Occident's nostalgia and desire for a commodified Orientalist fantasy, it is precisely because she is a figure that translates across and between these spaces that they begin to break down around her body. The nostalgia evoked within Dengue Fever's performance practice works less to reify fixed notions of race, gender, place, and time than to destabilize them. This allows Dengue Fever to conjure these harmful fantasies on the stage at the very moment that they begin to self-destruct, creating a space in which the band can work with these elements in a reparative fashion, piecing the deconstructed fragments back together to imagine and stage other conditions of possibility. Mediated by the figure of Chhom's native informant, Dengue Fever's Orientalist nostalgia lets the band achieve what Gayatri Gopinath discovers in the work of Asian British band Cornershop, a performance of "nostalgia not to evoke lost homelands or a fantasized imperial past but rather to offer a different vision of history, collectivity, and cultural genealogy."[13] Thus, the ironic, indie-rock, pastiche aesthetic that structures Dengue Fever's deployment of the native informant toys with notions of racial, national, and temporal authenticity, allowing for the emergence of new sets of critical possibility.

The band does not merely perform nostalgia to meet the tastes of the dominant consumer. It also issues nuanced performances of nostalgia from Chhom's immigrant perspective. In songs such as "Uku," for example, Chhom performs the affective dimensions of diasporic experiences that are often elided by a dominant, anti-immigrant logic that refuses the singularity of immigrant experiences in order to absorb the immigrant into a faceless and voiceless "illegal" mass. "Uku" begins with a winding arpeggio played by Zac Holtzman on a double-necked guitar, which is a combination of the *chaipei* (a traditional Cambodian string instrument) and the electric guitar. Bells and a flute introduce Chhom's voice, which enters as a harmonic wail (not unlike the one that grounds "Sni Bong"), before the rest of the band joins the song. The harmony is introduced, first, through Chhom's nonlinguistic wail, before she gives way to language. Singing in Khmer, she narrates an immigrant's experience with displacement and longing:

> The windy seasons makes me think of my village
> I think of the old people, young people, aunts and uncles.
> We used to run and play, hide and seek
> But now we are far apart.
> Far apart.[14]

This is the only verse in the song, repeated three times. As Chhom repeats the line "far apart" at the end of each verse, her voice gives way to another stunning, nonlinguistic wail, which is borne up by an explosion of syncopated sound from the band.

How are we to understand the significance of the wail in songs such as "Sni Bong" and "Uku"? A wail is explosive. It breaks away from the limits of language into something else that has to be signified but cannot be spoken. If the racialization of Asian immigrants reduces them to a set of limited coordinates predetermined by the dominant culture, I want to suggest that Chhom's wail pushes back, against, and beyond such limits. Here, I am thinking through the wail in a fashion similar to Fred Moten's understanding of the scream or the moan within the sonic aesthetics of the black radical tradition. For Moten, the moan is an improvisatory act that disrupts conditions of political limit.[15] The scream is similarly theorized as that which disrupts the political subordination of the raced, subaltern body. Whereas Spivak observes the foreclosure of subaltern speech, Moten understands the scream as "opening tonal and grammatical fissures that mark the space of the very globe-girdling, nationalist-under-erasure political agency and theoretical interven- tion . . . for which and from which Spivak calls."[16] If the immigrant is reduced to a foreclosed subject position by the yoking of her name to illegality, the wail explodes the conditions of this reduction as her voice articulates a political subjectivity that reaches out beyond the limits of racialized inscription.

In "Uku," Chhom's character emerges between this politically perfor- mative wail and the lyrical repetition of an immigrant's nostalgic com- plaint. Doing so, she centralizes a performance of the Cambodian-immi- grant subject position as a figure that cannot be rent from her affective particularity by the reduction of her body to a foreclosed and racialized illegal subjectivity. Utilizing her signature wail, Chhom opens "tonal and grammatical fissures" that make way for the sounding of a subjectivity- in-difference that is political precisely because of its irreducibility. Cen- tralizing the immigrant in her performance practice, Chhom's perfor- mances serve decreasingly to authenticate the logic that would maintain discrete racial and national subject positions. Instead, her performances as a native informant move across these spaces, constructing an audioto- pia that ultimately unleashes difference as that which pushes against the limits imposed by the racialization of the Cambodian-immigrant and Cambodian American body.

## The Politics of Remembering Cambodia

In this section, I consider how Dengue Fever's nostalgic gestures to the past refuse the forms of political amnesia that produce the Cambodian American and Cambodian immigrant as always already illegal. In order to do so, we need to discuss the elided political histories that set the stage for the band's antiamnesiac performances. Given the significant amount of violence the US military inflicted on Cambodia during the Cambodia Campaign of the Vietnam War, the virtual absence of the recent his- tory of Cambodia from public memory in the United States is a prime example of imperial amnesia. In 1969, President Richard Nixon autho- rized the US military to begin strategic bombing strikes within Cam- bodian borders in order to target Vietnamese troops suspected of oper- ating within eastern Cambodia. That same year, the State Department played a tacit role in militarist Lon Nol's coup against the government of Prince Norodom Sihanouk, resulting in the establishment of a brutal dictatorial regime.[17] US support for the unpopular Lon Nol regime and the continued bombings in the provinces became a primary source of propaganda used by the Communist rebels, dubbed the "Khmer Rouge" by Sihanouk, to turn public sentiment against Lon Nol and to recruit troops to their cause. The bombardment of Cambodia concluded in 1973, when Congress halted President Nixon's aggression in the region, but only after 150,000 innocent Cambodian civilians were dead, with countless more wounded and displaced from their homes and villages.

The sudden abandonment of Cambodia produced a massive power vacuum in the country, allowing the Communist Party of Kampuchea (CPK / Khmer Rouge) to overtake Lon Nol's Republican Army, gaining control of the state and nearly every aspect of Cambodian life. Renamed Democratic Kampuchea (DK), Cambodia sustained tragedies under the CPK that are well known and too complex to explain here.[18] Briefly summarized, in a matter of hours after claiming victory, the Khmer Rouge transformed the entire nation into a labor camp. As part of its revolutionary program, the CPK set out to destroy the cultural, social, and political history of the previous regime, isolating Cambodia from the rest of the world (with the partial exception of China). From 1975 to 1979, between one and two million of Cambodia's population of five million died.[19] Ethnic minorities such as the Cham, Thai, and Vietnamese and social groups including former Lon Nol government officials, monks, intellectuals, and artists were all at particular risk for elimination.

From 1979 on, US policy toward Cambodia was mercurial and comprised calculated acts of repression, short-term memory, and enforced amnesia. The Nixon, Ford, and Carter administrations all took the official position that Democratic Kampuchea was a puppet of the Vietnamese government while quietly tolerating the Khmer Rouge in deference to a fragile new relationship with China.[20] The US government denied reports of atrocities coming from Cambodia during the four years of Khmer Rouge rule, characterizing refugees' survivor testimony as propaganda. When former Khmer Rouge rebels—backed by the Vietnamese—ousted the CPK in 1979, the United States made a quick about-face and threw its official support behind an antioccupation coalition that included Sihanouk and, most importantly, the Khmer Rouge. As such, the United States played a key role in keeping the Khmer Rouge government-in-exile as the diplomatically recognized government of Cambodia at the United Nations until 1991. Helping to maintain diplomatic recognition of the Khmer Rouge as a government-in-exile, the United States hampered international efforts to assist in the reconstruction process following the Khmer Rouge collapse, to deliver aid to Cambodia during the Vietnamese occupation, and to bring former Khmer Rouge leaders to justice.[21]

To this day, the US government is reticent to acknowledge its role in the series of crises that have rocked Cambodia since 1975. Similarly, Cambodian attempts to bring the Khmer Rouge to justice and to document and memorialize the events of the period are frequently met with resistance from a government largely populated by former Khmer Rouge cadre (including Prime Minister Hun Sen), who would be embarrassed to see their role in this history come to light. Thus, as scholar of modern Cambodian history Ben Kiernan observes, in Cambodia and the United States, "Both the creation of historical memory and its erasure depend upon contemporary politics as much as history itself."[22] The United States began to accept Cambodian refugees after 1979, but this move was coupled with an almost immediate national amnesia regarding the traumatic experience and humiliation of the Vietnam War. Cambodian refugees were framed as an unwelcome presence, if not former enemies who were located outside the normative and regulative domain of US law.

When Chhom enters the stage with the rest of Dengue Fever, both her voice and body index and reproduce Cambodian memories from this period, inviting audiences to engage with these complicated histories under erasure. If the violence inflicted on a range of Asian nations by the US government and military is often officially elided, various scholars have shown that Asian American cultural acts can deploy memory to combat such erasures.[23] In an environment where political and diplomatic interests commandeer public memory, the officially forgotten injustices caused by both the Vietnam War and DK periods continue to haunt Cambodian America. Artists and scholars such as dancer and Khmer Rouge survivor Sophiline Cheam Shapiro, scholar and survivor Boreth Ly, performance ethnographer Judith Hamera, literary theorist Cathy J. Schlund-Vials, and activist-playwright Catherine Filloux have argued that aesthetic performances of memory play a vital, if complicated, role in providing redress for survivors of the Khmer Rouge era and its aftermath.[24] I argue that musical performance plays a central role in this process because of the erasure of traditional and modern Cambodian musical traditions as a result of the CPK's violent cultural policies. Dengue Fever's nostalgic performances of memory within this context are thus marked by a political power that insists on acknowledging erased histories while challenging the forms of subjection that occur through the official acts of amnesia enacted by both the Khmer Rouge regime and (albeit to radically different effect) US law and policy.

## A Brief History of Cambodian Rock

As noted earlier, Dengue Fever did not invent performance practices that shuttle across cultural, geographical, and temporal borders;
it adopted them. Although potentially misunderstood as "authentically
Cambodian," the pre-DK-era music that the band covers resists catego-
rization as authentic or culturally pure by any means. This music drew
on a range of traditions born from Cambodia's position at the geopoliti-
cal crossroads of the Khmer, Spanish, French, Chinese, and US empires.
It is a popular music genre that began with the fusing of traditional
Cambodian dance and music (itself the product of various histories
of interregional conflict and conquest) with Latin and Afro-diasporic
music introduced as a result of the Philippine sea trade in the 1930s,
which came to be known as *phleng manil* (Manila music/songs).[25] French
cabaret music, introduced by French colonists, also contributed to the
emergence of a new popular music. King Norodom Sihanouk was a prolific composer and performer during the 1950s and 1960s. With his support, government-run schools that initially trained in the traditional arts
began to incorporate training in Western music theory.[26] The increased
US military presence in neighboring South Vietnam and Thailand in the
1960s led to the flourishing of a rock and pop music subculture that came
to its zenith in the late Sihanouk (1952–1969) and Lon Nol (1969–1975)
years. With the spread of affordable radio technology, many Cambodians were introduced to rock and roll as well as rhythm and blues on
pirated radio waves carrying the Voice of America and the United States
Armed Forces Radio, radically restructuring the type of popular music
produced within the nation's borders.

Of the artists covered by Dengue Fever, Ros Sereysothea and Sinn
Sisamouth reign supreme. Sinn had been a court musician in the 1960s
and became famous as a crooning balladeer easily compared to Nat King
Cole. His voice is stunningly smooth, marked by an evocative melancho-
lia that surges forth in original material as well as covers of popular Brit-
ish/US rock hits such as "Whiter Shade of Pale" and "Hey Jude." In 1965,
Sinn discovered young starlet Ros Serey working as a wedding performer
with her brother Ros Sothea in Battambang (Chhom's hometown). In
Phnom Penh, Serey adopted her brother's name, becoming Ros Sereysothea, and rose to superstardom. She performed a range of popular music
including songs influenced by Khmer folk traditions, duets with Sinn,
and reincarnated covers of Western hits such as "Proud Mary" and
"Louis Louis." Her voice is crystalline, and her range is unmatched by

any of her contemporaries (including her sometimes collaborator, the playful Pan Ron). Artists such as these became a cornerstone of Cambodian youth culture, their music the soundtrack of a tumultuous era.

On April seventeenth, 1975, the rock scene of Cambodia came grinding to a halt as the Khmer Rouge marched into Phnom Penh, taking control of Cambodia in its entirety. The laws of the previous regime were obliterated, and even though a new constitution was written and enacted, the legal provisions and protections that it assured existed only in a state of permanent suspension. The Khmer Rouge declared itself a democratic, constitutional state but ruled through a violent machinery of ubiquitous extrajuridical violence. In order to claim legitimacy, the CPK attempted to erase any trace of the state that preceded Democratic Kampuchea. A regime of forced forgetting began with overnight evacuations of the urban cities and the strategic dismantling and violent abolishment of those institutions most responsible for the transmission of history and memory: schools, family, religion, and the arts. The regime sought, in its own words, to "abolish, uproot, and disperse the cultural, literary, and artistic remnants of the imperialists, colonialists, and all the other oppressor classes."[27] The new society of the Khmer Rouge was achieved not merely by decrying the past but by erasing it completely, "smashing" any thing or person that the regime perceived to be compromised by it.

Unsurprisingly, performers and artists, who the Khmer Rouge thought to be contaminated by and vessels of the bourgeois tendencies of the previous society, were considered particularly dangerous. As performance studies theorists including Joseph Roach, Diana Taylor, Tavia Nyong'o, and Rebecca Schneider have all variously shown, performance functions as a central means for the embodiment and transmission of memory.[28] Popular music performers, with their roots in urban, middle-class culture, were particular targets for the agrarian revolutionary regime. As survivor Teeda Butt Mam wrote in 1996, to the Khmer Rouge, "former celebrities, the poets [were criminal]. These people carried bad memories of the old, corrupted Cambodia."[29] It is suspected that the majority of professional performers and musicians (popular and traditional) were killed during the regime, and the only songs that people were allowed to hear and sing during the DK era were CPK-sponsored anthems.[30] Music was seen as a primary means of educating and inspiring the masses. So while nearly all forms of autonomous cultural production came to a standstill from 1975 to 1979, the party pledged to continue the "strengthening and expanding of songs and poems" celebrating the revolution.[31] This was one of the few promises that the CPK kept. As survivor and

FIGURE 5.3. Memorial image of Pan, Sinn, and Ros at the Tuol Sleng Prison /
Genocide Museum, Phnom Penh, Cambodia, 2008. Photo by the author.

contemporary choreographer Sophiline Cheam Shapiro observed, this
was part of the CPK's systematic assumption of control over history
and memory: "The Khmer Rouge hoped to obliterate our history, and
in doing so, their songs have forged a significant place in it."[32] Some
formerly prominent musicians, Ros Sereysothea rumored to be among
them, were forced to record such music. By the time the Vietnamese
marched into Phnom Penh, simultaneously liberating and occupying
Cambodia in 1979, few of the musicians from the pre-DK era (including
Sinn Sisamouth and Ros Sereysothea) were still alive.[33]

The music of the pre-DK era has a sustained popularity in both Cambodia and its diaspora. Harnessing the power of performance in the face

of historical erasure, Dengue Fever returns to and revives the archive and catalogue of pre-DK music to offer an audiotopic sound of the world as it has been, as we wanted it to be, and as it could become. Reviving the music traditions of the pre-DK era, Dengue Fever foregrounds a history that has been virtually erased from the political and historical consciousness of many US audiences, while articulating this musical tradition's genesis less as linear progression from an origin than as a series of networked exchanges that defy linear temporality or geographic and cultural purity. Speaking with an English-language radio station in Phnom Penh, bassist Senon Williams described "Pow Pow," the band's cover of Ros Sereysothea's "Have You Seen My Love?," this way: "[It is] derived from surf music, from the sixties.... It goes from like this,... like, kinda US, California—where we're from—surf music, and then it comes all the way over here to Cambodia and then [is] rewritten with Cambodian melodies."[34] Certainly, Williams's trajectory speaks to the cultural imperialism of popular culture from the United States. But the genealogy of the pre–Khmer Rouge rock scene that I have put forth here suggests that the movement was indicative of more than simple colonial mimicry. It was a profoundly generative way of responding to a number of colonial histories by way of the production of a polyvocal musical tradition. As the product of these preexisting networks of cross-cultural exchange, the legacy of colonialism, and the modern Cambodian diaspora, Dengue Fever's music directly challenges the possibility of "return" by defying the notion that the music of the pre-DK era was "original" or "authentic" to begin with. If there is a "return" that happens in Dengue Fever's performances, then, it is most likely the return of the repressed histories of US imperialism and its role in the Khmer Rouge era.

## "No, I've Not Forgotten": Refusing Amnesia in Cambodian America

The politics of forgetting the US role in the rise of the Khmer Rouge are structured by the nation's impulse to repress its own imperial history. As Sarita Echavez See argues, in a study of Filipino American art and performance, US "empire not only forgets imperialism, producing the historiographical amnesia constitutive of Filipino American invisibility. In the realm of the aesthetic, American empire also forgets that it forgets imperialism."[35] Deploying aesthetic means to draw attention to the Filipino American body as archive and legacy of US imperialism, these artists "respond to a matrix of historical, psychic, and cultural dispossession" in a fashion that not only signals the return of the (doubly) repressed but has the capacity to "'disarticulate' the empire [from] its radical interior."[36] Although the differences between the United States' colonization of the Philippines and its role in the history of mainland Southeast Asia are significant, the latter history was structured by imperial overtures that resulted in a similar double forgetting about the empire's role in the Second Indochinese War, resulting in a parallel amnesia structuring (among others) Cambodian American, Vietnamese American, Laotian American, Hmong American, and Thai American "invisibility." When Chhom places her body before an audience as she performs music that invites the listener to travel back through this set of elided histories, her native informant is embodied less as a figure that represents and translates indigenous knowledge than as a transitional medium that conjures and gives flesh to forgotten legacies of US imperialism and military aggression in Southeast Asia.

In 2008, Dengue Fever returned to New York to perform at the Central Park SummerStage. Between songs, and near the middle of the set, Chhom looked out over the audience, the boys milled about behind her, and the humid summer air floated above us. She moved to the left side of the stage and caught Zac's eye. He nodded and tore into his guitar to sound off a raunchy set of chords. The band responded in kind, and the outdoor amphitheater was immediately filled with tension. They repeated this call and response one more time before launching into their cover of "Have You Seen My Love? / Pow Pow." As the audience began to dance along, Chhom took up the mike to add her voice, singing with a piercing urgency:

> Have you seen my boyfriend?
> Who picked up my love?
> Who has the guts to snatch my love?
> Please let me have him back.[37]

In Ros's original recording of the song, her vocals are slow and melancholic, embedded in a determined arrangement featuring a psychedelic organ, smooth sax, and ragged wah-wah guitar. She ascends into her upper register with a twinkling vibrato while delivering the lower notes with a confident sense of control. But the tragedies that the Khmer Rouge inflicted on Cambodia a few years after the song was recorded inscribe a haunting resonance into these otherwise forgettable lyrics. In the wake of the Khmer Rouge atrocities, the pleading figure takes on a historical urgency as she asks, "Have you seen my boyfriend?" The disappearance of loved ones (for interrogation, torture, and murder) was a common occurrence during the Khmer Rouge era, leaving survivors to endlessly ask about kidnapped and murdered lovers, family members, and friends. Chhom's performance of the song thus draws it into the present, without discarding the ways in which it is overdetermined by the past.

In many ways, the character staged by "Have You Seen My Love?" is also reflective of broader survival strategies performed by Cambodian immigrants who found themselves subject to the often contradictory regulatory regimes of immigration law and neoliberal welfare policy. Here, I want to be clear that I am not attempting to reduce Dengue Fever's songs into tidy political symbols. In other words, I am not trying to prove that the band's music always directly and consciously represents the political circumstances here discussed. Rather, I want to suggest that the band's self-conscious engagement with music from Cambodia's past serves as a point of entry into this elided history for its audiences. Keenly aware of the importance of memory in relation to Cambodian and US entanglement, the band performs the past in a way that invites audiences to listen to the resonances imposed on a song such as "Have You Seen My Love? / Pow Pow" by the burden of history. The erased legacy of the Vietnam War and Khmer Rouge eras are not the explicit content of Dengue Fever's music. But there are implicit resonances that occur when the band plays music from this past. Aware of this fact, the band often capitalizes on these resonances in order to issue accompanying performances of political and historical pedagogy.

Near the middle of *Sleepwalking through the Mekong*, for example, a documentary that tracks the band on a tour of Cambodia, Chhom discusses the support she received from people in Cambodia after Dengue Fever performed on a televised variety show: "I received a lot of phone calls after the performance, with people saying the performance was from the heart of Khmer rock-and-roll music—Sinn Sisamouth and Ros Sereysothea—especially with the older generations who grew up with this music. It made them very happy and supportive of us."[38] She narrates the band as bridging prewar traditions into the present, giving voice to memories once silenced through political and legal erasure. This sequence is immediately followed by a voice-over from an unidentified male band member who articulates the stakes of performing these memories in front of US American audiences: "What a lot of people don't realize is that Cambodia suffered more than any other country as a result of America's war with Vietnam. The war allowed the Khmer Rouge to come to power, and under Pol Pot's leadership, about one-third of the population died. . . . Cambodia's entire culture came close to disappearing."[39] For the remainder of the film, Dengue Fever collaborates with Cambodian Living Arts, a Phnom Penh–based nongovernmental organization committed to the preservation of threatened cultural traditions within Cambodia. Given the band's commitment to performing a legacy threatened by erasure, it does not take much to hear resonances between the narrative in "Have You Seen My Love?" and the losses experienced by Cambodians at home and in the diaspora in the post-DK era.

If memory was placed under erasure during the Khmer Rouge regime, the legal regulation of Cambodian immigrants in the United States has achieved similarly traumatic effects. It is important to understand this context in order to be able to register the significance of the performance of memory enacted by Dengue Fever. A significant number of Cambodian refugees to the United States were deposited in unlikely places such as Minnesota or urban areas such as San Francisco. Subject to conditions of urban poverty, the subjection of Cambodian America was occurring not only on the terrain of international law and immigration law but on the parallel terrain of welfare policy. Welfare and immigration policy required new Cambodian immigrants to become proper subjects by comporting to the norms of the neoliberal state. Aihwa Ong argues that medical and welfare institutions increasingly required Cambodian immigrants to perform the role of the "depressed Cambodian": "Being sick became a state induced by the health system itself, rather than by causes recognizable by the biomedical model. . . . Engaging in such institutional practices was an unavoidable set of rituals and routines for impoverished newcomers along their road to learning and resetting the terms of belonging."[40] As a result, Cambodian immigrants were trained to perform a constant turn to the past as a means of becoming recognizable to the state, even if it was as a "depressed Cambodian." This allowed them to negotiate with the complicated demands of neoliberal governmentality.

The compulsory mimeticism that requires Cambodian American immigrants to perform themselves in the role of sick victims who are locked in the past contradicts and collides with welfare reforms that require new citizens to place the traumatic effects of surviving the Khmer Rouge and immigrating to the United States under erasure. This latter imperative was structured to ensure that immigrants would perform their role as a self-managing, productive source of labor power on the new terrain of the neoliberal nation. Though not a refugee, Chhom articulates her own immigration experience in the following fashion:

"Living in America, I had to be self-sufficient. I had no help. It was one depending on oneself. . . . I did everything for myself. . . . I was my own boss. It was a struggle having to wait for my citizenship papers for three years. I had to be patient. I endured having less. I worked and went to school. . . . In America, when one sings or works, it is only enough for oneself."[41] Comparing her experience of immigration to her life in Cambodia, where she was supported by and able to support a large family, Chhom describes the erasure of these larger bonds in order to achieve status as a self-sustaining individual. This act of "depending on oneself" was in keeping with neoliberal policies that literally demand that immigrants and refugees "take responsibility" for (or "forget" and "get over") their circumstances, regardless of the historical and systemic conditions responsible for them.

Just over fifteen years after the largest numbers of Cambodian refugees arrived in the United States, President William Jefferson Clinton signed into law the Personal Responsibility and Work Opportunity Reconciliation Act (PRWORA), radically restructuring the nation's welfare system.[42] As Lisa Duggan argues, the law fostered both the maintenance and the production of a subclass of often racialized and gendered laborers, while withholding assistance from them unless they fell into accordance with (often impossible) neoliberal ideals of self-management and "personal responsibility."[43] Adding insult to injury, the PRAWORA excluded noncitizens from eligibility for social support, disproportionately affecting Asian- and Latino-immigrant communities.[44] Cambodian immigrants were thus located outside the assurances of social support within the welfare state (in other words, outside the law) while simultaneously subject to the demands of neoliberal subjectivity in order to become proper national subjects. They were required to perform contradictory and simultaneous embodiments of an inability to detach from the past (the "depressed Cambodian") and amnesia (the "personally responsible" immigrant). The audiotopic space of Dengue Fever's music allows us to explore the law's contradictory demands on the Cambodian American immigrant as these contradictions are allowed to coexist in the band's music in a politically productive fashion.

Refusing amnesia in "Have You Seen My Love?" Chhom's character insists on holding on to the past, but she does so less as a condition of damaged subjectivity than as an act that defiantly gives sound to an officially silenced history. Commanding the stage in Central Park, her voice is less longing than the voice in Ros's version of the song. Instead, it is forceful and fierce, embellished with strong wails of anger. She bounds around the stage in a vintage gold dress, making eye contact with her fans as she sings,

No, I can't forget.
I see a man and thought he was you.
I soared up and was about to embrace him.
I yelled out, "Bong! Bong!"
But I was completely mistaken.[45]

Here, she describes the phantasm of a lost lover, one that inspires the narrator to call out his name, only to discover that her longing has betrayed her: that which has been taken remains lost to her. Still, in a stark rejoinder to an unspoken imperative to leave him behind, she opens up the verse with the statement "No, I can't forget." Her commanding delivery suggests an alternative to the normalizing production of the "depressed Cambodian" immigrant, who is forced to submit to the norms of the state's neoliberal imperatives. This *refusal* to forget, signified by the song's repetition of "No, I can't forget," deploys the temporal transgressions of the native informant to hold on to a past that is threatened with erasure. As in the ritual of lighting a candle in Echo Park, this song becomes a public performance of the refusal to let go of a past that remains unmourned and unacknowledged. Through Chhom's defiant vocalization of immigrant memory, the past, its erasure, and the refusal of this erasure emerge and coexist on Dengue Fever's audiotopic stage.

If Chhom's character *"can't* forget," her performance in "Have You Seen My Love? / Pow Pow" refuses to allow the audience the luxury of amnesia. As noted earlier, the band actively seeks out the opportunity to use this mode of performance to engage in audience education. This subtle pedagogy is performed through a range of practices, from the documentary to the Echo Park ritual to public interviews in which band members draw attention to the history of US and Cambodian military entanglement. Performing classic songs by Ros or Sinn, the band manifests the sentiment at the heart of "Pow Pow" by refusing to forget the significance of this legacy, inviting its audience to do the same as we listen and dance along. Performing an attachment to the past through the revival of the pre-DK catalogue might then be understood as an articulated strategy that becomes a condition of political possibility that forces audiences in the present to listen to the sounds of a politically and legally silenced history. Doing so radically complicates the figuration of the immigrant as illegal, by giving context and texture to his or her presence within the United States. This is a theme that surfaces in some of the band's original work as well.

"Seeing Hands," an original song on *Venus on Earth*, tells the story of a vengeful lover. In the song's music video, the story of a lover who refuses to relinquish the past is politicized through a visual vocabulary that references contemporary symbols of immigration and US military imperialism. In the opening shot, we see a van piled high with people. This is a sight not uncommon in the streets of a developing urban center such as Phnom Penh but also seems to gesture to the ways in which day laborers in the United States (often immigrants) pile on top of trucks on the way to and from work sites. As the van approaches, we see that the crowd is a pile of the male members of Dengue Fever, with Zac Holtzman prominently crucified on the windshield, his long beard blowing in his face as the car speeds down the highway. Wearing a poncho and a small black hat, Williams rides behind the truck on a rickety bicycle. Chhom drives the car in a shimmering silver dress. There is a critical inversion here: band members—wearing clothing associated with migrant Mexican laborers—draw into relief the exploitation and subjection of immigrants in the contemporary United States. In turn, Chhom, the only immigrant member of the band, is meticulously styled to reflect a Hollywood ideal that is exported wholesale across the world.

The camera cuts between shots of industrial buildings and footage of a stealth bomber in flight, reminding us of the heavy concentration of military installations throughout California. Linking a picture of migration to the technologies of military imperialism, the video visualizes what US immigration and welfare policy places under erasure: that refugee immigrant populations in the United States are often produced as a direct result of US military intervention abroad. If this is what the band articulates as the thing "that a lot of people don't realize" about the Vietnam War, the video subtly refuses to abet this erasure. Staged in the unmistakable present, this convergence of material realities connects the war in Vietnam to the ongoing constellation of wars that erupted at the dawn of the twenty-first century.

## "22 Nights": Caught in the War on Terror

Dengue Fever began to record its first album in 2002. Around this same time, the Bush administration's newly formed Department of Homeland Security introduced a color-coded terror-alert system. During one of the first orange alerts, Chhom was stopped in a "routine check by immigration agents," discovered with a lapsed green card, and placed in an Immigration and Naturalization Service (INS) detention center for twenty-two days.[46] "22 Nights," one of the songs on the album, captures Chhom and the band's response to this event. In "22 Nights," the listener is taken to a place where Chhom's body is literally caught up in the legal apparatuses of the national security state. Reflecting Chhom's experiences in a detention center, the beginning of "22 Nights" evokes the loneliness of time spent in a cell. The song opens on a minimalist soundscape, evoking isolation and alienation. Chhom's voice is alone, with the plaintively strumming guitar and an erratic, mournful flute playing a haunting melody. She sounds sad and lonely, as a ghostly organ enters and exits beneath the melody. As the song continues, however, each member of the band begins to surge forth with a forceful passion, and the raw emotion of Chhom's voice steps in to guide the listener through the song's rough terrain. The chorus is a heart-wrenching explosion as Chhom's wails over saxophone riffs that take over when the voice, exhausted, can no longer go on. Indeed, the song is full of sounds that shatter through the figurative walls of the song's detention center. The "tonal and grammatical fissures" opened by Chhom's wail in "22 Nights" create a "musical space of difference" that pushes out and against the state's total claim to the Cambodian immigrant's body.

The Department of Homeland Security's color-coded system is symptomatic of a system of governmentality amplified in the post-9/11 period, whereby the Bush administration attempted to organize difference in a fashion that would support the total imperatives of the national security state. As Brian Massumi argues, the alert system was "introduced to calibrate the public's anxiety. . . . Jacked into the same modulation of feeling, bodies reacted in unison without necessarily acting alike."[47] Tellingly, between 2002 and 2011, the alert system oscillated between yellow (elevated risk) and orange (high risk), the third- and fourth-highest of five options. Given that the blue (guarded) and green (low) levels were never declared, in 2011 the spectrum was replaced with a system that simply baselines at yellow.[48] In other words, the US nation is "jacked into" a constant state of paranoid fear. Arguably, "brown" functions as an unofficial color on the alert system's continuum, given that the state now apprehends the brown body as a heightened risk to national security in the post-9/11 era.

Within the racial imaginary of the national security state, brown bodies that are or can be (mis)perceived as Muslim are profiled as terrorists, represented and received by the dominant culture as elevated security risks.[49] This form of anti-immigrant racism, producing the brown body as a national security threat in the post-9/11 period, has also been projected onto Southeast Asian bodies. I close this chapter by showing how Dengue Fever's staging of Chhom's experience in a detention cell in "22 Nights" unleashes the range of "contradictions and conflicts" that push back against the racialization of the immigrant body as always already illegal, affirming a space for difference otherwise denied by the totalizing apparatuses of the national security state. In order to make this case, I first need to historicize the racialization of Cambodian American immigrants in the era of the GWOT.

Chhom's detention occurred during a period when US law and public culture was organizing the specter of immigrant difference into a homogeneous mass that is understood as an elevated threat to national security. As noted in chapter 1, the Illegal Immigrant Reform and Immigrant Responsibility Act of 1996 (IIRAIRA) included a provision that required the deportation of noncitizen immigrants (including permanent resident aliens) convicted of aggravated felony, even if they had already completed the terms of their sentence.[50] Beyond codifying the "illegal immigrant" as a term of law, IIRAIRA disproportionately affected Cambodian American immigrants because of the fraught relationship between the US government and its former "enemies" from the Vietnam War (Cambodia, Laos, and Vietnam). As a result of the US government's refusal to recognize the governments of the Vietnamese-occupied People's Republic of Kampuchea and later the independent State of Cambodia (1979–1993) until 1991, the terms of most diplomatic relations had yet to be fully defined by the time of IIRAIRA's enactment. No treaty of reciprocity (allowing the repatriation of immigrants to Cambodia) existed between the United States and Cambodia. As a result, hundreds of Cambodians under arrest, many of them refugees who entered the United States as small children, were held indefinitely in INS detention centers as the State Department had nowhere to send them "back" to.[51]

Kim Ho Ma, a Cambodian refugee, was raised in the United States from the age of seven. He was convicted of gang violence at the age of seventeen and prepared for deportation, subject to the demands of IIRAIRA. Held indefinitely in a detention center when Cambodia refused to accept him, Kim Ho Ma challenged his case all the way to the Supreme Court in *Ashcroft v. Kim Ho Ma*.[52] During oral arguments, the justices and government lawyers reified the performative construction of the Cambodian-immigrant body as located outside the law, as they tangled over a practice in immigration law known as the entry fiction. The entry fiction occurs when an alien who is legally excluded from the United States but has been allowed on US soil for humanitarian or administrative reasons remains, in the words of Justice Oliver Wendell Holmes, "in theory of law at the boundary line" of the nation.[53] In other words, the immigrant is conceptually located outside the country and outside the law, despite his or her physical presence within national borders.

At first, the justices drew on precedent from the Asian-exclusion period (including and especially *Chae Chan Ping*) to argue that the entry fiction was established, precisely, to allow the US government to exclude and deport targeted immigrants.[54] Soon, Justice Ruth Bader Ginsburg interceded to point out that one of the "benign" aspects of the entry fiction was to protect excluded immigrants from a capricious exposure to statelessness: "In other words, this person has no right to set foot on US land, but we're going to be kind to this person and not dump them in the sea. We could say, you're excludable, . . . but . . . we're going to treat you as though you never came in, and that's a fiction, but it's a benign fiction, because the alternative is, we dump you in the sea."[55] To this, Deputy United States Solicitor General Edwin S. Kneedler astonishingly replied, "The United States would not do this, but one way to remove the alien from the United States would be to put him on a boat, or to insist that he find a country and, unless he finds a country he will be detained here."[56] Both Kneedler and Ginsburg used the ocean as a metaphor for the immigrant's juridical status. According to ancient maritime traditions that remain binding in contemporary international law, the ocean is a space that is free from claims of national sovereignty or jurisdiction.[57] Thus, progressive justice and Bush-administration lawyer alike conceived of the immigrant's body as spatially within the nation while technically outside the law (or out to sea).

Justice Stephen G. Breyer's majority opinion for the Court rejected the government's position, ordering the prisoners released after a "reasonable" period of time, but only after carving out an exception that specified that this right of release did not apply to a "small segment of particularly dangerous individuals, say suspected terrorists."[58] Breyer left open the question of whether indefinite detention under the auspices of national security was permissible under the Constitution. Shortly after the Court issued this ruling, the events of 9/11 occurred. Chhom was detained a few months later, as the discursive spaces between "immigrant" and "illegal" and "terrorist" began to blend together.

The US government, in an effort to theatricalize its attempt to secure national borders in the wake of 9/11, began forceful implementation of

IIRAIRA. This act was significant of what Wendy Brown describes as an increased anxiety over border security that reifies the slippage between the "image of immigrant hordes" and "the figure of the terrorist," such that the government demonstrates its commitment to national security by closing "porous borders, . . . figured as the scrim through which terror slips."[59] Ceding to these imperatives, the US State Department successfully pressured Cambodia to begin accepting the return of Cambodian immigrants. Fifteen thousand Cambodian American immigrants caught in the net of IIRAIRA and the security exigencies of the GWOT were prepared for deportation. Many of these, like Kim Ho Ma, were raised in the United States and have few memories of Cambodia, let alone Khmer language skills or even a place to live.[60] Others, like Chhom, were rounded up and threatened with deportation.

In the era of the GWOT, the national security state racializes the Cambodian American immigrant as always already illegal, located outside the law or the nation. "22 Nights" refocuses the listener's attention on the immigrant's body as it is caught up in the law. The song centralizes the immigrant's experience at the precise moment that she is rendered illegal through the process of detention and potential deportation. That the lyrics are sung in Khmer, and thus inaccessible for most US American listeners, does not render the articulation of the immigrant's voice any less powerful. Throughout the song, Chhom pushes into her upper register, at a high volume approaching a wail. In the final minutes of the song, as Chhom completes the last chorus, her voice is angry, even furious. The band continues to build a condensing cloud of sound. At this point, in the background, we hear Chhom's distant wail. This wail starts with a haunting intensity at first but becomes more prevalent. It is distorted; it echoes underneath the band as cymbals and saxophone crash against each other. In the last few seconds, this wail hums like an ambient scream in the background.

I have suggested that Chhom's wail is a political articulation of a refusal to accept the limits that are projected onto the racialized immigrant's body. This is akin to Danielle Goldman's description of Abbey Lincoln's famous scream in *The Freedom Now Suite*, whereby "screaming . . . is bound with real life horror that is racialized, gendered, sexualized, and frequently played out on the body."[61] The wailing that dominates the final minutes of "22 Nights" is evidence of the powerful role that aesthetic performances may play in responding to legal processes of racialization. If for no other reason, "22 Nights" evidences the ability for an immigrant's otherwise foreclosed voice to shatter the assumption of total control that is performed by and imposed on the brown body by the national security state. In the case of Dengue Fever, these aesthetic practices are bound up in Chhom's refusal of the racializing logic of the law.

One might argue that the law worked in Chhom's favor, as with the help of lawyers, she was able to secure relief from detention and to repair the process leading to "proper" (or "legal") documentation. Doing so would ignore any range of problems including the potential trauma of being apprehended as a national security threat, held for nearly a month in an INS prison, and the economic impact that the event had on an immigrant and artist who was already struggling to make ends meet long before the arrest. But what is important here is the direct role that Dengue Fever's performance practice played in Chhom's negotiation with the law. Following Chhom's release from the INS detention center, she was forced to pick up extra work as a nightclub singer at the Dragon House (the Long Beach Cambodian nightspot referenced in the band's second album title) to make money so that she could pay off her legal fees. The band also mounted benefit performances. As a result, it was not only through the aesthetic performance of the wail in "22 Nights" that Chhom was able to refuse the law's regulative claim to her body. It was through her work as a musical performer that she was able to generate the economic and social capital to negotiate the legal system and eventually to establish legal residency.

## Last Track

Initially a figure meant to translate across stratified social subject positions, the playful figure of the immigrant-as-native-informant has the potential for the destabilization of racial, national, cultural, and temporal categories that contribute to the racialization, subordination, and subjection of Asian immigrants and Asian Americans. In this chapter, I have shown how Chhom and the band deploy this figure to refuse the amnesia that registers the Cambodian American refugee as an unwelcome and illegal presence within the United States. I have also argued that this figure is mobilized to criticize and refuse the racialization of the Cambodian immigrant and Cambodian American as a national security threat in the era of the GWOT. The band's intervention utilizes the audiotopic nature of musical performance to affirm difference through the mediating figure of the native informant. In so doing, it both refuses and reimagines the limits of racialization imposed on the Cambodian American and Cambodian immigrant through security, immigration, and welfare law.

Chhom's experiences in an INS detention center were no doubt traumatic, and her release is a laudable triumph. But we do well to remember that many immigrants continue to wait in prisons and detention centers; others—such as Kim Ho Ma—have been exiled to places that they never knew as home, while still more prisoners who have been unjustly classified as "enemy combatants" remain hidden away in military prisons such as Guantánamo. Recognizing performance as a powerful means for criticizing, documenting, and challenging these practices, we must continue to push forward as we disrupt and dismantle the national security state, capitalism's exploitation of immigrant labor, the processes of Asian American racialization, and the systemic conditions that produce racial subordination within the sphere of US law. As Dengue Fever and many of the artists and activists discussed throughout this book evidence, performance (both aesthetic and quotidian) can be a central means of moving toward such a seemingly impossible goal. At the very least, it is the space in which we can imagine the possibility of its realization and the construction of a more just world beyond the limits of the racialized present.

# Conclusion: Virtually Legal

Since 2002, artist Hasan M. Elahi has been constantly performing under the watchful eyes of US law enforcement. If you go to his website, *Tracking Transience* (http://trackingtransience.com/), you find a rectangular screen, split in half horizontally. The top half of the screen is usually a photograph of a location: a lecture hall, church, or hallway. The bottom half of the screen is a shot from Google Maps, featuring an aerial-view, satellite photograph of a landscape. Along the top half of the map is a series of black and red squares that, if clicked, zoom in or out of the map. Somewhere on the map is a flashing black-and-red arrow indicating Elahi's location. In small white script, just beneath the series of squares at the top of the panel, are the words "Present location as of . . ." followed by a date and time which Elahi's GPS (global positioning system) regularly updates.

After about forty seconds, this horizontal diptych gives way to a panel of sixty-four thumbnail images. These thumbnail sets are usually organized by type—for example, sixty-four views from airplane windows, airline meals, gas stations, parking lots, bowls of soup, tacos, dashboard captures of the highway with green-and-white road signs hanging above, produce in supermarkets, toilets, or empty and unmade hotel beds. Clicking on a thumbnail takes you to the full-sized image. If you do nothing, the screen automatically gives way to random photographs drawn from the sets. Sometimes the images are accompanied by a date or time. At other times, one simply gets a black screen with white text. This can be location coordinates or even a virtual receipt with the date, name of the

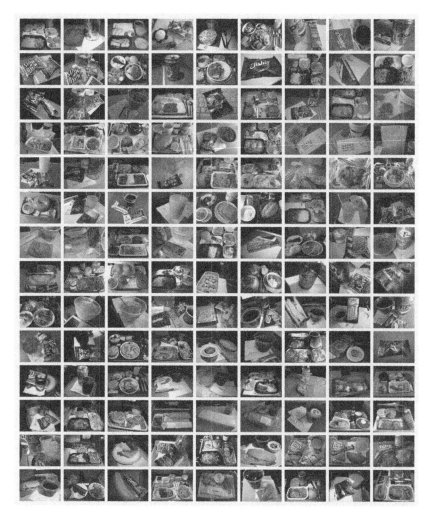

FIGURE 6.1. Hasan Elahi. "Tracking Transience: Altitude v3.0," C-print. Courtesy of the artist.

business, and amount of charge, such as "January 15 / Wal-Mart #3589 Salt Lake City UT / $135.23" The website is a giant archive of every place Elahi has been, every meal he has consumed, purchase he has made, and bed he has slept in, and so on. It is a virtual record of a life lived under constant surveillance.

Elahi is a multimedia artist, born in Rangpur, Bangladesh, and raised in New York City. In June 2002, he was returning from a trip to the

Netherlands when he was briefly detained in Detroit Metro Airport and questioned by the Federal Bureau of Investigation as a terror suspect. A few months earlier, Elahi rented a storage unit in Tampa, Florida, after which the manager reported seeing a "Middle Eastern man carrying explosives and fleeing the area."[1] The storage facility manager's charges were never verified, but Elahi was placed on a list of terror suspects and interrogated by the FBI a number of times following his initial Detroit detention. These interrogations included nine lie-detector tests, all of which the artist passed. He was given a phone number and instructed to inform the FBI of any future travel plans. As an academic and an artist who regularly travels internationally for work, Elahi took the government's request to the next level.

He began by sharing his whereabouts, travel plans, and personal information with the FBI via email and weblinks. Then he developed a system for constant self-surveillance, transforming his cell phone into a permanent tracking device and uploading as much information from his daily routine as possible onto the *Tracking Transience* website, "so anyone, including the FBI, would know where [he] was at any given moment."[2] Now, every moment of every day of Elahi's life is tracked, documented, and displayed for the national security state. The state has responded accordingly. Elahi reports hits on his site that trace variously to the FBI, the Central Intelligence Agency, and even the Office of the President of the United States.[3]

Understanding law enforcement's interest in him as being based on a regime of racial profiling, Elahi articulates his racialization as a South Asian American man thus: "They had received an erroneous report that an Arab man had fled on September twelfth [and] was hoarding explosives. Now, never mind I'm not Arab, never mind it wasn't the twelfth, never mind there were no explosives there. But, you know, we're going under this approach that, well, if you have a Muslim name, then you must be Arab. And if you're Arab, then you must have explosives."[4] The artist articulates a slippage from a South Asian body (misrecognized as Arab) to a Muslim name to the threat of terrorism. This slippage is predicated on misrecognition, as racial interpellation almost always is, and is indicative of the contemporary racialization of Muslims Americans and South Asian Americans. This occurs across various types of bodies, organized under the "unitary figure" of the Muslim, whereby racial and religious differences collapse into each other. As Junaid Rana argues, "The system of policing that targets Arab, Muslim, and South Asian immigrants for detention and deportation, as exemplified by the placement of 'the Muslim' in the U.S. racial formation under the Bush administration's War on Terror, is crafted through a broad logic of anti-immigrant racism."[5] Thus, the body of the perceived "Muslim" is made a spectacle, marked by the name of terrorist and, accordingly, placed outside the law at the very moment that it is rendered vulnerable to surveillance and legal regulation.

As Elahi discusses the FBI's continued refusal to issue proof of his clearance, he speaks of his encounter in the language of legal suspension: "In order to be formally cleared, you have to be formally charged. In America, we tend to think that we have these proper rights and these proper legal procedures. But when it comes to terrorism and national security, frankly, all that goes out the window. And, in this case, there was no law."[6] Elahi acknowledges that the situation prefigured the enactment of a regulatory regime to deal with cases of misrecognition by stating that "there was no law." But in saying this, he also suggests that the result of racial profiling places his body outside the normative rule of law. Indeed, legislature such as the USA Patriot Act reified this exceptional suspension of the law by giving the federal government unprecedented powers to use broad, potentially unconstitutional surveillance techniques against subjects both within and beyond the United States.

*Tracking Transience* is a performance both *of* the law and *for* the law. First, it stages the surveillance techniques of the national security state as they concentrate on the artist's racialized body. Second, the site is a pixelated record of the artist's performance *for* the law. That is, *Tracking Transience* documents Elahi's internalization and then exhibition of the law's profiling, racialization, and regulation of his body. A meditation on *Tracking Transience* is thus the perfect place to conclude *A Race So Different*. On the one hand, it demonstrates the links between law and performance in the process of racialization. On the other, it serves as a prime site across which we might think about the relationship between the historical racialization of Asian immigrants and Asian Americans and comparatively related forms of racialization in the present.

It is as a work of virtual performance that *Tracking Transience* allows Elahi to address and complicate his racialization through the state's practices of profiling and surveillance. I characterize Elahi's piece as a virtual performance for a number of reasons. Although the website is the interface through which the audience encounters the artist, and photography is the primary visual medium through which he documents his daily activities, the piece is organized around the location of the artist's body as it moves through space and time. This theorization is akin to

Marcela A. Fuentes's description of tactical media performances that utilize "tactical media practice and mobile technologies to raise questions about the interdiction to movement [for migrant bodies] through the very networks that exalt (or proclaim) connectivity and access."[7] Both virtual performances and tactical media performances are significant of contemporary performance forms that utilize technology to mediate embodied practices. Like tactical media performance, Elahi's use of technology draws attention to the ways in which state surveillance organizes and impacts the movement of the racialized body within the national security state.

Elahi's work can also be situated within recognizable traditions of endurance art, body art, and performance art. *Tracking Transience* starts with the assumption that people will be watching Elahi's body over a durational period. In this way, it can be read alongside the work of Tehching Hsieh or Marina Abramovic, who put their everyday activities under public and medial forms of surveillance.[8] The piece has political and formal resonances with Iraqi-born artist Wafaa Bilal's 2007 *Domestic Tension*. In this piece, a response to the death of his brother and father in the second Iraq War, Bilal put his body on display in a Chicago gallery for thirty days while spectators shot at him with paintballs through an online interface.[9] *Tracking Transience* also draws on the tradition of body artists, such as Hanna Wilke, Yoko Ono, Chris Burden, Cindy Sherman, and Karen Finley, who use the body in performance to stage, in the words of Amelia Jones, a "dislocation of normative subjectivity, reconfiguring identity politics (the way in which the subject comes to meaning in the social) and the very parameters of subjectivity itself."[10] Elahi's work differs from these artists, however, insofar as the spectator's attention is routinely drawn to a body that is constantly referenced but never actually given figural form.

While Elahi's body is the permanent referent that grounds the piece, its figuration is absent from the entire project. On the one hand, *Tracking Transience* is predicated on the idea that the artist's body is present and on display, both for the regulatory eye of the law and for the interested spectator. But on the other, Elahi literally dislocates this central referent from the spectator's experience of the work, as never in the library of images that make up *Tracking Transience* do we see Elahi. Ostensibly, the spectator goes to the website to "watch" him, but when he or she arrives at the website, the artist inverts this expectation. Browsing through the thousands of pictures, we see everything *but* the artist's body. This refusal to represent his body lends the work a disidentificatory status similar to

FIGURE 6.2. Hasan Elahi. "Tracking Transience: Stay v1.0," C-print. Courtesy of the artist.

what José Esteban Muñoz locates in the work of Félix González-Torres, "through the determined negation of direct representational routes [and] a turn toward a strategic obliquity that is anti-identitarian in the service of a reconstructed identity politics."[11]

Importantly, everything that we see is from the artist's perspective. As such, *Tracking Transience* invites spectators to take part in Elahi's surveillance, but only allows us to join in this act of self-surveillance if we are willing to see the world through his eyes. In picture after picture, we look out the windows of planes, across airport corridors, into plates of food and bowls of soup, across lecture halls and empty church pews, or down lonely highways. Over time, it is entirely possible that the viewer forgets, altogether, that he or she is supposed to be watching Elahi, as, instead, the spectator starts to view the world along with Elahi and even through his cell phone's camera lens. Viewing Elahi's world through his eyes, it becomes clear that the piece is as conceptually sophisticated as it is formally compelling. The different panels of thumbnails start to look like studies in shape, line, and color. A panel of meals, for example, draws the audience's eye to the interplay of circular, square, and rectangular plates, accented by vibrant splashes of red, brown, and green (the food). The photographs of empty beds evoke conceptual artists who have centralized the empty bed in the photographic frame (as in the work of González-Torres and Sophie Calle) as well as formal studies in perspective. Each photograph of a bed features the end of the bed in the image's foreground as the mattress withdraws to the background, with the headboard or wall blocking the disappearing point. Given the almost obsessive organization of these photographic sets (food, airport hallways, toilets, empty beds, street signs, graffiti, etc.), the site starts to take on the air of a vast survey.

Elahi's body is the referent that constitutes meaning in *Tracking Transience*. By withholding it from the visual frame, the artist forces the spectator (whether FBI agent or art enthusiast) to rehearse the ways in which racial knowledge is produced in and on his indexed but absent body. This is the only way to make sense of the piece and to situate it as a response to the racial profiling and surveillance techniques of the national security state. Formally and strategically, the project is an act of what Joan Kee describes as "visual reconnaissance": "The military provenance of this term alludes to the strategic nature of many works that seek to covertly uncover various phenomena of power external to the work ... by having the viewer reveal his or her allegiance to them."[12] Visual reconnaissance "forces the critic to deduce his or her evaluation from a visible, confirmable body of evidence accessible to all viewers."[13] In *Tracking Transience*, the spectator is forced to "reveal his or her allegiance to" (and role in) the process of racialization by making meaning vis-à-vis the profiling of the singular piece of evidence that is referenced but visually inaccessible to all viewers: Elahi's body.

The multitude of images on *Tracking Transience* are documents of the intimate minutiae that make up Elahi's life. At times picturesque but mostly mundane and even boring, collectively none of them lead one to the conclusion that Elahi is a terrorist or in any way worthy of the resources and scrutiny the US government continues to exhaust in profiling and watching him. Importantly, however, none of them disprove the charges either, as what we do not see in the images is as important as what we do. Elahi withholds any pictures of the people in his life, from students and co-workers to partners and friends. Instead, what we are viewing is a life boiled down to raw data, devoid of personal relationships or intimacy, a blank slate on which the spectator projects his or her desires and anxieties. In order to give meaning to the work, viewers are forced to situate their relationship and potential allegiance to the "various phenomena of power" that result in the profiling and racialization of Elahi's missing body; they are asked to reflect on the subtle role that they might unwittingly play in this process.

In this book's introduction, I cited a legal brief issued by Fred Korematsu that referred to the "all-too-familiar" resemblance between the government's suspension of civil rights for Japanese Americans during World War Two and the ways in which the law goes "out the window" for racialized subjects in the GWOT. *Tracking Transience* provides a platform for a discussion of these "all-too-familiar" resemblances, as well as a means of articulating their points of divergence. In this sense, *Tracking Transience* shares a conceptual resonance with some of the images in the Moriyuki Shimada scrapbook, discussed in chapter 4. Many of Shimada's photographs feature the Nikkei body as it performed before the state's regulatory apparatuses in the form of a guard tower. Similarly, *Tracking Transience* follows Elahi's display of his body for the watchful eye of the state. But if Shimada and his photographic subjects were already within the camp, Elahi's performance piece is partially predicated on the idea that his performance and disclosure for the state's optic might serve as an insurance policy against being disappeared into the camp. That is, if the profiling of brown and Muslim bodies in the GWOT leads to their misrecognition as terrorists or "enemy combatants," which in turn leads to detention in a place such as Guantánamo, Elahi's willingness to place his body on constant display for the national security state is partially intended to disrupt this process. At the very least, by making his whereabouts readily available to anyone who wants to know, Elahi makes it that much more difficult for the government to disappear him without anyone noticing.

In this way, *Tracking Transience* offers us an entry point into a discussion of the profiling and racialization of South Asian, Southeast Asian, Central Asian, Arab, and Muslim subjects in the contemporary moment. It also allows us to situate this process in relation to the racialization of Asian immigrants and Asian Americans over the past century and a half. It is thus useful to read Elahi's performance *of* and *for* the law in relation to emergent national security jurisprudence about the status of racially profiled "enemy combatants." I take as my example two cases involving a group of innocent Uighur refugees (an oppressed Muslim minority from western China) detained at Guantánamo: *Parhat v. Gates* and *Kiyemba v. Obama*.[14]

In June 2002, twenty-two Uighur refugees were imprisoned at Guantánamo Bay. Huzaifa Parhat and twenty-one other Uighur men were living in a refugee camp in Afghanistan in 2001 after fleeing persecution by the Chinese government. At the beginning of the Afghanistan War (October 2001), US aerial strikes destroyed the camp, and the group fled across the border to Pakistan. Pakistani authorities delivered the refugees to the US military for payment, and they were transferred to Guantánamo. In 2003, the Uighur refugees were ruled enemy combatants by the Combatant Status Review Tribunals (military courts established by the Bush administration's Department of Defense) despite scant evidence to justify the classification. Advocates for the Uighurs began to challenge their detention in US courts, and in 2008, the appeals court of the DC Circuit ruled, in *Parhat v. Gates*, that the Uighur refugees had been inaccurately classified as "enemy combatants" and, as such, wrongly detained. Although unstated, the inference was that their misclassification was the result of a system of racial and religious profiling.

After *Parhat*, the US State Department was not willing to return the men to China, where Uighurs are subject to political repression. Moreover, few other countries were willing to accept prisoners from a place that the US government spent nearly a decade trying to convince the world was a holding cell for the "worst of the worst."[15] After the Uighurs had spent almost half a decade in Guantánamo, their lawyers asked the courts to decide (a) whether the United States can indefinitely detain the men, given that they have nowhere else to go, or (b) whether because it is the government's fault for improperly classifying them in the first place, the United States has a responsibility to release them and grant them entry to the United States. In *Kiyemba v. Obama*, the judges sustained the State Department's refusal of entry to the United States, effectively permitting the US government to detain the Uighurs in Guantánamo indefinitely despite their uncontested innocence.

Clearly, *Kiyemba* has eerie resonances with many of the historical cases studied throughout this book. The case was haunted by the period of Asian exclusion, as a group of ethnic Asian men were once again banned from setting foot on US soil. Judge A. Raymond Randolph drew on no less than six Asian exclusion cases to support the court's opinion.[16] Randolph argued, "Ever since the decision in the *Chinese Exclusion Case*, the Court has, without exception, sustained the exclusive power of the political branches to decide which aliens may, and which aliens may not, enter the United States, and on what terms."[17] Although Randolph concluded that the United States had "insufficient evidence to classify [the Uighurs] as enemy combatants," he absolved the government of any responsibility to end the detention by accepting the Uighurs if no one else would: "their detention at Guantanamo for many years [does not] entitle them to enter the United States."[18] That the only alternative was for the men to remain in the prison indefinitely was simply not the judiciary's concern.[19]

Reading *Kiyemba* alongside *Tracking Transience* can help us to understand how contemporary forms of profiling, exclusion, and even indefinite detention are built on a juridical and social architecture that reaches back to cases such as *Chae Chan Ping*. In this way, Elahi's project allows us to see the important role that Asian Americanist criticism and cultural production may play in historicizing, contextualizing, and challenging the forms of comparative racialization and legal subjection occurring in a purportedly "postracial" moment. An Asian Americanist critical and cultural insurgency against the tactics of the national security state has to account for the ways in which these tactics are played out in and on the body, through forms of performance and subjection that confuse the distinction between voluntary and coerced acts.

The history of Asian American racialization is, thus, not simply a story of legal performatives that produce knowledge about racial difference. It is a story of speech acts that compel and inspire Asian Americans to perform in response to and *for* the law—as staged by *Tracking Transience*. Furthermore, in a moment characterized by the advent of multiracial conservatism, it is not simply that the law is written onto and embodied *by* Asian Americans: Asian Americans sometimes write the law. For example, the infamous Bush-administration torture memo, determining that enhanced interrogation is legal, was coauthored by Korean American lawyer John Yoo; the USA Patriot Act was written by a Vietnamese American lawyer, Viet Dinh. The US government's profiling of Elahi and the Uighur refugees, and detention of the latter, is thus intimately tied to the history of Asian American racialization as well as legal performatives about and even issued by Asian Americans.

If, as I have argued throughout this book, the interaction between performance and law is partially responsible for the processes of racialization, *Tracking Transience* reminds us that Asian American performance (both quotidian and aesthetic) is a critical means for disrupting and reformatting the process of subjectification. Engaging in a war of positions, Elahi uses a seemingly weak tactical position, as a racialized Bangladeshi American under the suspicious eye of the government, to his benefit. That is, if the state is watching him *because* he is a racialized subject, he builds on the fact that he has a captive audience for his virtual performance. Turning over more data about his life than his official watchers could ever want, he stages a public statement that radically undercuts the national security state's claim to his body. Obviously, the majority of immigrants caught within the web of the national security state do not have the resources to mount such a response. Neither do those who are already deeply integrated into these regulatory legal apparatuses, as in the case of the Uighur refugees. It is, thus, as a work of aesthetics that *Tracking Transience* reveals its true power.

What is significant is not that the performance has, by and large, relieved Elahi of the burden of government interference in his everyday life. (Although, no doubt, he appreciates no longer having to be interrogated every time he wants to catch a plane—a small victory that should not be undervalued.) Rather, the power of *Tracking Transience* and Elahi's performance *of* and *for* the constant optic of the law is its ability to attack the very logic that legitimizes the indiscriminate profiling and legal regulation of racialized subjects under the auspices of national security. Perhaps as importantly, the piece gives Elahi a platform to raise the issue publicly. Interest in *Tracking Transience* has resulted in highly publicized profiles of and interviews with the artist in *Wired* magazine, on National Public Radio, and on Comedy Central's popular political satire *The Colbert Report*.[20]

Like many of the performances studied in this book, *Tracking Transience* is a testament to the legal and political power of aesthetic practices. It is also a sobering reminder of chapter 4's discussion of the ways in which visibility can become a trap. In order for Elahi to "free" himself of FBI intrusion into his personal life, he has made his entire life a spectacle for public surveillance and consumption. He transforms his body from being a target of power into the organ of its operation and the means of power's articulation. At the same time, by refusing to allow spectators to access the figure of his body or specific and intimate details about his life, he reminds us that it may be in the act of withdrawing from the field of the visible or the domain of recognizable subjectivity that we are most capable of accessing emancipation or liberation.

My hope is that the conversations contained in *A Race So Different* create a foundation for thinking about the unique relationship between law and performance in the making and potential unmaking of racialized subjects. I have argued that Asian American racialization is a process that incorporates a unity of various and seemingly paradoxical opposites, consolidating them within the Asian American body and compelling this body to perform in a fashion that fosters the maintenance of dominant norms. But perhaps most importantly, I have engaged with artists and performers who demonstrate the power of performance as a strategically useful means for challenging the processes of racialization while staging alternative world-making possibilities. At the very least, such practices—and forms of critical

engagement with them—allow us to hold up a candle for future generations. In this way, this book is a document of the insurgent impulses
contained in performances (both quotidian and aesthetic) that rise up
against the limits of racialization in the present and rehearse freedom
from these limits for the future.

# Notes

## Introduction

1. Frances Ya-Chu Cowhig, *Lidless* (London: Metheun, 2011), 37.
2. Ibid., 8.
3. Ibid.
4. Ibid., 10.
5. Here, I am gesturing to important work by Jasbir Puar on the construction of the racialized "terrorist" body as queer and, thus, subject to forms of exceptional sexual violence. See Jasbir K. Puar, *Terrorist Assemblages: Homonationalism in Queer Times* (Durham: Duke University Press, 2007).
6. Cowhig, *Lidless*, 38, 46.
7. Ibid., 60.
8. This book covers various examples of Asian American racialization, including the Japanese American concentration camps of World War Two, the Chinese-exclusion era, and the Cambodian deportation cases of the early twenty-first century.
9. I would provisionally locate *Lidless* within a tradition that includes, but is not limited to, works such as a Wakako Yamauchi's *12-1-A* (about Japanese American internment), Genny Lim's *Paper Angels* (about Chinese immigrants caught up in a restrictive immigration system), and Velina Hasu Houston's *Kokoro (True Heart)* (about the use of the cultural defense for Asian immigrant defendants). Wakako Yamauchi, "12-1-A," in *The Politics of Life*, ed. Velina Hasu Houston (Philadelphia: Temple University Press, 1993); Genny Lim, "Paper Angels," in *Unbroken Thread*, ed. Roberta Uno (Amherst: University of Massachusetts Press, 1993); Velina Hasu Houston, "Kokoro (True Heart)," in *But Still, Like Air, I'll Rise: New Asian American Plays*, ed. Velina Hasu Houston (Philadelphia: Temple University Press, 1997).
10. Robert S. Chang, *Disoriented: Asian Americans, Law, and the Nation-State* (New York: NYU Press, 1999), 1.
11. Michael Omi and Howard Winant, *Racial Formation in the United States: From the 1960s to the 1990s*, 2nd ed. (New York: Routledge, 1994), 56.

12. See, for example, Robert M. Jarvis, Steven E. Chaikelson, Christine A. Corcos, et al., *Theater Law: Cases and Materials* (Durham: Carolina Academic Press, 2004).

13. Catherine Cole, *Performing South Africa's Truth Commission: Stages of Transition* (Bloomington: Indiana University Press, 2009); Tony Perucci, *Paul Robeson and the Cold War Performance Complex: Race, Madness, Activism* (Ann Arbor: University of Michigan Press, 2012). Joseph Roach's work has also been foundational to my own interest in the intersection between law and performance, most profoundly in his historicization of and accounting for the relationship between law and performance in the New Orleans Mardi Gras: Joseph Roach, "Carnival and the Law in New Orleans," *TDR: The Drama Review* 37, no. 3 (1993); Roach, *Cities of the Dead: Circum-Atlantic Performance* (New York: Columbia University Press, 1996), 239–82. See also Shane Vogel, "Where Are We Now? Queer World Making and Cabaret Performance," *GLQ: A Journal of Gay and Lesbian Studies* 6, no. 1 (2000); Luke Wilson, *Theaters of Intention: Drama and the Law in Early Modern England* (Stanford: Stanford University Press, 2000); Paul Siegel, "A Right to Boogie Queerly: The First Amendment on the Dance Floor," in *Dancing Desires: Choreographing Sexualities on and off the Stage*, ed. Jane C. Desmond (Madison: University of Wisconsin Press, 2001).

14. Perucci, *Paul Robeson*, 4, 86.

15. Catherine Cole, "Performance, Transitional Justice, and the Law: South Africa's Truth and Reconciliation Commission," *Theatre Journal* 59, no. 2 (2007): 186.

16. The final chapter of Cole's monograph does turn to analysis of an aesthetic response to the TRC, but her project is overwhelmingly concerned with analysis of the TRC proper: Cole, *Performing South Africa's Truth Commission*, 121–58.

17. David Palumbo-Liu, *Asian/American: Historical Crossings of a Racial Frontier* (Stanford: Stanford University Press, 1999); Karen Shimakawa, *National Abjection: The Asian American Body Onstage* (Durham: Duke University Press, 2002); Mae M. Ngai, *Impossible Subjects: Illegal Aliens and the Making of Modern America* (Princeton: Princeton University Press, 2004).

18. Erving Goffman, *The Presentation of Self in Everyday Life* (New York: Anchor Books, 1959), 15.

19. *Boumediene v. Bush*, 553 U.S. 723 (2008).

20. *Brief for Petitioner El-Banna et al. in Al Odah v. United States*, No. 06-1196, Supreme Court of the United States (2007). In a later interview with the Associated Press, one of the lawyers, Thomas B. Wilner, complained, "Anyone, including a federal official, who violates the Endangered Species Act by harming an iguana at (Guantanamo), can be fined and prosecuted. . . . Yet the government argues that U.S. law does not apply to protect the human prisoners there. . . . Pretty absurd." A public affairs office at Guantánamo confirmed as much in the same article: "There is a very consistent effort by the command to protect the iguanas and other exotic species here, which I assume is partially driven by the federal law": Associated Press, "More Rights for Gitmo's Lizards than Detainees? Supreme Court Mulls What Protections Apply to Prisoners in 'Law-Free Zone,'" *NBCNews.com* (December 8, 2007), http://www.nbcnews.com/id/22161810/ns/world_news-terrorism/t/more-rights-gitmos-lizards-detainees/#.UQqwRkrDSKM.

21. *Brief for Petitioner El-Banna et al. in Al Odah v. United States*, 2.

22. *Brief of Amicus Curiae Fred Korematsu in Support of Petitioners Al Odah, et al., v. United States*, No. 03-334, Supreme Court of the United States (2003), 1.

23. Ibid., 2.

24. *Plessy v. Ferguson*, 163 U.S. 537, at 559 (1896), Harlan, J., dissenting.

25. See Kimberlé Crenshaw, "Mapping the Margins: Intersectionality, Identity Politics, and Violence against Women of Color," in *Critical Race Theory: The Key Writings That Formed the Movement*, ed. Kimberlé Crenshaw, Neil Gotanda, Gary Peller, and Kendall Thomas (New York: New Press, 1995); Neil Gotanda, "A Critique of 'Our Constitution Is Color-Blind,'" in ibid.; David L. Eng, *The Feeling of Kinship: Queer Liberalism and the Racialization of Intimacy* (Durham: Duke University Press, 2010), 7–8; Joshua Takano Chambers-Letson, "Embodying Justice: The Making of Justice Sonia Sotomayor," *Women and Performance: A Journal of Feminist Theory* 20, no. 2 (2010).

26. *Plessy v. Ferguson*, 163 U.S. at 561.

27. Chinese Exclusion Act, I (1882).

28. *Chae Chan Ping v. United States*, 130 U.S. 581 (1889).

29. As I briefly discuss later, my use of the term *racial exception* is drawn from a synthesis of the work of Carl Schmitt, Walter Benjamin, and Giorgio Agamben. *Racial exception*, as a term, is hardly a neologism, insofar as a number of different scholars, writing in different contexts, give spontaneous use to the phrase. See, for example, Scott Michaelsen, "Between Japanese American Internment and the USA Patriot Act: The Borderlands and the Permanent State of Racial Exception," *Aztlán: The Journal of Chicano Studies* 30, no. 2 (2005); Tavia Nyong'o, *The Amalgamation Waltz: Race, Performance, and the Ruses of Memory* (Minneapolis: University of Minnesota Press, 2009), 47–54.

30. Palumbo-Liu, *Asian/American*, 21.

31. Shimakawa, *National Abjection*, 9.

32. Ibid., 3.

33. Carl Schmitt, *Political Theology: Four Chapters on the Concept of Sovereignty* (1922), trans. George Schwab (Chicago: University of Chicago Press, 2005).

34. Schmitt strategically refused to articulate the effects that such a state may have on subjects who are already vulnerable to forms of state violence, an omission that had disastrous effects in Nazi Germany. For more on the intellectual and political legacy of Schmitt, see Gopal Balakrishnan, *The Enemy: An Intellectual Portrait of Carl Schmitt* (New York: Verso, 2000); Ellen Kennedy, *Constitutional Failure: Carl Schmitt in Weimar* (Durham: Duke University Press, 2004).

35. Walter Benjamin, "Theses on the Philosophy of History," trans. Harry Zohn, in *Illuminations: Essays and Reflections*, ed. Hannah Arendt (New York: Harcourt, 1988), 257.

36. This phrasing is drawn from Didier Fassin and Mariella Pandolfi's reading of contemporary deployments of the "emergency" in humanitarian interventions: "Walter Benjamin's well-known formula, 'that the "state of emergency" in which we live is not the exception but the rule,' should be understood here as signaling not an indefinite extension of the state of exception, but rather the now indefinite extension of the possibility of it": Didier Fassin and Mariella Pandolfi, "Introduction: Military and Humanitarian Government in the Age of Intervention," in *Contemporary States of Emergency: The Politics of Military and Humanitarian Interventions*, ed. Didier Fassin and Mariella Pandolfi (New York: Zone Books, 2010), 22.

37. See Junaid Akram Rana, *Terrifying Muslims: Race and Labor in the South Asian Diaspora* (Durham: Duke University Press, 2011).

38. See Alexander Hamilton, John Jay, and James Madison, *The Federalist: A Commentary on the Constitution of the United States* (1788), ed. Robert Scigliano (New York: Modern Library, 2000), 349; John Adams, "Letter to Abigail Adams: April 14, 1776," in *Founding America: Documents from the Revolution to the Bill of Rights*, ed. Jack N. Rakove (New York: Barnes and Nobles Classics, 2006).

39. *Minor v. Happersett*, 88 U.S. 162 (1874); *Dred Scott v. Sandford*, 60 U.S. 294 (1856); *Cherokee Nation v. Georgia*, 31 U.S. 1 (1831).

40. Thurgood Marshall, "Reflections on the Bicentennial of the United States Constitution," in *Thurgood Marshall: His Speeches, Writings, Arguments, Opinions, and Reminiscences*, ed. Mark V. Tushnet (Chicago: Lawrence Hill Books, 2001), 282.

41. J. Kēhaulani Kauanui, *Hawaiian Blood: Colonialism and the Politics of Sovereignty and Indigeneity* (Durham: Duke University Press, 2008), 25.

42. Schmitt, *Political Theology*, 6.

43. A specific study of the exceptional nature of Latino racialization is beyond the scope of the present study, because of time and space constraints. Clearly, the racialization of Latino immigrants has occurred hand in hand with the racialization of Asian immigrants. See Ngai, *Impossible Subjects*.

44. Giorgio Agamben, *Homo Sacer: Sovereign Power and Bare Life*, trans. Daniel Heller-Roazen (Stanford: Stanford University Press, 1998), 51.

45. In turn, the genocidal logic that differentially governs indigenous racialization amplified fragmentation for Native Americans with the first articulation of blood-quantum classifications in the 1887 Dawes Act.

46. J. L. Austin, *How to Do Things with Words* (Cambridge: Harvard University Press, 1962), 5.

47. Ibid.

48. Ibid., 154.

49. Ibid., 4n. 2.

50. Jacques Derrida, "Declarations of Independence," *New Political Science* 15 (Summer 1986): 9.

51. Andrew Parker and Eve Kosofsky Sedgwick, "Introduction: Performativity and Performance," in *Performativity and Performance*, ed. Andrew Parker and Eve Kosofsky Sedgwick (New York: Routledge, 1995), 4.

52. Louis Althusser, "Ideology and Ideological State Apparatuses," in *Lenin and Philosophy, and Other Essays* (1971; reprint, New York: Monthly Review Press, 2001), 89.

53. Ibid., 96.

54. Ibid., 118; Louis Althusser, "Idéologie et appareils idéologiques d'état (Notes pour une recherche)," in *Sur la reproduction* (Paris: Presses Universitaires de France, 1995), 305.

55. Althusser, "Ideology and Ideological State Apparatuses," 118.

56. Ibid.; Althusser, "Idéologie et appareils idéologiques d'état," 306.

57. Karl Marx, *Capital: Volume 1*, trans. Ben Fowkes (New York: Penguin, 1990), 206, 47, 164; Marx, "The Eighteenth Brumaire of Louis Bonaparte" (1869), in *Marx's "Eighteenth Brumaire": (Post)modern Interpretations*, ed. Mark Cowling and James Martin (London: Pluto, 2002), 19.

58. Louis Althusser, "The 'Piccolo Teatro': Bertolazzi and Brecht," trans. Ben Brewster, in *For Marx* (1965; reprint, New York: Verso, 1999), 151.

59. Judith Butler, *The Psychic Life of Power: Theories in Subjection* (Stanford: Stanford University Press, 1997), 112.

60. Cowhig, *Lidless*, 46.

61. Ibid. Clearly, this scenario has resonances with what Homi K. Bhabha describes as the ambivalent and "*ironic* compromise" that occurs in the scene of colonial mimicry: Homi Bhabha, "Of Mimicry and Man: The Ambivalence of Colonial Discourse," in *The Location of Culture* (New York: Routledge, 1994), 122.

62. Cowhig, *Lidless*, 47.

63. Rey Chow, *The Protestant Ethnic and the Spirit of Capitalism* (New York: Columbia University Press, 2002), 115.

64. Antonio Viego, *Dead Subjects: Toward a Politics of Loss in Latino Studies* (Durham: Duke University Press, 2007), 105.

65. Louis D. Brandeis, "The Living Law," *Illinois Law Review* 10 (1916). See also Marshall, "Reflections on the Bicentennial of the United States Constitution"; Stephen G. Breyer, *Active Liberty: Interpreting Our Democratic Constitution* (New York: Knopf, 2005); Laurence H. Tribe, *The Invisible Constitution* (New York: Oxford University Press, 2008); Joshua Takano Chambers-Letson, "Contracting Justice: The Viral Strategy of Felix González-Torres," *Criticism: A Quarterly for Literature and the Arts* 51, no. 4 (2009–2010).

66. Schmitt, *Political Theology*, 13.

67. Ibid., 31.

68. Thomas Hobbes, *Leviathan* (1651), ed. J. C. A. Gaskin (New York: Oxford University Press, 1998), 179.

69. Ibid., 106.

70. Ibid.

71. Plato's famous complaint against impersonation or mimesis occurs in *The Republic*: Plato, *The Republic and Other Works*, trans. and ed. Benjamin Jowett (New York: Anchor Books, 1973), 81–85.

72. Hobbes, *Leviathan*, 106–7.

73. Ibid., 109.

74. Mark P. Denbeaux and Jonathan Hafetz, introduction to *The Guantánamo Lawyers: Inside a Prison Outside the Law*, ed. Mark P. Denbeaux and Jonathan Hafetz (New York: NYU Press, 2009), 1.

75. Juana María Rodríguez, *Queer Latinidad: Identity Practices, Discursive Spaces* (New York: NYU Press, 2003), 87.

76. Max Horkheimer and Theodor W. Adorno, *Dialectic of Enlightenment*, trans. John Cumming (New York: Continuum, 1972), 147.

77. Shoshana Felman, *The Juridical Unconscious: Trials and Traumas in the Twentieth Century* (Cambridge: Harvard University Press, 2002), 107.

78. Jacques Rancière, *The Emancipated Spectator*, trans. Gregory Elliot (New York: Verso, 2009), 17.

79. Shimakawa, *National Abjection*, 18.

80. Ernst Bloch, "The Stage Regarded as a Paradigmatic Institution and the Decision within It," in *The Utopian Function of Art and Literature: Selected Essays*, trans. Jack Zipes and Frank Mecklenburg (Cambridge: MIT Press, 1988).

81. Ibid., 225.

82. Ibid., 230.

83. Dorinne K. Kondo, *About Face: Performing Race in Fashion and Theater* (New York: Routledge, 1997), 256–57.

84. Josephine D. Lee, *Performing Asian America: Race and Ethnicity on the Contemporary Stage* (Philadelphia: Temple University Press, 1997); Shimakawa, *National Abjection*; Esther Kim Lee, *A History of Asian American Theater* (Cambridge: Cambridge University Press, 2006); Sarita Echavez See, *The Decolonized Eye: Filipino American Art and Performance* (Minneapolis: University of Minnesota Press, 2009); Lucy Mae San Pablo Burns, *Puro Arte: Filipinos on the Stages of Empire* (New York: NYU Press, 2012); Christine Bacareza Balance, "Notorious Kin: Filipino America Reimagines Andrew Cunanan," *Journal of Asian American Studies* 11, no. 1 (2008).

## 1 / "That May Be Japanese Law, but Not in My Country"

1. *Nguyen v. INS*, 533 U.S. 53, 68 (2001).

2. Emily Bazelon, "The Place of Women on the Court," *New York Times*, July 7, 2009, 47.

3. For clarity, I use the term *Madame Butterfly* to refer to the narrative in general, as well as the novella and the play. *Madama Butterfly* is used to refer to the opera only. Similarly, I refer to "Cho-Cho-San" when referencing the book and play and "Cio-Cio-San" when discussing the opera.

4. For scholarship on the different versions of *Madame Butterfly* (including *M. Butterfly*), see Ping Hui Liao, "'Of Writing Words for Music Which Is Already Made': 'Madama Butterfly,' 'Turandot,' and Orientalism," *Cultural Critique* 16 (1990); Angela Pao, "The Eyes of the Storm: Gender, Genre and Cross-Casting in *Miss Saigon*," *Text and Performance Quarterly* 12, no. 1 (1992); Gina Marchetti, *Romance and the "Yellow Peril": Race, Sex, and Discursive Strategies in Hollywood Fiction* (Berkeley: University of California Press, 1993), 78–108; James S. Moy, *Marginal Sights: Staging the Chinese in America* (Iowa City: University of Iowa Press, 1993), 82–94; Kondo, *About Face*, 31–54; Rey Chow, *Ethics after Idealism: Theory, Culture, Ethnicity, Reading* (Bloomington: Indiana University Press, 1998), 74–97; David L. Eng, *Racial Castration: Managing Masculinity in Asian America* (Durham: Duke University Press, 2001), 137–66; Maureen Honey and Jean Lee Cole, introduction to *"Madame Butterfly" and "A Japanese Nightingale": Two Orientalist Texts*, ed. Maureen Honey and Jean Lee Cole (New Brunswick: Rutgers University Press, 2002), 1–22; Shimakawa, *National Abjection*, 23–56; Jonathan Wisenthal, Sherrill Grace, Melinda Boyd, Brian McIlroy, and Vera Micznik, eds., *A Vision of the Orient: Texts, Intertexts, and Contexts of Madame Butterfly* (Toronto: University of Toronto Press, 2006); Seung Ah Oh, *Recontextualizing Asian American Domesticity: From "Madame Butterfly" to "My American Wife!"* (Lanham, MD: Lexington Books, 2008).

5. Fredric Jameson, *The Political Unconscious: Narrative as a Socially Symbolic Act* (Ithaca: Cornell University Press, 1981), 34. Shoshana Felman uses the term "juridical unconscious" in a later text, although she refrains from engaging with Jameson directly: Felman, *The Juridical Unconcsious*.

6. David Henry Hwang, *M. Butterfly* (New York: New American Library, 1989); Claude-Michel Schönberg, Alain Boublil, and Richard Maltby, *Miss Saigon: Original London Cast Recording* (Geffen, 1990), CD.

7. The ur-text for Long's novella is generally considered to be the French novel *Madame Chrysanthemum*, published in 1885 by Pierre Loti. This semiautobiographical

text was based on Loti's experiences as a naval officer stationed in Japan, beginning in 1885. Because I am focusing directly on the question of Butterfly in US law and culture as related to the Asian American body, I exclude analysis of Loti's novella from this chapter. For an excellent analysis of Loti's novel and, in particular, the homoeroticism of *Madame Chrysanthemum*, see Joy James, "Madame Butterfly: Behind Every Great Woman . . . ," in Wisenthal et al., *A Vision of the Orient*.

8. Rebecca Bailey-Harris, "Madame Butterfly and the Conflict of Laws," *American Journal of Comparative Law* 39, no. 1 (1991): 157–77.

9. Ibid., 160, 157.

10. See Lisa Lowe, *Immigrant Acts: On Asian American Cultural Politics* (Durham: Duke University Press, 1996).

11. Lucy Mae San Pablo Burns, "'Splendid Dancing': Filipino 'Exceptionalism' in Taxi Dancehalls," *Dance Research Journal* 40, no. 2 (2008): 32.

12. See Arthur Groos, "Madame Butterfly: The Story," *Cambridge Opera Journal* 3, no. 2 (1991).

13. Harry Ransom Humanities Research Center, "Biographical Sketch of John Luther Long," in *John Luther Long: An Inventory of His Papers at the Harry Ransom Humanities Research Center*, http://research.hrc.utexas.edu:8080/hrcxtf/view?docId=ead/00080.xml (accessed Septebember 15, 2012).

14. "This 'Butterfly' a Winged Jewel: Belasco's Little Play Earns Distinct Success," *New York Press*, March 6, 1900, New York Public Library for the Performing Arts / Billy Rose Theatre Division, Series X, Scrapbooks, microfilm r.5.

15. "'Mme. Butterfly' a Great Success: Tumult of Applause Greets Mr. Belasco's New Play," *Morning Telegraph*, March 6, 1900, New York Public Library for the Performing Arts / Billy Rose Theatre Division, Series X, Scrapbooks, microfilm r.5.

16. "Various Dramatic Topics," *New York Times*, March 11, 1900, 16.

17. "'Mme. Butterfly' Gives Blanche Bates an Opportunity," *New York Times*, March 6, 1900, New York Public Library for the Performing Arts / Billy Rose Theatre Division, Series X, Scrapbooks, microfilm r.5.

18. Honey and Cole, introduction to *"Madame Butterfly" and "A Japanese Nightingale,"* 4. Newspaper reviewers worried that "it is bad to make the spectators feel that they, too, are waiting": "'Mme. Butterfly' Gives Blanche Bates an Opportunity." As a later reporter commented, "The representation of the silent passage of a night is a risky device in a piece designed for popular entertainment, but there can be no two sane opinions of the power in repose of Miss Bates' acting in that scene or of the pathos of her representation of Cho-Cho-San's death": Edward A. Dithmar, "At the Play with the Players," *New York Times*, March 11, 1900.

19. Alan Dale, "Alan Dale Says: 'Mme. Butterfly' Is a Gem, and Advises Everyone to See It," *The Journal*, March 8, 1900.

20. *Illustrated Sporting & Dramatic News* (London), July 7, 1900, New York Public Library for the Performing Arts / Billy Rose Theatre Division, Series X, Scrapbooks, microfilm r.5; "Green-Room Chatter," *Pictorial Life*, June 30, 1900, New York Public Library for the Performing Arts / Billy Rose Theatre Division, Series X, Scrapbooks, microfilm r.5.

21. Mosco Carner, *Puccini: A Critical Biography*, 3rd ed. (New York: Holmes and Meier, 1958), 135–56.

22. John Luther Long, *Madame Butterfly*, in Honey and Cole, *"Madame Butterfly" and "A Japanese Nightingale,"* 31.

23. Ibid.

24. Michio Kitahara, "Commodore Perry and the Japanese: A Study in the Dramaturgy of Power," *Symbolic Interaction* 9, no. 1 (1986): 54.

25. Ruskola Teemu, "Canton Is Not Boston: The Invention of American Imperial Sovereignty," *American Quarterly* 57, no. 3 (2005): 881.

26. Seung Ah Oh offers a compelling reading of Long's novella, shifting attention from the nature of the interracial romance to the construction of national domesticity in *Madame Butterfly*. For Oh, Long's novella follows Cho-Cho-San's transition into a space that is both interior and exterior to national and racial belonging, constructed through tropes of domesticity: Oh, *Recontextualizing Asian American Domesticity*.

27. Aihwa Ong, *Flexible Citizenship: The Cultural Logics of Transnationality* (Durham: Duke University Press, 1999), 5.

28. Ramón H. Rivera-Servera and Harvey Young, "Introduction: Border Moves," in *Performance in the Borderlands*, ed. Ramón H. Rivera-Servera and Harvey Young (New York: Palgrave Macmillan, 2011), 7.

29. Ibid.

30. Long, *Madame Butterfly*, 31.

31. Ibid.

32. See Ngai, *Impossible Subjects*, 37–50; Sucheng Chan, *Asian Americans: An Interpretive History* (New York: Twayne, 1991), 3–23.

33. Shirley Hune, "Politics of Chinese Exclusion: Legislative-Executive Conflict: 1876–1882," *Amerasia Journal* 9, no. 1 (1982): 23.

34. *Chae Chan Ping v. United States*.

35. "Chan Ping Leaves US: He Refuses to Pay His Fare and the Company Takes Him as Guest," *New York Times*, September 2, 1889.

36. Ibid.

37. Ibid.

38. *Chae Chan Ping v. United States*, 130 U.S. at 603.

39. *Nishimura Ekiu v. United States*, 142 U.S. 651 (1892).

40. Ibid., 659.

41. *United States v. Jung Ah Lung*, 124 U.S. 621 (1888).

42. As Justice Harlan noted in his dissent, this loophole allowed Chinese subjects who were expressly barred entry to continue to find ways into the nation's borders: ibid., 635–39, Harlan, J., dissenting.

43. *Ng Fung Ho v. White*, 259 U.S. 276, 281 (1922).

44. Overwhelmingly, US standards of feminine beauty were compared to fantasies of Japanese femininity. One reviewer complained that Bates was "made up like a far more beautiful Japanese girl than any upon whom it has been the privilege of the writer to gaze," as others complained that Bates was "too big and brainy a woman for a Geisha": "'Mme. Butterfly' a Great Success"; "This 'Butterfly' a Winged Jewel." The fiction of Butterfly was enough to overwrite their reservations, and if nearly everyone agreed that Bates was physically too large, they were also in concurrence that "that was a mere detail which was instantly forgotten in the charm of her performance": "David Belasco Scores Another Great Success," *Evening Sun*, March 6, 1900, New York Public Library for the Performing Arts / Billy Rose Theatre Division, Series X, Scrapbooks, microfilm r.5.

45. Edward A. Dithmar, "Various Dramatic Topics," *New York Times*, March 11, 1900.

46. "Her Japanese Masquerade," *New York Times*, May 1, 1904.

47. Ibid.

48. David Belasco, *Madame Butterfly*, in *Six Plays* (Boston: Little, Brown, 1928), 14.

49. Ibid., 13.

50. Ibid., 14.

51. Long, *Madame Butterfly*, 38, 39.

52. Ibid., 39.

53. "Chan Ping Leaves US."

54. Eric Lott, *Love and Theft: Blackface Minstrelsy and the American Working Class* (New York: Oxford University Press, 1993).

55. Ibid., 122.

56. Krystyn R. Moon, *Yellowface: Creating the Chinese in American Popular Music and Performance, 1850s–1920s* (New Brunswick: Rutgers University Press, 2005), 87.

57. Julia H. Lee, *Interracial Encounters: Reciprocal Representations in African American and Asian American Literatures, 1896–1937* (New York: NYU Press, 2011), 25.

58. Dithmar, "At the Play with the Players." If you think this a quaint feature of the turn-of-the-century audience, however, one need only remind the reader that audiences still delight in cultural representations of speaking Asian subjects incapable of mastering the English tongue. We find this in "Mrs. Swan" of *Mad TV*, "Ting Ting Macadengdong" of the popular BBC/HBO comedy series *Little Britain*, or even Margaret Cho's more progressive (but no-less-Orientalizing) hyperbolic embodiments of her Korean immigrant mother. For more on the relationship between Asian American racialization and dialect, see Angela Chia-yi Pao, "False Accents: Embodied Dialects and the Characterization of Ethnicity and Nationality," *Theatre Topics* 14, no. 1 (2004).

59. Belasco, *Madame Butterfly*, 31.

60. Long, *Madame Butterfly*, 31.

61. Belasco, *Madame Butterfly*, 14.

62. Indeed, as Bailey-Harris demonstrates, under the Japanese Civil Code of 1898, the state introduced judicial divorce and allowed nonjudicial divorce *only* if mutually agreed on by both parties: Bailey-Harris, "Madame Butterfly and the Conflict of Laws," 167. Additionally, the *Horei*, governing international law, would not have recognized Pinkerton as having grounds for a judicial divorce: ibid., 168.

63. Belasco, *Madame Butterfly*, 21.

64. Long, *Madame Butterfly*, 33.

65. Giacomo Puccini, Luigi Illica, and Giuseppe Giacosa, *Madam Butterfly: A Japanese Tragedy*, trans. R. H. Elkin (New York: Boosey, 1905), 46.

66. Thanks to Yves Winter for the direct translation of these lyrics. All other translations are drawn from the libretto, cited in note 65.

67. "Chan Ping Leaves US."

68. Ibid. (emphasis added).

69. Ethnomusicologist Ping-hui Liao notes that the structure of the music generally reflects the opera's Orientalist ideology: "This distinction [between the United States and Japan] is also noticeable in Puccini's different composition styles, of *Japonais* versus Western, of pentatonic versus harmonic system": Liao, "Of Writing Words for Music Which Is Already Made," 46.

70. Puccini, Illica, and Giacosa, *Madam Butterfly*, 46.

71. Ibid. The play and the novel have similar scenes. In Belasco's 1900 dramatic adaptation, Butterfly delivers a condensed but otherwise verbatim version of the speech from Long's novella.

72. J. Peter Euben, "Justice and the Oresteia," *American Political Science Review* 76, no. 1 (1982): 23.

73. Schmitt, *Political Theology*, 16–35. Indeed, Schmitt explicitly links, but differentiates, the realm of the juristic and the aesthetic by enigmatically stating that the "form of aesthetic production . . . knows no decision": ibid., 35.

74. Euben, "Justice and the Oresteia," 23.

75. Schmitt, *Political Theology*, 6.

76. California Civil Practice Act (April 29, 1851); California Criminal Act (April 29, 1851).

77. *People of California v. Hall*, 4 Cal. 399, 402 (1854).

78. *State of Oregon v. Mah Jim*, 13 Ore. 235, 236 (1886).

79. *State of Oregon v. Ching Ling*, 16 Ore. 419, 423 (1888).

80. Ibid., 425.

81. Puccini, Illica, and Giacosa, *Madam Butterfly*, 46–47.

82. *State of Oregon v. Ching Ling*, 16 Ore. at 426.

83. *State of Oregon v. Mah Jim*, 13 Ore. at 237.

84. *State of Oregon v. Ching Ling*, 16 Ore. at 426.

85. Long, *Madame Butterfly*, 34.

86. Ibid., 36.

87. Ann Laura Stoler, *Race and the Education of Desire: Foucault's History of Sexuality and the Colonial Order of Things* (Durham: Duke University Press, 1995), 135.

88. See Chan, *Asian Americans*, 45–62; David A. Wolff, *Industrializing the Rockies: Growth, Competition, and Turmoil in the Coalfields of Colorado and Wyoming, 1868–1914* (Boulder: University Press of Colorado, 2003), 101–3.

89. Lee, *Performing Asian America*, 192.

90. Moy, *Marginal Sights*, 84.

91. Long, *Madame Butterfly*, 78 (emphasis added).

92. Ibid.

93. Ibid., 79.

94. Ibid.

95. Belasco, *Madame Butterfly*, 32.

96. "'Mme. Butterfly' Gives Blanche Bates an Opportunity" (emphasis added).

97. Long, *Madame Butterfly*, 36.

98. Nicole Loraux, *The Children of Athena: Athenian Ideas about Citizenship and the Division between the Sexes*, trans. Caroline Levine (Princeton: Princeton University Press, 1993), 26.

99. Hortense J. Spillers, *Black, White, and in Color: Essays on American Literature and Culture* (Chicago: University of Chicago Press, 2003), 214–15.

100. Ibid., 217.

101. Long, *Madame Butterfly*, 75. Likewise, in Puccini's 1907 opera, Kate offers to take possession of the child, encouraging Cio-Cio-San to "take this step for his welfare": Puccini, Illica, and Giacosa, *Madam Butterfly*, 70.

102. Belasco, *Madame Butterfly*, 31.

103. *In re Knight*, 171 F. 299 (1909). See also *In re Camille*, 6 F. 256 (1880).

104. *In re North Pacific Presbyterian Board of Missions v. Ah Won and Ah Tie*, 18 Ore. 339, 349 (1890).

105. Ibid., 348.

106. Ibid., 347–48.

107. Ibid., 349.

108. Belasco, *Madame Butterfly*, 32.

109. Matthew Gurewitsch, "Madama Butterfly Is Ready for Her Close-Up," *New York Times*, September 24, 2006.

110. Ibid.

111. *Miller v. Albright*, 523 U.S. 420, 486 (1998), Breyer, J., dissenting.

112. Ong, *Flexible Citizenship*, 186.

113. Ibid.

## 2 / "Justice for My Son"

1. Kirk Semple, "Sergeant Acquitted of Driving a Suicide," *New York Times*, July 30, 2012.

2. Kirk Semple, "Army Charges 8 in Wake of Death of a Fellow G.I.," *New York Times*, December 21, 2011.

3. Ibid.

4. Kirk Semple, "Most Serious Charge in a Private's Death May Be Dropped," *New York Times*, January 23, 2012.

5. Semple, "Sergeant Acquitted of Driving a Suicide."

6. Marx and Engels best identify this problem when they argue that bourgeois "jurisprudence is but the will of your [the bourgeois] class made into a law for all": Karl Marx and Friedrich Engels, *The Communist Manifesto* (1848; New York: Penguin, 2004), 27.

7. See, for example, Gotanda, "A Critique of 'Our Constitution Is Color-Blind'"; Alan David Freeman, "Legitimizing Racial Discrimination through Antidiscrimination Law: A Critical Review of Supreme Court Doctrine," in Crenshaw et al., *Critical Race Theory*; Mari J. Matsuda, "Looking to the Bottom: Critical Legal Studies and Reparations," in ibid.

8. Lowe, *Immigrant Acts*, 22.

9. In making these observations, I am not trying to do away with the blur between law and performance that I discussed in the introduction. Indeed, much of this chapter continues to explore this blur. I simply mean to point out that there are formal differences between the two phenomena, leading to different possibilities and outcomes for both.

10. Ping Chong, *The East/West Quartet* (New York: TCG, 2004), 64.

11. See Melanie Klein, "Love, Guilt and Reparation," in *Love, Hate and Reparation*, by Melanie Klein and Joan Riviere (New York: Norton, 1937), 123–51; Eve Kosofsky Sedgwick, *Touching Feeling: Affect, Pedagogy, Performativity* (Durham: Duke University Press, 2003). I have explored the concept of reparation in relation to feminism and postcolonial theory elsewhere: Joshua Chambers-Letson, "Introduction: Reparative Feminisms, Repairing Feminism—Reparation, Postcolonial Violence, and Feminism," *Women and Performance* 16, no. 2 (2006).

12. Melanie Klein, "Infantile Anxiety Situations Reflected in a Work of Art and in the Creative Impulse (1929)," in *The Selected Melanie Klein*, ed. Juliet Mitchell (New York: Free Press, 1987), 93.

13. Sedgwick, *Touching Feeling*, 128.

14. Chong, it should be noted, publicly rejects the label "Asian American artist": "I'm not going to allow myself to be ghettoized as an Asian-American artist. I'm an *American* artist": Cathy Madison, "Writing Home: Interviews with Suzan-Lori Parks, Christopher Durang, Eduardo Machado, Ping Chong, and Migdalia Cruz," *American Theatre* 8, no. 7 (1991): 41. I am sympathetic with and even invested in Chong's avowed desire to undo Asian American subjectivity. As such, I turn to *Chinoiserie* as a means of exploring how the play accounts for the historical *making* of Chinese American subjectivity, not in order to describe it as in any way a "celebration" of Asian American identity as such.

15. Sedgwick, *Touching Feeling*, 150–51.

16. Theodore Shank, *Beyond the Boundaries: American Alternative Theatre* (Ann Arbor: University of Michigan Press, 2002), 256.

17. The petitioners in *Brown v. Board of Education* cited the concept in their petitioners brief, and though it is not explicitly cited, its logic is affirmed by Justice Warren's ruling: *Brown v. Board of Education 1*, 347 U.S. 483 (1954). In recent years, it has expanded beyond the realm of racial justice into gay and lesbian jurisprudence. See *Lawrence v. Texas*, 539 U.S. 558, 584 (2003).

18. See, for example, *Parents Involved in Community Schools v. Seattle School District No. 1*, 551 U.S. 701, 731, 782, 788 (2007); *Rice v. Cayetano*, 528 U.S. 495 (2000).

19. Angela C. Pao, "Changing Faces: Recasting National Identity in All-Asian(-) American Dramas," *Theatre Journal* 53, no. 3 (2001): 391; Pao, *No Safe Spaces: Recasting Race, Ethnicity, and Nationality in American Theater* (Ann Arbor: University of Michigan Press, 2010), 3–10.

20. Pao, "Changing Faces," 409.

21. Chong, *The East/West Quartet*, 80.

22. Ibid., 83.

23. Ibid., 73.

24. Ibid.

25. Benjamin, "Theses on the Philosophy of History."

26. Ibid., 257.

27. Ibid., 263.

28. Chong, *The East/West Quartet*, 74.

29. Ibid.

30. Roach, *Cities of the Dead*, 205.

31. Declaration of Independence (1776).

32. Chong, *The East/West Quartet*, 75.

33. Ibid., 86.

34. Henry Grimm, *The Chinese Must Go: A Farce in Four Acts* (San Francisco: A. L. Bancroft, 1879), 3.

35. Sean Metzger, "Charles Parsloe's Chinese Fetish: An Example of Yellowface Performance in Nineteenth-Century American Melodrama," *Theatre Journal* 56, no. 4 (2004): 628.

36. Chong, *The East/West Quartet*, 89.

37. Moon, *Yellowface*, 168.

38. Chong, *The East/West Quartet*, 61.

39. See Kathryn Kish Sklar, *Women's Rights Emerges within the Anti-slavery Movement, 1830–1870: A Brief History with Documents* (Boston: Bedford / St. Martin's, 2000).

40. George Anthony Peffer, "Forbidden Families: Emigration Experiences of Chinese Women under the Page Law, 1875–1882," *Journal of American Ethnic History* 6, no. 1 (1986): 29.

41. Laura Hyun Yi Kang, *Compositional Subjects: Enfiguring Asian/American Women* (Durham: Duke University Press, 2002), 114–15.

42. See Chan, *Asian Americans*, 59–61. For a succinct, general history of marriage and immigration law, see *Miller v. Albright*, 523 U.S. at 463–64, Ginsburg, J., dissenting.

43. Grimm, *The Chinese Must Go*, 20.

44. Ibid., 4.

45. Chong, *The East/West Quartet*, 91–92.

46. Moon-Ho Jung, *Coolies and Cane: Race, Labor, and Sugar in the Age of Emancipation* (Baltimore: Johns Hopkins University Press, 2006), 5.

47. Chong, *The East/West Quartet*, 1–57 (*Deshima: A Poetic Documentary*).

48. Ibid., 118.

49. Ibid., 119.

50. Ibid., 120.

51. Ibid.

52. Ibid., 91.

53. Ibid., 94. I have adjusted the text slightly from the published version, as based on the documentation of the BAM production.

54. *United States v. Ebens*, 800 F.2d 1422, 1427 (1986).

55. Ibid.

56. Ibid., 1430.

57. Ibid., 1434.

58. *State of Oregon v. Ching Ling*, 16 Ore. at 425.

59. Chong, *The East/West Quartet*, 113–14.

60. Fred Moten, *In the Break: The Aesthetics of the Black Radical Tradition* (Minneapolis: University of Minnesota Press, 2003), 4.

61. Ibid., 5.

62. Chong, *The East/West Quartet*, 115–17.

63. Shimakawa, *National Abjection*, 156.

64. Victoria Abrash, "An Interview with Ping Chong," in Chong, *The East/West Quartet*, xxiv.

65. Chong, *The East/West Quartet*, 122.

66. Ibid.

67. José Esteban Muñoz, *Cruising Utopia: The Then and There of Queer Futurity* (New York: NYU Press, 2009), 64.

## 3 / Pledge of Allegiance

1. Denise Uyehara, "Big Head," in *Maps of City and Body: Shedding Light on the Performances of Denise Uyehara* (New York: Kaya, 2003).

2. Omi and Winant, *Racial Formation in the United States*, 201n. 65.

3. See Tetsuden Kashima, *Judgment without Trial: Japanese American Imprisonment during World War II* (Seattle: University of Washington Press, 2003); Shimakawa, *National Abjection*, 10–11, 78–82; Eng, *Racial Castration*, 104–36; Emily Roxworthy, *The Spectacle of Japanese American Trauma: Racial Performativity and World War II* (Honolulu: University of Hawaii Press, 2008); Elena Tajima Creef, *Imaging Japanese*

*America: The Visual Construction of Citizenship, Nation, and the Body* (New York: NYU Press, 2004); Caroline Chung Simpson, *An Absent Presence: Japanese Americans in Postwar American Culture, 1945–1960* (Durham: Duke University Press, 2001); Rea Tajiri, *History and Memory* (Women Make Movies, 1991), DVD; Kandice Chuh, *Imagine Otherwise: On Asian Americanist Critique* (Durham: Duke University Press, 2003), 58–84.

4. Simpson, *An Absent Presence*, 1.

5. Agamben, *Homo Sacer*, 119–88.

6. Giorgio Agamben, *State of Exception*, trans. Kevin Attell (Chicago: University of Chicago Press, 2005), 22.

7. Goffman, *The Presentation of Self in Everyday Life*.

8. Franklin D. Roosevelt, Executive Order 9066 (1952). A reprint of the order, dispensed to residents of the Presidio in San Francisco on April 1, 1942, can be found in Jean Yu-Wen Shen Wu and Min Song, eds., *Asian American Studies: A Reader* (New Brunswick: Rutgers University Press, 2004), 93–94.

9. Some of the more prominent prerequisite cases are *In re Ah Yup*, 1 F. Cas. 223 (1878); *In re Camille*; *In re Kanaka Nian*, 6 Utah 259 (1889); *In re Rodriguez*, 81 F. 337 (1897); *Ozawa v. United States*, 260 U.S. 178 (1922); *United States v. Thind*, 261 U.S. 204 (1923); *United States v. Cartozian*, 6 F.2d 919 (1925); the exclusion case is *Chae Chan Ping v. United States*; and the Alien Land Law cases consist of *Frick v. Webb*, 263 U.S. 326 (1923); *Porterfield v. Webb*, 263 U.S. 225 (1923); *Terrace v. Thompson*, 263 U.S. 197 (1923); *Webb v. O'Brien*, 263 U.S. 313 (1923).

10. Congressional Record—House, vol. 88, part 2 (February 18, 1942; publication date Feburary 24, 1942), 1420.

11. Manzanar Committee, *Reflections in Three Self-Guided Tours of Manzanar* (Los Angeles: Manzanar Committee, 1998), iii–iv.

12. Brian Niiya, ed., *Encyclopedia of Japanese American History: An A-to-Z Reference from 1868 to the Present*, updated ed. (New York: Checkmark Books, 2001), 266, 190.

13. Although the word *internment* is commonly used to describe the camps, this term is somewhat inaccurate—technically and historically. The ten camps administered by the War Relocation Authority were euphemistically called "relocation centers." "Internment camps," on the other hand, were administered by the Justice Department, detaining enemy aliens during World War Two whom the Justice Department considered dangerous. The qualifications for detention were somewhat loose, including many Issei community leaders, church workers, and even artists. "Assembly centers" were temporary detention centers established as interim holding areas while the "relocation centers" were being built. Following the recommendations of historian Tetsuden Kashima, I use *internment* to refer to the Justice Department camps, and I use *imprisonment, incarceration*, and *concentration camps* in reference to the WRA "relocation centers." I describe *assembly centers* as named: Kashima, *Judgment without Trial*, 9. See also Audrie Girdner and Anne Loftis, *The Great Betrayal: The Evacuation of the Japanese-Americans during World War II* (New York: Macmillan, 1969); Commission on Wartime Relocation and Internment of Civilians, *Personal Justice Denied: Report of the Commission on Wartime Relocation and Internment of Civilians* (Washington, DC: Civil Liberties Public Education Fund / University of Washington Press, 1997); Maisie Conrat, Richard Conrat, Dorothea Lange, and

California Historical Society, *Executive Order 9066: The Internment of 110,000 Japanese Americans* (Cambridge: MIT Press for the California Historical Society, 1972); Gary Y. Okihiro, "An American Story," in *Impounded: Dorothea Lange and the Censored Images of Japanese American Internment*, ed. Linda Gordon and Gary Y. Okihiro (New York: Norton, 2006).

14. Austin, *How to Do Things with Words*, 109.

15. Eve Kosofsky Sedgwick, *The Weather in Proust*, ed. Jonathan Goldberg (Durham: Duke University Press, 2012), 15.

16. Bill Hosokawa, *Nisei: The Quiet Americans* (New York: Morrow, 1969).

17. Mike Masaoka and Bill Hosokawa, *They Call Me Moses Masaoka: An American Saga* (New York: Morrow, 1987), 92.

18. Ibid., 122.

19. Ralph P. Merritt, "America in the War and America in the Peace," May 13, 1944, UCLA Charles E. Young Research Library / Ansel Adams Papers, box 2.

20. Michel Foucault, *Discipline and Punish: The Birth of the Prison*, trans. Alan Sheridan (New York: Pantheon Books, 1977).

21. Merritt, "America in the War and America in the Peace," 3.

22. Althusser, "Ideology and Ideological State Apparatuses," 89.

23. Goffman, *The Presentation of Self in Everyday Life*, 35.

24. Eric Owens, dir., *Remembering Manzanar* (US National Parks Service, 2004), DVD.

25. Carl Schmitt, *Constitutional Theory* (1928), trans. Jeffrey Seitzer (Durham: Duke University Press, 2008), 60.

26. Balakrishnan, *The Enemy*, 263.

27. "The Pledge of Allegiance," *Music Educators Journal* 29, no. 2 (1942).

28. Laurie Allen Gallancy, "Teachers and the Pledge of Allegiance," *University of Chicago Law Review* 57, no. 3 (1990).

29. Ngai, *Impossible Subjects*, 21–55.

30. Minxin Pei, "The Paradoxes of American Nationalism," *Foreign Policy* 136 (2003): 33.

31. Derrida, "Declarations of Independence."

32. During the debates of June 4, 1788: Jonathan Elliot, ed., *The Debates in the Several State Conventions on the Adoption of the Federal Constitution*, vol. 3 (Philadelphia: Lippincott, 1876), 22.

33. *Minersville School District v. Gobitis*, 210 U.S. 586 (1940).

34. Ibid. (emphasis added).

35. *West Virginia State Board of Education v. Barnette*, 319 U.S. 624 (1943).

36. André Lepecki, *Exhausting Dance: Performance and the Politics of Movement* (New York: Routledge, 2006), 63.

37. Owens, *Remembering Manzanar*.

38. *Korematsu v. United States*, 323 U.S. 214, 223 (1944).

39. Ibid.

40. Chuh, *Imagine Otherwise*, 59.

41. *Korematsu v. United States*, 323 U.S. at 216.

42. Ibid., 219.

43. Ibid.

44. Ibid.

45. Althusser, "Ideology and Ideological State Apparatuses," 118.

46. "Our World, 1943–1944, Manzanar High Yearbook," 1944, UCLA Charles E. Young Research Library / Special Collections, Manzanar War Relocation Center Records, 1942–1946, box 59, folder 3, 42.

47. Ibid.

48. Ibid.

49. Roxworthy, *The Spectacle of Japanese American Trauma*, 157.

50. Michael Paul Rogin, *Blackface, White Noise: Jewish Immigrants in the Hollywood Melting Pot* (Berkeley: University of California Press, 1996), 5.

51. Gayatri Chakravorty Spivak, *Outside in the Teaching Machine* (New York: Routledge, 1993), 262.

52. Philip Joseph Deloria, *Playing Indian* (New Haven: Yale University Press, 1998), 182.

53. Cedric J. Robinson, *Black Marxism: The Making of the Black Radical Tradition* (1983; reprint, Chapel Hill: University of North Carolina Press, 2000), 186.

54. Ibid., 187.

55. Frank Chin, "Introduction to Frank Emi and James Omura," in *Frontiers of Asian American Studies: Writing, Research, and Commentary*, ed. Gail M. Nomura, Russell Endo, Stephen H. Sumida, and Russell C. Leong (Pullman: Washington State University Press, 1989).

56. Frank Seishi Emi, "Draft Resistance at the Heart Mountain Concentration Camp and the Fair Play Committee," in Nomura et al., *Frontiers of Asian American Studies*, 42.

57. Eric L. Muller, *Free to Die for Their Country: The Story of the Japanese American Draft Resisters in World War II* (Chicago: University of Chicago Press, 2001), 100–124.

58. Emi, "Draft Resistance," 41.

59. Frank Chin, *Born in the U.S.A.: A Story of Japanese America, 1889–1947* (New York: Rowman and Littlefield, 2002), 72–74.

60. Quoted in Kashima, *Judgment without Trial*, 161.

61. See Ngai, *Impossible Subjects*, 199–201.

62. Emi, "Draft Resistance," 42.

63. Stanley Hayami, "Stanley Hayami Diary, 1941–1944" (gift from the Estate of Frank Naoichi and Asano Hayami, parents of Stanley Hayami, Japanese American National Museum, Hirasaki National Resource Center Archives, Los Angeles, 1941–1944).

64. John Okada, *No-No Boy* (Seattle: University of Washington Press, 1981).

65. Dennis Hevesi, "Frank Emi, Defiant World War II Internee, Dies at 94," *New York Times*, December 19, 2010.

66. This is, of course, a reference to the hero of Melville's tragic short story "Bartleby, the Scrivener," in which the title character refuses a definitive answer to nearly all requests, saying instead, "I prefer not to": Herman Melville, "Bartleby, the Scrivener," in *Billy Budd and Other Stories* (New York: Penguin, 1986).

67. Emi, "Draft Resistance," 42.

68. Sedgwick, *Touching Feeling*, 68.

69. Sedgwick, *The Weather in Proust*, 55.

70. Austin, *How to Do Things with Words*, 22.

71. Rebecca Schneider, *The Explicit Body in Performance* (New York: Routledge, 1997), 7.

72. Frank Abe, dir., *Conscience and the Constitution* (Transit Media, 2000), DVD.

73. Muller, *Free to Die for Their Country*, 90.

74. Emi, "Draft Resistance," 62. All quotations from the hearing are drawn from transcripts reprinted in ibid.

75. Ibid.

76. A. Naomi Paik, "Testifying to Rightlessness: Hatian Refugees Speaking from Guantánamo," *Social Text* 28, no. 3 (2010): 41.

77. Emi, "Draft Resistance."

78. Ibid., 64–65.

79. Ibid., 54.

80. Ibid.

81. Ibid., 55.

82. Ibid., 54 (emphasis added).

83. Ibid.

84. Ibid., 62.

85. Ibid., 54.

86. Ibid.

87. Ibid., 62.

88. Ibid., 56 (emphasis added).

89. Chuh, *Imagine Otherwise*, 22.

90. Emi, "Draft Resistance," 58.

91. Ibid. (emphasis added).

92. Ibid.

93. Ibid.

94. Ibid., 64.

95. Michel Foucault, "Two Lectures," in *Power/Knowledge: Selected Interviews and Other Writings, 1972–1977*, ed. Colin Gordon (New York: Pantheon Books, 1980), 98.

96. Austin, *How to Do Things with Words*, 106.

## 4 / The Nail That Stands Out

1. Emily Hanako Momohara, "The Camps (Artist Statement)" (unpublished paper, on file with the author, 2002).

2. D. Soyini Madison, "Dressing Out-of-Place: From Ghana to Obama Commemorative Cloth on the American Red Carpet," in *African Dress: Fashion, Agency, Performance*, ed. Karen Tranberg Hansen and D. Soyini Madison (New York: Bloomsbury, 2013), 218.

3. Roland Barthes, *Camera Lucida: Reflections on Photography*, trans. Richard Howard (New York: Hill and Wang, 1981).

4. For more on the staging of violence during slavery, see Saidiya V. Hartman, *Scenes of Subjection: Terror, Slavery, and Self-Making in Nineteenth-Century America* (New York: Oxford University Press, 1997). On cinema and ethnographic spectacle, see Fatimah Tobing Rony, *The Third Eye: Race, Cinema, and Ethnographic Spectacle* (Durham: Duke University Press, 1996); Coco Fusco, "The Other History of Intercultural Performance," in *English Is Broken Here: Notes on Cultural Fusion in the Americas* (New York: New Press, 1995); Barbara Kirshenblatt-Gimblett, *Destination Culture: Tourism, Museums, and Heritage* (Berkeley: University of California Press, 1998), 17–78. On performing racial stereotype in popular performance, see bell hooks,

*Black Looks: Race and Representation* (Boston: South End, 1992); Lott, *Love and Theft*; Moon, *Yellowface*; Deloria, *Playing Indian*; Tavia Nyong'o, "Racial Kitsch and Black Performance," in *The Spike Lee Reader*, ed. Paula Massood (Philadelphia: Temple University Press, 2008).

5. Creef, *Imaging Japanese America*, 9.

6. Frantz Fanon, *Black Skin, White Masks*, trans. Charles Lam Markmann (New York: Grove, 1967), 112.

7. Ibid., 111–12.

8. Ibid., 110–11.

9. US Congress, "Act of March 26, 1790" (1790).

10. Of twelve cases between 1878 and 1909, nine involved Asian, mixed Asian, or Asian Hawaiian petitioners. Central and South Asian petitioners sought to expand the definition of whiteness by relying on nineteenth-century raciology, asserting that descent from the Aryan races and the Caucasus qualified one as "white." Nearly all such petitions were denied, with the exception of Armenian petitioners in 1925: *United States v. Cartozian*. For more, see Ian F. Haney-López, *White by Law: The Legal Construction of Race* (New York: NYU Press, 1996).

11. *In re Ah Yup*.

12. Ibid., 221.

13. *In re Camille*, 6 F. at 257.

14. *In re Kanaka Nian*, 6 Utah at 263; *In re Camille*, 6 F. at 257.

15. *United States v. Dolla*, 177 F. 101, 102 (1910).

16. *Ozawa v. United States*; *United States v. Thind*.

17. Quoted in Haney-López, *White by Law*, 80.

18. *Ozawa v. United States*, 260 U.S. at 189.

19. Justice Stewart's original phrase was in an obscenity case involving the French film *The Lovers*: "I shall not today attempt further to define the kinds of material I understand to be [pornography]; and perhaps I could never succeed in intelligibly doing so. But I know it when I see it, and the motion picture involved in this case is not that": *Jacobellis v. Ohio*, 378 U.S. 184, 197 (1964).

20. *Ozawa v. United States*, 260 U.S. at 197.

21. See Adrian Piper, "Passing for White, Passing for Black," in *New Feminist Criticism: Art, Identity, Action*, ed. Joanna Frueh, Cassndra L. Langer, and Arlene Raven (New York: IconEditions, 1994); Kip Fulbeck, *Part Asian/100% Hapa* (San Francisco: Chronicle Books, 2006).

22. *Ozawa v. United States*, 260 U.S. at 197.

23. *United States v. Thind*, 261 U.S. at 209.

24. Rony, *The Third Eye*, 9.

25. Eng, *Racial Castration*, 104.

26. "How to Tell Japs from the Chinese," *Life*, December 1941.

27. Ibid.

28. Ibid.

29. Peter Irons, *Justice at War* (New York: Oxford University Press, 1983), 203.

30. Transcript of Arguments on Coram Nobis Petitions, U.S. District Court for the Northern District of California, *Korematsu v. United States* (10 November 1983), reprinted in *Justice Delayed: The Record of the Japanese American Internment Cases*, ed. Peter Irons (Middletown, CT: Wesleyan University Press, 1989), 220–21 (emphasis added).

31. Commission on Wartime Relocation and Internment of Civilians, *Personal Justice Denied*, 390n. 100.

32. Linda Gordon, "Dorothea Lange Photographs the Japanese American Internment," in *Impounded: Dorothea Lange and the Censored Images of Japanese American Internment*, ed. Linda Gordon and Gary Y. Okihiro (New York: Norton, 2006), 21.

33. Gerald H. Robinson, *Elusive Truth: Four Photographers at Manzanar* (Nevada City, CA: Carl Mautz, 2002); Dorothea Lange, *Impounded: Dorothea Lange and the Censored Images of Japanese American Internment*, ed. Linda Gordon and Gary Y. Okihiro (New York: Norton, 2006).

34. Dorothea Lange to Ansel Adams, November 12, 1943, UCLA Charles E. Young Research Library / Ansel Adams Collection, box 2.

35. Ansel Adams, *Born Free and Equal: Photographs of the Loyal Japanese-Americans at Manzanar Relocation Center, Inyo County, California* (New York: US Camera, 1944).

36. US War Relocation Authority, *A Challenge to Democracy* (War Relocation Authority in cooperation with the Office of War Information and the Office of Strategic Services, 1943), film.

37. Archie Miyatake, "Manzanar Remembered," in *Born Free and Equal*, ed. Wynne Benti (Bishop, CA: Spotted Dog, 2001), 17. The elder Miyatake's utilization of Japanese suggests an articulate strategy that was realized in his photographic practice. While Japanese was by no means banned in the camps, it was certainly discouraged. Japanese language and writing instruction was banned in Manzanar, for example, and adult classes were under strict scrutiny of the project director: "Japanese Language Schools Prohibited," *Manzanar Free Press*, August 5, 1944, Archives of the Hirasaki Resource Center / Japanese American National Museum, microfilm, 3.

38. Barthes, *Camera Lucida*, 76.

39. Rancière, *The Emancipated Spectator*, 72.

40. Barthes, *Camera Lucida*, 20.

41. Ibid., 31.

42. Ibid., 32.

43. Ibid., 30.

44. Ibid., 27.

45. Ibid.

46. Ibid., 59.

47. Ibid., 10.

48. Ibid., 44–45.

49. Ibid., 109.

50. Foucault, *Discipline and Punish*, 200.

51. Ibid. For an excellent analysis of this moment in Foucault and, in particular, its relationship to questions posed by the Eurocentric scope of Foucault's analysis, see Rey Chow, *Entanglements, or Transmedial Thinking about Capture* (Durham: Duke University Press, 2012), 151–68.

52. Foucault, *Discipline and Punish*, 201.

53. Brian Niiya, "Gila River," in Niiya, *Encyclopedia of Japanese American History*.

54. Fanon, *Black Skin, White Masks*, 140.

55. Mari J. Matsuda, *Where Is Your Body? And Other Essays on Race, Gender, and the Law* (Boston: Beacon, 1996), 163.

56. Ibid., 164–69.

57. Rey Chow, *Primitive Passions: Visuality, Sexuality, Ethnography, and Contemporary Chinese Cinema* (New York: Columbia University Press, 1995), 9.

58. Chow, *Ethics after Idealism*, 23.

59. Madison, "Dressing Out-of-Place," 217–230.

60. Ibid., 218.

61. Rancière, *The Emancipated Spectator*, 75.

## 5 / Illegal Immigrant Acts

1. Rana, *Terrifying Muslims*, 140.

2. Ngai, *Impossible Subjects*, 8.

3. Notable exceptions include Cathy J. Schlund-Vials's monograph about the relationship between memory and Cambodian American cultural production. I deeply regret that Schlund-Vials's book's publication came too late in this book's revision process to allow more sustained engagement with it: Cathy J. Schlund-Vials, *War, Genocide, and Justice: Cambodian American Memory Work* (Minneapolis: University of Minnesota Press, 2012). See also Aihwa Ong, *Buddha Is Hiding: Refugees, Citizenship, the New America* (Berkeley: University of California Press, 2003).

4. Lowe, *Immigrant Acts*, 17.

5. It would be worth interrogating the name of the band as, indeed, there is a long tradition of discursively constructing the spread of ethnic and minoritarian cultural production as a form of epidemiological contagion, an argument brilliantly argued by Barbara Browning and something that I have discussed elsewhere. See Barbara Browning, *Infectious Rhythm: Metaphors of Contagion and the Spread of African Culture* (New York: Routledge, 1998); Chambers-Letson, "Contracting Justice."

6. Dengue Fever, *Dengue Fever* (Mimicry, 2003), CD; Dengue Fever, *Escape from Dragon House* (BRG, 2005), CD; Dengue Fever, *Venus on Earth* (M80, 2008), CD; Dengue Fever, *Sleepwalking through the Mekong* (M80, 2009), CD; Dengue Fever, *Dengue Fever Presents: Electric Cambodia* (Minsky Records, 2010), mp4; Dengue Fever, *Cannibal Courtship* (Fantasy, 2011), mp4.

7. Gayatri Chakravorty Spivak, *A Critique of Postcolonial Reason: Toward a History of the Vanishing Present* (Cambridge: Harvard University Press, 1999), 6.

8. E. Patrick Johnson, *Appropriating Blackness: Performance and the Politics of Authenticity* (Durham: Duke University Press, 2003), 192.

9. Matt Gross, "All the World, Onstage: A Night Out with Dengue Fever," *New York Times*, October 1, 2006.

10. Johnson, *Appropriating Blackness*, 197.

11. Josh Kun, *Audiotopia: Music, Race, and America* (Berkeley: University of California Press, 2005), 23.

12. Dengue Fever, "Sni Bong," on *Escape from Dragon House*.

13. Gayatri Gopinath, *Impossible Desires: Queer Diasporas and South Asian Public Cultures* (Durham: Duke University Press, 2005), 39.

14. Dengue Fever, "Uku," on *Cannibal Courtship*.

15. Moten, *In the Break*, 210.

16. Ibid., 213. See also Gayatri Chakravorty Spivak, "Can the Subaltern Speak?," in *Marxism and the Interpretation of Culture*, ed. Cary Nelson and Larry Grossberg (Urbana: University of Illinois Press, 1988).

17. Elizabeth Becker, *When the War Was Over: The Voices of Cambodia's Revolution and Its People*, 2nd ed. (New York: Simon and Schuster, 1998), 112.

18. For more on this period, see Michael Vickery, *Cambodia, 1975–1982* (Boston: South End, 1984); David P. Chandler, *Voices from S-21: Terror and History in Pol Pot's Secret Prison* (Berkeley: University of California Press, 1999); Chandler, *Brother Number One: A Political Biography of Pol Pot*, rev. ed. (Boulder, CO: Westview, 1999); Ben Kiernan, *The Pol Pot Regime: Race, Power, and Genocide in Cambodia under the Khmer Rouge, 1975–79*, 2nd ed. (New Haven: Yale University Press, 2002).

19. Kiernan, *The Pol Pot Regime*, 456–60; Patrick Heuveline, "Between One and Three Million: Towards the Demographic Reconstruction of Cambodian History (1970–1979)," *Population Studies* 52, no. 1 (1998); Damien De Walque, "Selective Mortality during the Khmer Rouge Period in Cambodia," *Population and Development Review* 31, no. 2 (2005).

20. In a private meeting in 1975, US Secretary of State Henry Kissinger said to the Thai foreign minister, Chatichai Choonhavan, "You should also tell the Cambodians that we will be friends with them. They are murderous thugs, but we won't let that stand in our way. We are prepared to improve relations with them": US Department of State, "Memorandum of Conversation: Secretary's Meeting with Foreign Minister Chatichai of Thailand" (November 26, 1975; declassified July 27, 2004), 19, available at http://www.gwu.edu/~nsarchiv/NSAEBB/NSAEBB193/HAK-11-26-75.pdf (accessed February 11, 2010).

21. See Vickery, *Cambodia*, 202–318; Becker, *When the War Was Over*, 437–507; Chandler, *Brother Number One*, 157–88; Stephen Heder and Brian D. Tittemore, *Seven Candidates for Prosecution: Accountability for the Crimes of the Khmer Rouge* (Phnom Penh: Documentation Center of Cambodia, 2004); John D. Ciorciari, ed., *The Khmer Rouge Tribunal* (Phnom Penh: Documentation Center of Cambodia, 2006); Ben Kiernan, *Genocide and Resistance in Southeast Asia: Documentation, Denial and Justice in Cambodia and East Timor* (New Brunswick, NJ: Transaction, 2008).

22. Kiernan, *Genocide and Resistance in Southeast Asia*, 237.

23. See, for example, Lowe, *Immigrant Acts*; Grace M. Cho, *Haunting the Korean Diaspora: Shame, Secrecy, and the Forgotten War* (Minneapolis: University of Minnesota Press, 2008); Vincent K. Her and Mary Louise Buley-Meissner, "Hmong Voices and Memories: An Exploration of Identity, Culture, and History through *Bamboo among the Oaks*: Contemporary Writing by Hmong Americans," *Journal of Asian American Studies* 13, no. 1 (2010).

24. Sophiline Cheam Shapiro, "Songs My Enemies Taught Me," in *Children of Cambodia's Killing Fields: Memoirs by Survivors*, ed. Pran Dith and Kim DePaul (New Haven: Yale University Press, 1997); Boreth Ly, "Devastated Vision(s): The Khmer Rouge Scopic Regime in Cambodia," *Art Journal* 61, no. 1 (2003); Judith Hamera, "An Answerability of Memory: 'Saving' Khmer Classical Dance," *TDR: The Drama Review* 46, no. 4 (2002); Schlund-Vials, *War, Genocide, and Justice*; Catherine Filloux, "Ten Gems on a Thread," *Manoa* 16, no. 1 (2004); Filloux, "Ten Gems on a Thread 2," *TDR: The Drama Review* 48, no. 4 (2004).

25. Stephen Mamula, "Starting from Nowhere? Popular Music in Cambodia after the Khmer Rouge," *Asian Music*, Winter–Spring 2008, 29–31.

26. Ly Daravuth and Ingrid Muan, *Cultures of Independence: An Introduction to Cambodian Arts and Culture in the 1950's and 1960's* (Phnom Penh, Cambodia: Reyum, 2001), 190–237.

27. CPK, Party Center, "The Party's Four-Year Plan to Build Socialism in All Fields, 1977–1980," trans. Cahanthou Boua, in *Pol Pot Plans the Future: Confidential Leadership Documents from Democratic Kampuchea, 1976–1977*, ed. David P. Chandler, Ben Kiernan, and Chanthou Boua (New Haven: Yale Center for International and Area Studies, 1988), 113.

28. Roach, *Cities of the Dead*; Diana Taylor, *The Archive and the Repertoire: Performing Cultural Memory in the Americas* (Durham: Duke University Press, 2003); Nyong'o, *The Amalgamation Waltz*; Rebecca Schneider, *Performing Remains: Art and War in Times of Theatrical Reenactment* (New York: Routledge, 2011).

29. Teeda Butt Mam, "Worms from Our Skin," in *Children of Cambodia's Killing Fields: Memoirs by Survivors*, ed. Pran Dith and Kim DePaul (New Haven: Yale University Press, 1997), 13.

30. Kiernan, *The Pol Pot Regime*, 246–50.

31. CPK, "The Party's Four-Year Plan," 113.

32. Shapiro, "Songs My Enemies Taught Me," 5.

33. It is generally assumed that Sinn, Ros, Pan, and Lieu perished at the hands of the Khmer Rouge, or at least as a direct result of its policies: Kiernan, *The Pol Pot Regime*, 198.

34. John Pirozzi, dir., *Sleepwalking through the Mekong* (M80/Film 101 Productions, 2009), DVD.

35. See, *The Decolonized Eye*, 45.

36. Ibid., xviii.

37. Dengue Fever, "Have You Seen My Love? / Pow Pow," on *Dengue Fever*. Translations, though slightly amended for clarity, are drawn from the liner notes to the compilation album *Cambodian Rocks*, vol. 4 (Khmer Rocks, 2005), CD. The liner notes credit translations collectively to Sar K., Tony C., Srey Da, Sopheak Chhouy, and Vatthana Lim.

38. Pirozzi, *Sleepwalking through the Mekong*.

39. Ibid.

40. Ong, *Buddha Is Hiding*, 118–19.

41. Pirozzi, *Sleepwalking through the Mekong*.

42. Personal Responsibility and Work Opportunity Reconciliation Act, Pub. L. 104-193, 104th Congress.

43. Such laws are significant of neoliberalism as "a broader cultural project of legitimating the redistribution of resources upward . . . [that] depended, for its cultural effectiveness, on coded hierarchies of race, gender, and sexuality—especially as they affect women and children": Lisa Duggan, *The Twilight of Equality? Neoliberalism, Cultural Politics, and the Attack on Democracy* (Boston: Beacon, 2003), 15.

44. See Ancheta, *Race, Rights, and the Asian American Experience*, 38–39.

45. Dengue Fever, "Have You Seen My Love? / Pow Pow."

46. R. J. Smith, "They've Got Those Mekong Blues Again," *New York Times*, January 20, 2008.

47. Brian Massumi, "Fear (the Spectrum Said)," *Positions: East Asia Cultures Critique* 13, no. 1 (2005): 33.

48. US Department of Homeland Security, Office of the Press Secretary, "Secretary Napolitano Announces Implementation of National Terrorism Advisory System" (April 20, 2011), http://www.dhs.gov/news/2011/04/20/

secretary-napolitano-announces-implementation-national-terrorism-advisory-system (accessed October 15, 2012).

49. See Puar, *Terrorist Assemblages*, 166–202; Rana, *Terrifying Muslims*.

50. IIRAIRA was passed only a few months before House Speaker Newt Gingrich (R-GA) introduced the Anti-Terrorism and Effective Death Penalty Act (AEDP), responding to the terrorist bombing on a federal building in Oklahoma City. The coterminous passage of both bills at the same time suggests a link between the figure of the "illegal immigrant" and the "terrorist" in the legislative unconscious of Congress.

51. See Linda K. Kerber, "Toward a History of Statelessness in America," *American Quarterly* 57, no. 3 (2005): 741.

52. *Zadvydas v. INS, Ashcroft v. Kim Ho Ma*, 533 U.S. 678 (2001).

53. *Kaplan v. Tod*, 267 U.S. 228, 230 (1925).

54. This argument surfaced in Justice Antonin Scalia's dissenting opinion in the case, in which he cited both *Nishimura Ekiu v. United States* and *Chae Chang Ping*. See *Zadvydas v. INS, Ashcroft v. Kim Ho Ma*, 533 U.S. at 703, Scalia, J., dissenting.

55. *Zadvydas v. Davi, Ashcroft v. Kim Ho Ma*, No. 99-7791, Supreme Court of the United States, oral arguments, June 28, 2001.

56. Ibid.

57. See Justinian, *The Digest of Justinian*, trans. Alan Watson, ed. Theodor Mommsen and Paul Krueger, 4 vols. (Philadelphia: University of Pennsylvania Press, 1985), 1:24; Hugo Grotius, *The Free Sea* (1609), trans. Richard Hakluyt, ed. David Armitage (Indianapolis: Liberty Fund, 2004); Carl Schmitt, *The Nomos of the Earth in the International Law of the Jus Publicum Europaeum*, trans. G. L. Ulmen (New York: Telos, 2003), 172.

58. *Zadvydas v. INS, Ashcroft v. Kim Ho Ma*, 533 U.S. at 691 (internal quotations removed).

59. Wendy Brown, *Walled States, Waning Sovereignty* (New York: Zone Books, 2010), 68–69.

60. See David Grabias and Nicole Newnham, *Sentenced Home* (Indiepix, 2008), film.

61. Danielle Goldman, "Sound Gestures: Posing Questions for Music and Dance," *Women and Performance: A Journal of Feminist Theory* 17, no. 2 (2007): 131.

## Conclusion

1. Joseph Keehn II, "Hasan Elahi," in *Rethinking Contemporary Art and Multicultural Education*, ed. Eungie Joo and Joseph Keehn II, with Jenny Ham-Roberts (New York: Routledge, 2011), 91.

2. Brooke Gladstone, "The Art of Self-Surveillance," *On the Media* (WNYC Radio and NPR, November 11, 2011).

3. Ibid.

4. Ibid.

5. Rana, *Terrifying Muslims*, 9.

6. Gladstone, "The Art of Self-Surveillance."

7. Marcela A. Fuentes, "Zooming In and Out: Tactical Media Performance in Transnational Contexts," in *Performance, Politics, and Activism*, ed. John Rouse and Peter Lichtenfels (London: Palgrave Macmillan, 2013), 38.

8. See Adrian Heathfield, *Out of Now: The Lifeworks of Tehching Hsieh* (Cambridge: MIT Press, 2008); Marina Abramovic, *The Artist Is Present*, ed. Klaus Biesenbach (New York: Museum of Modern Art, 2010).

9. Wafaa Bilal and Kari Lydersen, *Shoot an Iraqi: Art, Life and Resistance under the Gun* (San Francisco: City Lights, 2008).

10. Amelia Jones, *Body Art / Performing the Subject* (Minneapolis: University of Minnesota Press, 1998). See also Schneider, *The Explicit Body in Performance*; Yoko Ono, Alexandra Munroe, and Jon Hendricks, *Yes: Yoko Ono* (New York: Japan Society / H. N. Abrams, 2000); Midori Yoshimoto, *Into Performance: Japanese Women Artists in New York* (New Brunswick: Rutgers University Press, 2005).

11. José Esteban Muñoz, *Disidentifications: Queers of Color and the Performance of Politics* (Minneapolis: University of Minnesota Press, 1999), 176.

12. Joan Kee, "Visual Reconnaissance," in *Alien Encounters: Popular Culture in Asian America*, ed. Mimi Thi Nguyen and Thuy Linh N. Tu (Durham: Duke University Press, 2007), 136.

13. Ibid.

14. *Parhat v. Gates*, 532 F.3d 834 (2008); *Kiyemba v. Obama*, 555 F.3d 1022 (2009).

15. Associated Press, "Cheney: Gitmo Holds 'Worst of the Worst': Former Vice President Says Killing Suspects Was Only Other Option," *NBCNews.com* (June 1, 2009), http://www.nbcnews.com/id/31052241/ns/world_news-terrorism/t/cheney-gitmo-holds-worst-worst/#.UQ_oHo66esg (accessed October 31, 2012).

16. The court cited *Chae Chan Ping v. United States*; *Nishimura Ekiu v. United States*; *Fong Yue Ting v. United States*, 149 U.S. 698 (1893); *Lem Moon Sing v. United States*, 158 U.S. 538 (1895); *Wong Wing v. United States*, 163 U.S. 237 (1896); and *Fok Yung Yo v. United States*, 185 U.S. 296 (1902).

17. *Kiyemba v. Obama*, 555 F.3d at 1025.

18. Ibid., 1029.

19. The Supreme Court agreed to hear the Uighurs' appeal during the 2009–2010 term. Days before the oral arguments, the Obama administration secured a deal with Switzerland to take the remaining detainees, and the High Court dropped the case. Three years later, at the time of writing, at least two of the men remain at Guantánamo.

20. Clive Thompson, "The Visible Man: An FBI Target Puts His Whole Life Online," *Wired* 15.06 (May 22, 2007), http://www.wired.com/techbiz/people/magazine/15-06/ps_transparency (accessed May 14, 2012); Gladstone, "The Art of Self-Surveillance."

# Bibliography

Abe, Frank, dir. *Conscience and the Constitution.* 56 mins. Transit Media, 2000. DVD.

Abramovic, Marina. *The Artist Is Present.* Edited by Klaus Biesenbach. New York: Museum of Modern Art, 2010.

Abrash, Victoria. "An Interview with Ping Chong." In *The East/West Quartet*, by Ping Chong, xv–xxxv. New York: TCG, 2004.

Adams, Ansel. *Born Free and Equal: Photographs of the Loyal Japanese-Americans at Manzanar Relocation Center, Inyo County, California.* New York: US Camera, 1944.

Adams, John. "Letter to Abigail Adams: April 14, 1776." In *Founding America: Documents from the Revolution to the Bill of Rights*, edited by Jack N. Rakove, 70–72. New York: Barnes and Nobles Classics, 2006.

Agamben, Giorgio. *Homo Sacer: Sovereign Power and Bare Life.* Translated by Daniel Heller-Roazen. Stanford: Stanford University Press, 1998.

———. *State of Exception.* Translated by Kevin Attell. Chicago: University of Chicago Press, 2005.

Althusser, Louis. "Idéologie et appareils idéologiques d'état (Notes pour une recherche)." In *Sur la reproduction*, 269–314. Paris: Presses Universitaires de France, 1995.

———. "Ideology and Ideological State Apparatuses." In *Lenin and Philosophy, and Other Essays*, 85–126. 1971. Reprint, New York: Monthly Review Press, 2001.

———. "The 'Piccolo Teatro': Bertolazzi and Brecht." Translated by Ben Brewster. In *For Marx*, 129–52. 1965. Reprint, New York: Verso, 1999.

Ancheta, Angelo N. *Race, Rights, and the Asian American Experience*. 2nd ed. New Brunswick: Rutgers University Press, 2008.

Associated Press. "Cheney: Gitmo Holds 'Worst of the Worst': Former Vice President Says Killing Suspects Was Only Other Option." *NBCNews. com* (June 1, 2009). http://www.nbcnews.com/id/31052241/ns/world_news-terrorism/t/cheney-gitmo-holds-worst-worst/#.UQ_oHo66esg (accessed October 31, 2012).

———. "More Rights for Gitmo's Lizards than Detainees? Supreme Court Mulls What Protections Apply to Prisoners in 'Law-Free Zone.'" *NBCNews. com* (December 8, 2007). http://www.nbcnews.com/id/22161810/ns/world_news-terrorism/t/more-rights-gitmos-lizards-detainees/#.UQqwRkrDSKM.

Austin, J. L. *How to Do Things with Words*. Cambridge: Harvard University Press, 1962.

Bailey-Harris, Rebecca. "Madame Butterfly and the Conflict of Laws." *American Journal of Comparative Law* 39, no. 1 (1991): 157–77.

Balakrishnan, Gopal. *The Enemy: An Intellectual Portrait of Carl Schmitt*. New York: Verso, 2000.

Balance, Christine Bacareza. "Notorious Kin: Filipino America Re-imagines Andrew Cunanan." *Journal of Asian American Studies* 11, no. 1 (2008): 87–106.

Barthes, Roland. *Camera Lucida: Reflections on Photography*. Translated by Richard Howard. New York: Hill and Wang, 1981.

Bazelon, Emily. "The Place of Women on the Court." *New York Times*, July 7, 2009, 23–25, 46–47.

Becker, Elizabeth. *When the War Was Over: The Voices of Cambodia's Revolution and Its People*. 2nd ed. New York: Simon and Schuster, 1998.

Belasco, David. *Madame Butterfly*. In *Six Plays*, 12–32. Boston: Little, Brown, 1928.

Benjamin, Walter. "Theses on the Philosophy of History." Translated by Harry Zohn. In *Illuminations: Essays and Reflections*, edited by Hannah Arendt, 253–64. New York: Harcourt, 1988.

Bhabha, Homi. "Of Mimicry and Man: The Ambivalence of Colonial Discourse." In *The Location of Culture*, 85–92. New York: Routledge, 1994.

Bilal, Wafaa, and Kari Lydersen. *Shoot an Iraqi: Art, Life and Resistance under the Gun*. San Francisco: City Lights, 2008.

Bloch, Ernst. "The Stage Regarded as a Paradigmatic Institution and the Decision within It." In *The Utopian Function of Art and Literature: Selected Essays*, translated by Jack Zipes and Frank Mecklenburg, 224–44. Cambridge: MIT Press, 1988.

Brandeis, Louis D. "The Living Law." *Illinois Law Review* 10 (1916): 461.

Breyer, Stephen G. *Active Liberty: Interpreting Our Democratic Constitution*. New York: Knopf, 2005.

———. *Making Our Democracy Work: A Judge's View*. New York: Knopf, 2010.

Brown, Wendy. *Walled States, Waning Sovereignty.* New York: Zone Books, 2010.

Browning, Barbara. *Infectious Rhythm: Metaphors of Contagion and the Spread of African Culture.* New York: Routledge, 1998.

Burns, Lucy Mae San Pablo. *Puro Arte: Filipinos on the Stages of Empire.* New York: NYU Press, 2012.

———. "'Splendid Dancing': Filipino 'Exceptionalism' in Taxi Dancehalls." *Dance Research Journal* 40, no. 2 (2008): 23–40.

Butler, Judith. *The Psychic Life of Power: Theories in Subjection.* Stanford: Stanford University Press, 1997.

*Cambodian Rocks,* vol. 4. Khmer Rocks, 2005. CD.

Carner, Mosco. *Puccini: A Critical Biography.* 3rd ed. New York: Holmes and Meier, 1958.

Chambers-Letson, Joshua Takano. "Contracting Justice: The Viral Strategy of Felix González-Torres." *Criticism: A Quarterly for Literature and the Arts* 51, no. 4 (2009–2010): 559–87.

———. "Embodying Justice: The Making of Justice Sonia Sotomayor." *Women and Performance: A Journal of Feminist Theory* 20, no. 2 (2010): 149–73.

———. "Introduction: Reparative Feminisms, Repairing Feminism—Reparation, Postcolonial Violence, and Feminism." *Women and Performance* 16, no. 2 (2006): 169–91.

Chan, Sucheng. *Asian Americans: An Interpretive History.* New York: Twayne, 1991.

Chandler, David P. *Brother Number One: A Political Biography of Pol Pot.* Rev. ed. Boulder, CO: Westview, 1999.

———. *Voices from S-21: Terror and History in Pol Pot's Secret Prison.* Berkeley: University of California Press, 1999.

Chang, Robert S. *Disoriented: Asian Americans, Law, and the Nation-State.* New York: NYU Press, 1999.

"Chan Ping Leaves US: He Refuses to Pay His Fare and the Company Takes Him as Guest." *New York Times,* September 2, 1889, 3.

Chin, Frank. *Born in the U.S.A.: A Story of Japanese America. 1889–1947.* New York: Rowman and Littlefield, 2002.

———. "Introduction to Frank Emi and James Omura." In *Frontiers of Asian American Studies: Writing, Research, and Commentary,* edited by Gail M. Nomura, Russell Endo, Stephen H. Sumida, and Russell C. Leong, 39–40. Pullman: Washington State University Press, 1989.

Cho, Grace M. *Haunting the Korean Diaspora: Shame, Secrecy, and the Forgotten War.* Minneapolis: University of Minnesota Press, 2008.

Chong, Ping. *The East/West Quartet.* New York: TCG, 2004.

Chow, Rey. *Entanglements, or Transmedial Thinking about Capture.* Durham: Duke University Press, 2012.

———. *Ethics after Idealism: Theory, Culture, Ethnicity, Reading.* Bloomington: Indiana University Press, 1998.

———. *Primitive Passions: Visuality, Sexuality, Ethnography, and Contemporary Chinese Cinema*. New York: Columbia University Press, 1995.

———. *The Protestant Ethnic and the Spirit of Capitalism*. New York: Columbia University Press, 2002.

Chuh, Kandice. *Imagine Otherwise: On Asian Americanist Critique*. Durham: Duke University Press, 2003.

Ciorciari, John D., ed. *The Khmer Rouge Tribunal*. Phnom Penh: Documentation Center of Cambodia, 2006.

Cole, Catherine. "Performance, Transitional Justice, and the Law: South Africa's Truth and Reconciliation Commission." *Theatre Journal* 59, no. 2 (2007): 167–87.

———. *Performing South Africa's Truth Commission: Stages of Transition*. Bloomington: Indiana University Press, 2009.

Commission on Wartime Relocation and Internment of Civilians. *Personal Justice Denied: Report of the Commission on Wartime Relocation and Internment of Civilians*. Washington, DC: Civil Liberties Public Education Fund / University of Washington Press, 1997.

Conrat, Maisie, Richard Conrat, Dorothea Lange, and California Historical Society. *Executive Order 9066: The Internment of 110,000 Japanese Americans*. Cambridge: MIT Press for the California Historical Society, 1972.

Cowhig, Frances Ya-Chu. *Lidless*. London: Metheun, 2011.

CPK, Party Center. "The Party's Four-Year Plan to Build Socialism in All Fields, 1977–1980." Translated by Cahanthou Boua. In *Pol Pot Plans the Future: Confidential Leadership Documents from Democratic Kampuchea, 1976–1977*, edited by David P. Chandler, Ben Kiernan, and Chanthou Boua, 36–119. New Haven: Yale Center for International and Area Studies, 1988.

Creef, Elena Tajima. *Imaging Japanese America: The Visual Construction of Citizenship, Nation, and the Body*. New York: NYU Press, 2004.

Crenshaw, Kimberlé. "Mapping the Margins: Intersectionality, Identity Politics, and Violence against Women of Color." In *Critical Race Theory: The Key Writings That Formed the Movement*, edited by Kimberlé Crenshaw, Neil Gotanda, Gary Peller, and Kendall Thomas, 357–83. New York: New Press, 1995.

Dale, Alan. "Alan Dale Says: 'Mme. Butterfly' Is a Gem, and Advises Everyone to See It." *The Journal*, March 8, 1900.

Daravuth, Ly, and Ingrid Muan. *Cultures of Independence: An Introduction to Cambodian Arts and Culture in the 1950's and 1960's*. Phnom Penh, Cambodia: Reyum, 2001.

"David Belasco Scores Another Great Success." *Evening Sun*, March 6, 1900. New York Public Library for the Performing Arts / Billy Rose Theatre Division, Series X, Scrapbooks, microfilm r.5.

Deloria, Philip Joseph. *Playing Indian*. New Haven: Yale University Press, 1998.

Denbeaux, Mark P., and Jonathan Hafetz. Introduction to *The Guantánamo*

*Lawyers: Inside a Prison Outside the Law*, edited by Mark P. Denbeaux and Jonathan Hafetz. New York: NYU Press, 2009.

Dengue Fever. *Cannibal Courtship*. Fantasy, 2011. mp4.

———. *Dengue Fever*. Mimicry, 2003. CD.

———. *Dengue Fever Presents: Electric Cambodia*. Minsky Records, 2010. mp4.

———. *Escape from Dragon House*. BRG, 2005. CD.

———. *Sleepwalking through the Mekong*. M80, 2009. CD.

———. *Venus on Earth*. M80, 2008. CD.

Derrida, Jacques. "Declarations of Independence." *New Political Science* 15 (Summer 1986): 7–15.

De Walque, Damien. "Selective Mortality during the Khmer Rouge Period in Cambodia." *Population and Development Review* 31, no. 2 (2005): 351–68.

Dithmar, Edward A. "At the Play with the Players." *New York Times*, March 11, 1900, 16.

———. "Various Dramatic Topics." *New York Times*, March 11, 1900, 16.

Duggan, Lisa. *The Twilight of Equality? Neoliberalism, Cultural Politics, and the Attack on Democracy*. Boston: Beacon, 2003.

Elliot, Jonathan, ed. *The Debates in the Several State Conventions on the Adoption of the Federal Constitution*. Vol. 3. Philadelphia: Lippincott, 1876.

Emi, Frank Seishi. "Draft Resistance at the Heart Mountain Concentration Camp and the Fair Play Committee." In *Frontiers of Asian American Studies: Writing, Research, and Commentary*, edited by Gail M. Nomura, Russell Endo, Stephen H. Sumida, and Russell C. Leong, 41–69. Pullman: Washington State University Press, 1989.

Eng, David L. *The Feeling of Kinship: Queer Liberalism and the Racialization of Intimacy*. Durham: Duke University Press, 2010.

———. *Racial Castration: Managing Masculinity in Asian America*. Durham: Duke University Press, 2001.

Euben, J. Peter. "Justice and the Oresteia." *American Political Science Review* 76, no. 1 (1982): 22–33.

Fanon, Frantz. *Black Skin, White Masks*. Translated by Charles Lam Markmann. New York: Grove, 1967.

Fassin, Didier, and Mariella Pandolfi. "Introduction: Military and Humanitarian Government in the Age of Intervention." In *Contemporary States of Emergency: The Politics of Military and Humanitarian Interventions*, edited by Didier Fassin and Mariella Pandolfi. New York: Zone Books, 2010.

Felman, Shoshana. *The Juridical Unconscious: Trials and Traumas in the Twentieth Century*. Cambridge: Harvard University Press, 2002.

Filloux, Catherine. "Ten Gems on a Thread." *Manoa* 16, no. 1 (2004): 177–87.

———. "Ten Gems on a Thread 2." *TDR: The Drama Review* 48, no. 4 (2004): 58–71.

Foucault, Michel. *Discipline and Punish: The Birth of the Prison*. Translated by Alan Sheridan. New York: Pantheon Books, 1977.

———. "Two Lectures." In *Power/Knowledge: Selected Interviews and Other Writings, 1972–1977*, ed. Colin Gordon, 78–108. New York: Pantheon Books, 1980.

Freeman, Alan David. "Legitimizing Racial Discrimination through Antidiscrimination Law: A Critical Review of Supreme Court Doctrine." In *Critical Race Theory: The Key Writings That Formed the Movement*, edited by Kimberlé Crenshaw, Neil Gotanda, Gary Peller, and Kendall Thomas, 29–46. New York: New Press, 1995.

Fuentes, Marcela A. "Zooming In and Out: Tactical Media Performance in Transnational Contexts." In *Performance, Politics, and Activism*, edited by John Rouse and Peter Lichtenfels, 32–55. London: Palgrave Macmillan, 2013.

Fulbeck, Kip. *Part Asian/100% Hapa*. San Francisco: Chronicle Books, 2006.

Fusco, Coco. "The Other History of Intercultural Performance." In *English Is Broken Here: Notes on Cultural Fusion in the Americas*, 37–63. New York: New Press, 1995.

Gallancy, Laurie Allen. "Teachers and the Pledge of Allegiance." *University of Chicago Law Review* 57, no. 3 (1990): 929–54.

Girdner, Audrie, and Anne Loftis. *The Great Betrayal: The Evacuation of the Japanese-Americans during World War II*. New York: Macmillan, 1969.

Gladstone, Brooke. "The Art of Self-Surveillance." *On the Media*, November 11, 2011. WNYC Radio and NPR.

Goffman, Erving. *The Presentation of Self in Everyday Life*. New York: Anchor Books, 1959.

Goldman, Danielle. "Sound Gestures: Posing Questions for Music and Dance." *Women and Performance: A Journal of Feminist Theory* 17, no. 2 (2007): 123–38.

Gopinath, Gayatri. *Impossible Desires: Queer Diasporas and South Asian Public Cultures*. Durham: Duke University Press, 2005.

Gordon, Linda. "Dorothea Lange Photographs the Japanese American Internment." In *Impounded: Dorothea Lange and the Censored Images of Japanese American Internment*, edited by Linda Gordon and Gary Y. Okihiro, 5–39. New York: Norton, 2006.

Gotanda, Neil. "A Critique of 'Our Constitution Is Color-Blind.'" In *Critical Race Theory: The Key Writings That Formed the Movement*, edited by Kimberlé Crenshaw, Neil Gotanda, Gary Peller, and Kendall Thomas, 257–75. New York: New Press, 1995.

Grabias, David, and Nicole Newnham. *Sentenced Home*. 76 mins. Indiepix, 2008. Film.

"Green-Room Chatter." *Pictorial Life*, June 30, 1900. New York Public Library for the Performing Arts / Billy Rose Theatre Division, Series X, Scrapbooks, microfilm r.5.

Grimm, Henry. *The Chinese Must Go: A Farce in Four Acts*. San Francisco: A. L. Bancroft, 1879.

Groos, Arthur. "Madame Butterfly: The Story." *Cambridge Opera Journal* 3, no. 2 (1991): 125–58.

Gross, Matt. "All the World, Onstage: A Night Out with Dengue Fever." *New York Times*, October 1, 2006, 4.

Grotius, Hugo. *The Free Sea* (1609). Translated by Richard Hakluyt. Edited by David Armitage Indianapolis: Liberty Fund, 2004.

Gurewitsch, Matthew. "Madama Butterfly Is Ready for Her Close-Up." *New York Times*, September 24, 2006, 1.

Hamera, Judith. "An Answerability of Memory: 'Saving' Khmer Classical Dance." *TDR: The Drama Review* 46, no. 4 (2002): 65–85.

Hamilton, Alexander, John Jay, and James Madison. *The Federalist: A Commentary on the Constitution of the United States*. 1788. Edited by Robert Scigliano. New York: Modern Library, 2000.

Haney-López, Ian F. *White by Law: The Legal Construction of Race*. New York: NYU Press, 1996.

Harry Ransom Humanities Research Center. "Biographical Sketch of John Luther Long." In *John Luther Long: An Inventory of His Papers at the Harry Ransom Humanities Research Center*. http://research.hrc.utexas.edu:8080/hrcxtf/view?docId=ead/00080.xml (accessed September 15, 2012).

Hartman, Saidiya V. *Scenes of Subjection: Terror, Slavery, and Self-Making in Nineteenth-Century America*. New York: Oxford University Press, 1997.

Hayami, Stanley. "Stanley Hayami Diary, 1941–1944." Gift from the Estate of Frank Naoichi and Asano Hayami, parents of Stanley Hayami. Japanese American National Museum, Hirasaki National Resource Center Archives, 1941–1944, Los Angeles.

Heathfield, Adrian. *Out of Now: The Lifeworks of Tehching Hsieh* Cambridge: MIT Press, 2008.

Heder, Stephen, and Brian D. Tittemore. *Seven Candidates for Prosecution: Accountability for the Crimes of the Khmer Rouge*. Phnom Penh: Documentation Center of Cambodia, 2004.

Her, Vincent K., and Mary Louise Buley-Meissner. "Hmong Voices and Memories: An Exploration of Identity, Culture, and History through *Bamboo among the Oaks*: Contemporary Writing by Hmong Americans." *Journal of Asian American Studies* 13, no. 1 (2010): 35–58.

"Her Japanese Masquerade." *New York Times*, May 1, 1904, SM2.

Heuveline, Patrick. "Between One and Three Million: Towards the Demographic Reconstruction of Cambodian History (1970–1979)." *Population Studies* 52, no. 1 (1998): 49–65.

Hevesi, Dennis. "Frank Emi, Defiant World War II Internee, Dies at 94." *New York Times*, December 19, 2010.

Hobbes, Thomas. *Leviathan*. 1651. Edited by J. C. A. Gaskin. New York: Oxford University Press, 1998.

Honey, Maureen, and Jean Lee Cole. Introduction to *"Madame Butterfly" and "A Japanese Nightingale": Two Orientalist Texts*, edited by Maureen Honey and Jean Lee Cole, 1–22. New Brunswick: Rutgers University Press, 2002.

hooks, bell. *Black Looks: Race and Representation*. Boston: South End Press, 1992.

Horkheimer, Max, and Theodor W. Adorno. *Dialectic of Enlightenment*. Translated by John Cumming. New York: Continuum, 1972.

Hosokawa, Bill. *Nisei: The Quiet Americans*. New York: Morrow, 1969.

Houston, Velina Hasu. "Kokoro (True Heart)." In *But Still, Like Air, I'll Rise: New Asian American Plays*, edited by Velina Hasu Houston, 89–129. Philadelphia: Temple University Press, 1997.

"How to Tell Japs from the Chinese." *Life*, December 1941, 81–82.

Hune, Shirley. "Politics of Chinese Exclusion: Legislative-Executive Conflict: 1876–1882." *Amerasia Journal* 9, no. 1 (1982): 5–27.

Hwang, David Henry. *M. Butterfly*. New York: New American Library, 1989.

*Illustrated Sporting & Dramatic News* (London). July 7, 1900. New York Public Library for the Performing Arts / Billy Rose Theatre Division, Series X, Scrapbooks, microfilm r.5.

Irons, Peter. *Justice at War*. New York: Oxford University Press, 1983.

———, ed. *Justice Delayed: The Record of the Japanese American Internment Cases*. Middletown, CT: Wesleyan University Press, 1989.

James, Joy. "Madame Butterfly: Behind Every Great Woman . . ." In *A Vision of the Orient: Texts, Intertexts, and Contexts of Madame Butterfly*, edited by Jonathan Wisenthal, Sherrill Grace, Melinda Boyd, Brian McIlroy, and Vera Micznik, 196–226. Toronto: University of Toronto Press, 2006.

Jameson, Fredric. *The Political Unconscious: Narrative as a Socially Symbolic Act*. Ithaca: Cornell University Press, 1981.

"Japanese Language Schools Prohibited." *Manzanar Free Press*, August 5, 1944. Archives of the Hirasaki Resource Center / Japanese American National Museum, microfilm.

Jarvis, Robert M., Steven E. Chaikelson, Christine A. Corcos, et al. *Theater Law: Cases and Materials*. Durham: Carolina Academic Press, 2004.

Johnson, E. Patrick. *Appropriating Blackness: Performance and the Politics of Authenticity*. Durham: Duke University Press, 2003.

Jones, Amelia. *Body Art / Performing the Subject*. Minneapolis: University of Minnesota Press, 1998.

Jung, Moon-Ho. *Coolies and Cane: Race, Labor, and Sugar in the Age of Emancipation*. Baltimore: Johns Hopkins University Press, 2006.

Justinian. *The Digest of Justinian*. Translated by Alan Watson. Edited by Theodor Mommsen and Paul Krueger. 4 vols. Philadelphia: University of Pennsylvania Press, 1985.

Kang, Laura Hyun Yi. *Compositional Subjects: Enfiguring Asian/American Women*. Durham: Duke University Press, 2002.

Kashima, Tetsuden. *Judgment without Trial: Japanese American Imprisonment during World War II*. Seattle: University of Washington Press, 2003.

Kauanui, J. Kēhaulani. *Hawaiian Blood: Colonialism and the Politics of Sovereignty and Indigeneity*. Durham: Duke University Press, 2008.

Kee, Joan. "Visual Reconnaissance." In *Alien Encounters: Popular Culture in Asian America*, edited by Mimi Thi Nguyen and Thuy Linh N. Tu, 130–49. Durham: Duke University Press, 2007.

Keehn, Joseph, II. "Hasan Elahi." In *Rethinking Contemporary Art and Multicultural Education*, edited by Eungie Joo and Joseph Keehn II, with Jenny Ham-Roberts, 91–93. New York: Routledge, 2011.

Kennedy, Ellen. *Constitutional Failure: Carl Schmitt in Weimar*. Durham: Duke University Press, 2004.

Kerber, Linda K. "Toward a History of Statelessness in America." *American Quarterly* 57, no. 3 (2005): 727–50.

Kiernan, Ben. *Genocide and Resistance in Southeast Asia: Documentation, Denial and Justice in Cambodia and East Timor*. New Brunswick, NJ: Transaction, 2008.

———. *The Pol Pot Regime: Race, Power, and Genocide in Cambodia under the Khmer Rouge, 1975–79*. 2nd ed. New Haven: Yale University Press, 2002.

Kirshenblatt-Gimblett, Barbara. *Destination Culture: Tourism, Museums, and Heritage*. Berkeley: University of California Press, 1998.

Kitahara, Michio. "Commodore Perry and the Japanese: A Study in the Dramaturgy of Power." *Symbolic Interaction* 9, no. 1 (1986): 53–65.

Klein, Melanie. "Infantile Anxiety Situations Reflected in a Work of Art and in the Creative Impulse (1929)." In *The Selected Melanie Klein*, 84–94, edited by Juliet Mitchell. New York: Free Press, 1987.

———. "Love, Guilt and Reparation." In *Love, Hate and Reparation*, by Melanie Klein and Joan Riviere, 57–119. New York: Norton, 1937.

Kondo, Dorinne K. *About Face: Performing Race in Fashion and Theater*. New York: Routledge, 1997.

Kun, Josh. *Audiotopia: Music, Race, and America*. Berkeley: University of California Press, 2005.

Lange, Dorothea. *Impounded: Dorothea Lange and the Censored Images of Japanese American Internment*. Edited by Linda Gordon and Gary Y. Okihiro. New York: Norton, 2006.

Lee, Esther Kim. *A History of Asian American Theater*. Cambridge: Cambridge University Press, 2006.

Lee, Josephine D. *Performing Asian America: Race and Ethnicity on the Contemporary Stage*. Philadelphia: Temple University Press, 1997.

Lee, Julia H. *Interracial Encounters: Reciprocal Representations in African American and Asian American Literatures, 1896–1937*. New York: NYU Press, 2011.

Lepecki, André. *Exhausting Dance: Performance and the Politics of Movement.* New York: Routledge, 2006.

Liao, Ping Hui. "'Of Writing Words for Music Which Is Already Made': 'Madama Butterfly,' 'Turandot,' and Orientalism." *Cultural Critique* 16 (Autumn 1990): 31–59.

Lim, Genny. "Paper Angels." In *Unbroken Thread,* edited by Roberta Uno, 11–52. Amherst: University of Massachusetts Press, 1993.

Long, John Luther. *Madame Butterfly.* In *"Madame Butterfly" and "A Japanese Nightingale": Two Orientalist Texts,* edited by Maureen Honey and Jean Lee Cole, 25–79. New Brunswick: Rutgers University Press, 2002.

Loraux, Nicole. *The Children of Athena: Athenian Ideas about Citizenship and the Division between the Sexes.* Translated by Caroline Levine. Princeton: Princeton University Press, 1993.

Lott, Eric. *Love and Theft: Blackface Minstrelsy and the American Working Class.* New York: Oxford University Press, 1993.

Lowe, Lisa. *Immigrant Acts: On Asian American Cultural Politics.* Durham: Duke University Press, 1996.

Ly, Boreth. "Devastated Vision(s): The Khmer Rouge Scopic Regime in Cambodia." *Art Journal* 61, no. 1 (2003): 67–81.

Madison, Cathy. "Writing Home: Interviews with Suzan-Lori Parks, Christopher Durang, Eduardo Machado, Ping Chong, and Migdalia Cruz." *American Theatre* 8, no. 7 (1991): 36–42.

Madison, D. Soyini. "Dressing Out-of-Place: From Ghana to Obama Commemorative Cloth on the American Red Carpet." In *African Dress: Fashion, Agency, Performance,* edited by Karen Tranberg Hansen and D. Soyini Madison. New York: Bloomsbury, 2013: 217–230.

Mam, Teeda Butt. "Worms from Our Skin." In *Children of Cambodia's Killing Fields: Memoirs by Survivors,* edited by Pran Dith and Kim DePaul, 11–17. New Haven: Yale University Press, 1997.

Mamula, Stephen. "Starting from Nowhere? Popular Music in Cambodia after the Khmer Rouge." *Asian Music,* Winter–Spring 2008, 26–41.

Manzanar Committee. *Reflections in Three Self-Guided Tours of Manzanar.* Los Angeles: Manzanar Committee, 1998.

Marchetti, Gina. *Romance and the "Yellow Peril": Race, Sex, and Discursive Strategies in Hollywood Fiction.* Berkeley: University of California Press, 1993.

Marshall, Thurgood. "Reflections on the Bicentennial of the United States Constitution." In *Thurgood Marshall: His Speeches, Writings, Arguments, Opinions, and Reminiscences,* edited by Mark V. Tushnet, 281–85. Chicago: Lawrence Hill Books, 2001.

Marx, Karl. *Capital: Volume 1.* Translated by Ben Fowkes. New York: Penguin, 1990.

———. "The Eighteenth Brumaire of Louis Bonaparte" (1869). Translated by

Terrell Carver. In *Marx's "Eighteenth Brumaire": (Post)modern Interpretations*, edited by Mark Cowling and James Martin, 19–109. London: Pluto, 2002.

Marx, Karl, and Friedrich Engels. *The Communist Manifesto*. 1848. New York: Penguin, 2004.

Masaoka, Mike, and Bill Hosokawa. *They Call Me Moses Masaoka: An American Saga*. New York: Morrow, 1987.

Massumi, Brian. "Fear (the Spectrum Said)." *Positions: East Asia Cultures Critique* 13, no. 1 (2005): 31–38.

Matsuda, Mari J. "Looking to the Bottom: Critical Legal Studies and Reparations." In *Critical Race Theory: The Key Writings That Formed the Movement*, edited by Kimberlé Crenshaw, Neil Gotanda, Gary Peller, and Kendall Thomas, 63–79. New York: New Press, 1995.

———. *Where Is Your Body? And Other Essays on Race, Gender, and the Law*. Boston: Beacon, 1996.

Melville, Herman. "Bartelby, the Scrivener." In *Billy Budd and Other Stories*, 1–46. New York: Penguin, 1986.

Merritt, Ralph P. "America in the War and America in the Peace." May 13, 1944. UCLA Charles E. Young Research Library / Ansel Adams Papers, box 2.

Metzger, Sean. "Charles Parsloe's Chinese Fetish: An Example of Yellowface Performance in Nineteenth-Century American Melodrama." *Theatre Journal* 56, no. 4 (2004): 627–51.

Michaelsen, Scott. "Between Japanese American Internment and the USA Patriot Act: The Borderlands and the Permanent State of Racial Exception." *Aztlán: The Journal of Chicano Studies* 30, no. 2 (2005): 87–111.

Miyatake, Archie. "Manzanar Remembered." In *Born Free and Equal*, edited by Wynne Benti, 15–23. Bishop, CA: Spotted Dog, 2001.

"'Mme. Butterfly' a Great Success: Tumult of Applause Greets Mr. Belasco's New Play." *Morning Telegraph*, March 6, 1900, 1. New York Public Library for the Performing Arts / Billy Rose Theatre Division, Series X, Scrapbooks, microfilm r.5.

"'Mme. Butterfly' Gives Blanche Bates an Opportunity." *New York Times*, March 6, 1900. New York Public Library for the Performing Arts / Billy Rose Theatre Division, Series X, Scrapbooks, microfilm r.5.

Momohara, Emily Hanako. "The Camps (Artist Statement)." Unpublished paper, on file with the author, 2002.

Moon, Krystyn R. *Yellowface: Creating the Chinese in American Popular Music and Performance, 1850s–1920s*. New Brunswick: Rutgers University Press, 2005.

Moten, Fred. *In the Break: The Aesthetics of the Black Radical Tradition*. Minneapolis: University of Minnesota Press, 2003.

Moy, James S. *Marginal Sights: Staging the Chinese in America*. Iowa City: University of Iowa Press, 1993.

Muller, Eric L. *Free to Die for Their Country: The Story of the Japanese American Draft Resisters in World War II.* Chicago: University of Chicago Press, 2001.

Muñoz, José Esteban. *Cruising Utopia: The Then and There of Queer Futurity.* New York: NYU Press, 2009.

———. *Disidentifications: Queers of Color and the Performance of Politics.* Minneapolis: University of Minnesota Press, 1999.

Ngai, Mae M. *Impossible Subjects: Illegal Aliens and the Making of Modern America.* Princeton: Princeton University Press, 2004.

Niiya, Brian, ed. *Encyclopedia of Japanese American History: An A-to-Z Reference from 1868 to the Present.* Updated ed. New York: Checkmark Books, 2001.

Nyong'o, Tavia. *The Amalgamation Waltz: Race, Performance, and the Ruses of Memory.* Minneapolis: University of Minnesota Press, 2009.

———. "Racial Kitsch and Black Performance." In *The Spike Lee Reader,* edited by Paula Massood, 212–28. Philadelphia: Temple University Press, 2008.

Oh, Seung Ah. *Recontextualizing Asian American Domesticity: From "Madame Butterfly" to "My American Wife!"* Lanham, MD: Lexington Books, 2008.

Okada, John. *No-No Boy.* Seattle: University of Washington Press, 1981.

Okihiro, Gary Y. "An American Story." In *Impounded: Dorothea Lange and the Censored Images of Japanese American Internment,* edited by Linda Gordon and Gary Y. Okihiro, 47–84. New York: Norton, 2006.

Omi, Michael, and Howard Winant. *Racial Formation in the United States: From the 1960s to the 1990s.* 2nd ed. New York: Routledge, 1994.

Ong, Aihwa. *Buddha Is Hiding: Refugees, Citizenship, the New America.* Berkeley: University of California Press, 2003.

———. *Flexible Citizenship: The Cultural Logics of Transnationality.* Durham: Duke University Press, 1999.

Ono, Yoko, Alexandra Munroe, and Jon Hendricks. *Yes: Yoko Ono.* New York: Japan Society / H. N. Abrams, 2000.

"Our World, 1943–1944, Manzanar High Yearbook." 1944. UCLA Charles E. Young Research Library / Special Collections, Manzanar War Relocation Center Records, 1942–1946, box 59, folder 3.

Owens, Eric, dir. *Remembering Manzanar.* 22 mins. US National Parks Service, 2004. DVD.

Paik, A. Naomi. "Testifying to Rightlessness: Hatian Refugees Speaking from Guantánamo." *Social Text* 28, no. 3 (2010): 39–65.

Palumbo-Liu, David. *Asian/American: Historical Crossings of a Racial Frontier.* Stanford: Stanford University Press, 1999.

Pao, Angela Chia-yi. "Changing Faces: Recasting National Identity in All-Asian(-)American Dramas." *Theatre Journal* 53, no. 3 (2001): 389–409.

———. "The Eyes of the Storm: Gender, Genre and Cross-Casting in *Miss Saigon.*" *Text and Performance Quarterly* 12, no. 1 (1992): 21–39.

———. "False Accents: Embodied Dialects and the Characterization of Ethnicity and Nationality." *Theatre Topics* 14, no. 1 (2004): 353–72.

———. *No Safe Spaces: Re-casting Race, Ethnicity, and Nationality in American Theater*. Ann Arbor: University of Michigan Press, 2010.

Parker, Andrew, and Eve Kosofsky Sedgwick. "Introduction: Performativity and Performance." In *Performativity and Performance*, edited by Andrew Parker and Eve Kosofsky Sedgwick, 1–18. New York: Routledge, 1995.

Peffer, George Anthony. "Forbidden Families: Emigration Experiences of Chinese Women under the Page Law, 1875–1882." *Journal of American Ethnic History* 6, no. 1 (1986): 28–46.

Pei, Minxin. "The Paradoxes of American Nationalism." *Foreign Policy* 136 (2003): 30–37.

Perucci, Tony. *Paul Robeson and the Cold War Performance Complex: Race, Madness, Activism*. Ann Arbor: University of Michigan Press, 2012.

Piper, Adrian. "Passing for White, Passing for Black." In *New Feminist Criticism: Art, Identity, Action*, edited by Joanna Frueh, Cassndra L. Langer, and Arlene Raven, 216–47. New York: IconEditions, 1994.

Pirozzi, John, dir. *Sleepwalking through the Mekong*. M80/Film 101 Productions, 2009. DVD.

Plato. *The Republic and Other Works*. Translated and edited by Benjamin Jowett. New York: Anchor Books, 1973.

"Pledge of Allegiance, The." *Music Educators Journal* 29, no. 2 (1942): 23.

Puar, Jasbir K. *Terrorist Assemblages: Homonationalism in Queer Times*. Durham: Duke University Press, 2007.

Puccini, Giacomo, Luigi Illica, and Giuseppe Giacosa. *Madam Butterfly: A Japanese Tragedy*. Translated by R. H. Elkin. New York: Boosey, 1905.

Rana, Junaid Akram. *Terrifying Muslims: Race and Labor in the South Asian Diaspora*. Durham: Duke University Press, 2011.

Rancière, Jacques. *The Emancipated Spectator*. Translated by Gregory Elliot. New York: Verso, 2009.

Rivera-Servera, Ramón H., and Harvey Young. "Introduction: Border Moves." In *Performance in the Borderlands*, edited by Ramón H. Rivera-Servera and Harvey Young, 1–16. New York: Palgrave Macmillan, 2011.

Roach, Joseph. "Carnival and the Law in New Orleans." *TDR: The Drama Review* 37, no. 3 (1993): 42–75.

———. *Cities of the Dead: Circum-Atlantic Performance*. New York: Columbia University Press, 1996.

Robinson, Cedric J. *Black Marxism: The Making of the Black Radical Tradition*. 1983. Reprint, Chapel Hill: University of North Carolina Press, 2000.

Robinson, Gerald H. *Elusive Truth: Four Photographers at Manzanar*. Nevada City, CA: Carl Mautz, 2002.

Rodríguez, Juana María. *Queer Latinidad: Identity Practices, Discursive Spaces*. New York: NYU Press, 2003.

Rogin, Michael Paul. *Blackface, White Noise: Jewish Immigrants in the Hollywood Melting Pot*. Berkeley: University of California Press, 1996.

Rony, Fatimah Tobing. *The Third Eye: Race, Cinema, and Ethnographic Spectacle*. Durham: Duke University Press, 1996.

Roxworthy, Emily. *The Spectacle of Japanese American Trauma: Racial Performativity and World War II*. Honolulu: University of Hawaii Press, 2008.

Schlund-Vials, Cathy J. *War, Genocide, and Justice: Cambodian American Memory Work*. Minneapolis: University of Minnesota Press, 2012.

Schmitt, Carl. *Constitutional Theory*. 1928. Translated by Jeffrey Seitzer. Durham: Duke University Press, 2008.

———. *The Nomos of the Earth in the International Law of the Jus Publicum Europaeum*. Translated by G. L. Ulmen. New York: Telos Press, 2003.

———. *Political Theology: Four Chapters on the Concept of Sovereignty*. 1922. Translated by George Schwab. Chicago: University of Chicago Press, 2005.

Schneider, Rebecca. *The Explicit Body in Performance*. New York: Routledge, 1997.

———. *Performing Remains: Art and War in Times of Theatrical Reenactment*. New York: Routledge, 2011.

Schönberg, Claude-Michel, Alain Boublil, and Richard Maltby. *Miss Saigon: Original London Cast Recording*. Geffen, 1990. CD.

Sedgwick, Eve Kosofsky. *Touching Feeling: Affect, Pedagogy, Performativity*. Durham: Duke University Press, 2003.

———. *The Weather in Proust*. Edited by Jonathan Goldberg. Durham: Duke University Press, 2012.

See, Sarita Echavez. *The Decolonized Eye: Filipino American Art and Performance*. Minneapolis: University of Minnesota Press, 2009.

Semple, Kirk. "Army Charges 8 in Wake of Death of a Fellow G.I." *New York Times*, December 21, 2011.

———. "Most Serious Charge in a Private's Death May Be Dropped." *New York Times*, January 23, 2012.

———. "Sergeant Acquitted of Driving a Suicide." *New York Times*, July 30, 2012.

Shank, Theodore. *Beyond the Boundaries: American Alternative Theatre*. Ann Arbor: University of Michigan Press, 2002.

Shapiro, Sophiline Cheam. "Songs My Enemies Taught Me." In *Children of Cambodia's Killing Fields: Memoirs by Survivors*, edited by Pran Dith and Kim DePaul, 1–5. New Haven: Yale University Press, 1997.

Shimakawa, Karen. *National Abjection: The Asian American Body Onstage*. Durham: Duke University Press, 2002.

Siegel, Paul. "A Right to Boogie Queerly: The First Amendment on the Dance Floor." In *Dancing Desires: Choreographing Sexualities on and off the Stage*, edited by Jane C. Desmond, 267–84. Madison: University of Wisconsin Press, 2001.

Simpson, Caroline Chung. *An Absent Presence: Japanese Americans in Postwar American Culture, 1945–1960*. Durham: Duke University Press, 2001.

Sklar, Kathryn Kish. *Women's Rights Emerges within the Anti-Slavery Movement, 1830–1870: A Brief History with Documents*. Boston: Bedford / St. Martin's, 2000.

Smith, R. J. "They've Got Those Mekong Blues Again." *New York Times*, January 20, 2008, 21.

Spillers, Hortense J. *Black, White, and in Color: Essays on American Literature and Culture*. Chicago: University of Chicago Press, 2003.

Spivak, Gayatri Chakravorty. "Can the Subaltern Speak?" In *Marxism and the Interpretation of Culture*, edited by Cary Nelson and Larry Grossberg, 271–313. Urbana: University of Illinois Press, 1988.

———. *A Critique of Postcolonial Reason: Toward a History of the Vanishing Present*. Cambridge: Harvard University Press, 1999.

———. *Outside in the Teaching Machine*. New York: Routledge, 1993.

Stoler, Ann Laura. *Race and the Education of Desire: Foucault's History of Sexuality and the Colonial Order of Things*. Durham: Duke University Press, 1995.

Tajiri, Rea, dir. *History and Memory*. 32 mins. Women Make Movies, 1991. DVD

Taylor, Diana. *The Archive and the Repertoire: Performing Cultural Memory in the Americas*. Durham: Duke University Press, 2003.

Teemu, Ruskola. "Canton Is Not Boston: The Invention of American Imperial Sovereignty." *American Quarterly* 57, no. 3 (2005): 859–84.

"This 'Butterfly' a Winged Jewel: Belasco's Little Play Earns Distinct Success." *New York Press*, March 6, 1900. New York Public Library for the Performing Arts / Billy Rose Theatre Division, Series X, Scrapbooks, microfilm r.5.

Thompson, Clive. "The Visible Man: An FBI Target Puts His Whole Life Online." *Wired* 15.06 (May 22, 2007). http://www.wired.com/techbiz/people/magazine/15-06/ps_transparency (accessed May 14, 2012).

Tribe, Laurence H. *The Invisible Constitution*. New York: Oxford University Press, 2008.

US Department of Homeland Security, Office of the Press Secretary. "Secretary Napolitano Announces Implementation of National Terrorism Advisory System." April 20, 2011. http://www.dhs.gov/news/2011/04/20/secretary-napolitano-announces-implementation-national-terrorism-advisory-system (accessed October 15, 2012).

US Department of State. "Memorandum of Conversation: Secretary's Meeting with Foreign Minister Chatichai of Thailand." November 26, 1975. Declassified July 27, 2004. Available at http://www.gwu.edu/~nsarchiv/NSAEBB/NSAEBB193/HAK-11-26-75.pdf (accessed February 11, 2010).

US War Relocation Authority. *A Challenge to Democracy*. 20 mins. War Relocation Authority in cooperation with the Office of War Information and the Office of Strategic Services, 1943. Film.

Uyehara, Denise. "Big Head." In *Maps of City and Body: Shedding Light on the Performances of Denise Uyehara*, 21–59. New York: Kaya, 2003.

"Various Dramatic Topics." *New York Times*, March 11, 1900, 16.

Vickery, Michael. *Cambodia, 1975–1982.* Boston: South End, 1984.

Viego, Antonio. *Dead Subjects: Toward a Politics of Loss in Latino Studies.* Durham: Duke University Press, 2007.

Vogel, Shane. "Where Are We Now? Queer World Making and Cabaret Performance." *GLQ: A Journal of Gay and Lesbian Studies* 6, no. 1 (2000): 29–60.

Wilson, Luke. *Theaters of Intention: Drama and the Law in Early Modern England.* Stanford: Stanford University Press, 2000.

Wisenthal, Jonathan, Sherrill Grace, Melinda Boyd, Brian McIlroy, and Vera Micznik, eds. *A Vision of the Orient: Texts, Intertexts, and Contexts of Madame Butterfly.* Toronto: University of Toronto Press, 2006.

Wolff, David A. *Industrializing the Rockies: Growth, Competition, and Turmoil in the Coalfields of Colorado and Wyoming, 1868–1914.* Boulder: University Press of Colorado, 2003.

Wu, Jean Yu-Wen Shen, and Min Song, eds. *Asian American Studies: A Reader.* New Brunswick: Rutgers University Press, 2004.

Yamauchi, Wakako. "12-1-A." In *The Politics of Life,* edited by Velina Hasu Houston, 45–100. Philadelphia: Temple University Press, 1993.

Yoshimoto, Midori. *Into Performance: Japanese Women Artists in New York.* New Brunswick: Rutgers University Press, 2005.

## Legal Primary Sources (Cases, Briefs, and Oral Arguments)

*Al Odah v. United States,* No. 06-1196, Supreme Court of the United States (2007). Brief for Petitioner El-Banna, et al.

*Al Odah, et al., v. United States,* No. 03-334, Supreme Court of the United States (2003). Brief of Amicus Curiae Fred Korematsu in Support of Petitioners.

*Boumediene v. Bush,* 553 U.S. 723 (2008).

*Brown v. Board of Education 1,* 347 U.S. 483 (1954).

*Chae Chan Ping v. United States,* 130 U.S. 581 (1889).

*Cherokee Nation v. Georgia,* 31 U.S. 1 (1831).

*Dred Scott v. Sandford,* 60 U.S. 294 (1856).

*Fok Yung Yo v. United States,* 185 U.S. 296 (1902).

*Fong Yue Ting v. United States,* 149 U.S. 698 (1893).

*Frick v. Webb,* 263 U.S. 326 (1923).

*In re Ah Yup,* 1 F. Cas. 223 (1878).

*In re Camille,* 6 F. 256 (1880).

*In re Kanaka Nian,* 6 Utah 259 (1889).

*In re Knight,* 171 F. 299 (1909).

*In re North Pacific Presbyterian Board of Missions v. Ah Won and Ah Tie,* 18 Ore. 339 (1890).

*In re Rodriguez,* 81 F. 337 (1897).

*Jacobellis v. Ohio,* 378 U.S. 184 (1964).

*Kaplan v. Tod,* 267 U.S. 228 (1925).

*Kiyemba v. Obama,* 555 F.3d 1022 (2009).

*Korematsu v. United States*, 323 U.S. 214 (1944).

*Lawrence v. Texas*, 539 U.S. 558 (2003).

*Lem Moon Sing v. United States*, 158 U.S. 538 (1895).

*Miller v. Albright*, 523 U.S. 420 (1998).

*Minersville School District v. Gobitis*, 210 U.S. 586 (1940).

*Minor v. Happersett*, 88 U.S. 162 (1874).

*Ng Fung Ho v. White*, 259 U.S. 276 (1922).

*Nguyen v. INS*, 533 U.S. 53 (2001).

*Nishimura Ekiu v. United States*, 142 U.S. 651 (1892).

*Ozawa v. United States*, 260 U.S. 178 (1922).

*Parents Involved in Community Schools v. Seattle School District No. 1*, 551 U.S. 701 (2007).

*Parhat v. Gates*, 532 F.3d 834 (2008).

*People of California v. Hall*, 4 Cal. 399 (1854).

*Plessy v. Ferguson*, 163 U.S. 537 (1896).

*Porterfield v. Webb*, 263 U.S. 225 (1923).

*Rice v. Cayetano*, 528 U.S. 495 (2000).

*State of Oregon v. Ching Ling*, 16 Ore. 419 (1888).

*State of Oregon v. Mah Jim*, 13 Ore. 235 (1886).

*Terrace v. Thompson*, 263 U.S. 197 (1923).

*United States v. Cartozian*, 6 F.2d 919 (1925).

*United States v. Dolla*, 177 F. 101 (1910).

*United States v. Ebens*, 800 F.2d 1422 (1986).

*United States v. Jung Ah Lung*, 124 U.S. 621 (1888).

*United States v. Thind*, 261 U.S. 204 (1923).

*Webb v. O'Brien*, 263 U.S. 313 (1923).

*West Virginia State Board of Education v. Barnette*, 319 U.S. 624 (1943).

*Wong Wing v. United States*, 163 U.S. 237 (1896).

*Zadvydas v. Davis, Ashcroft v. Kim Ho Ma*, No. 99-7791, Supreme Court of the United States. Oral arguments. June 28, 2001.

*Zadvydas v. INS, Ashcroft v. Kim Ho Ma*, 533 U.S. 678 (2001).

# Index

## About the Author

**Joshua Takano Chambers-Letson** is Assistant Professor in the Department of Performance Studies in the School of Communications of Northwestern University.

Made in the USA
Las Vegas, NV
08 May 2022

48622864R00166